# GUILLOTINE

*Both the garden style called 'sentimental', and the
French Revolution, grew from Rousseau. The garden
trellis, and the guillotine, are alike entwined with
the honeysuckle of the new 'sensibility'.*

*Ian Hamilton Finlay, with Gary Hincks.* "BOTH THE GARDEN STYLE . . . ," *1987.*

# GUILLOTINE

## ITS LEGEND AND LORE

DANIEL GEROULD

BLAST BOOKS • NEW YORK

Library of Congress Cataloging-in-Publication Data

Gerould, Daniel Charles, 1928–
    Guillotine, its legend and lore / Daniel Gerould. — 1st ed.
        p.  cm.
    Includes bibliographical references.
    ISBN 0-922233-02-0
    1. Guillotine—History. 2. Guillotine in literature. I. Title.
HV8555.G47 1990
306.4—dc20                          90-32649


Author's acknowledgments: Paul Berman, Lenny Borger, Rex Butt, Harry Carlson, Marvin and Pat Carlson, Prudence Carlson, Ruby Cohn, Ed Dee, Guy Ducrey, Isabelle Ginot, Mel Gordon, Jan Heissenger, Peter Hill, Jane House, Marion Holt, Stanley and Laura Kauffmann, Jim Leverett, Jane McMahon, Miodini, Andre A. Moerman, Susan Newman, Richard Niles, Jeanine Plottel, Laurence Senelick, Lech Sokól, Giovanna Tomassucci, Scott Walters, Alyson Waters, Markus Wessendorf, David Willinger, Christine Burgin Gallery, The Graduate Center CUNY Library, Theatre de l'Eclipse, Ubu Repertory Theater, Victoria Miro Gallery, The Woodstock New York Library

The publishers gratefully acknowledge the help of Joe Coleman, Beth Escott, Alex Gendrano, Sergei Hasenecz, Linda Hayashi, Don Kennison, Scott Lindgren, Adam Parfrey, Charles Schneider, Kim Spurlock and J. G. Thirlwell.

Excerpts from *Explosion in a Cathedral* by Alejo Carpentier © 1962 Editions Gallimard under the title *Le Siècle des Lumières*. © 1963 English translation: Victor Gollancz Ltd.
"Four Patients of Dr. Deibler" by J. C. Longoni, printed 1970 by Lawrence & Wishart Ltd. reprinted by permission of Lawrence & Wishart Ltd.
Excerpts from *Fantômas* by Marcel Allain and Pierre Souvestre translation © 1986 by William Morrow & Company, Inc.
Excerpts from *Literary Reminiscences* by Ivan Turgenev, translated by David Magarshack. © 1958 by Farrar, Straus and Cudahy, Inc. Renewal © 1986 by Elise D. Magarshack. Reprinted by permission of Farrar, Straus and Giroux, Inc.
We have contacted copyright owners where known. Inquiries should be directed to Blast Books, P.O. Box 51, Cooper Station, New York, New York 10276-0051.

Cover and interior design by Beth Escott

Published by Blast Books, Inc.
        P.O. Box 51
        Cooper Station
        New York, NY 10276-0051

Manufactured in the United States of America

First Edition 1992

10 9 8 7 6 5 4 3 2 1

# CONTENTS

# GUILLOTINE

# INTRODUCTION

"**M**ONSIEUR, I HAVE A right to be curious. I have never seen it before," said Charlotte Corday to the executioner Sanson on first catching sight of the guillotine that would soon cut off her head. Do we, whose heads are not at risk, have a right to the same curiosity? Are we condoning the guillotine's bloody history when we delve into its past? Does the very act of studying this semiautomatic killing machine make us a party to the abominations it has been used to commit? Should we rather avert our gaze?

An invention born of humanitarian concern, the guillotine was designed to alleviate the suffering of those condemned to die, but it soon became an instrument of indiscriminate carnage. Instead of bringing order and equality to the outmoded legal system that had made the death penalty under the ancien régime so iniquitous, it unleashed lawless chaos. The very democratic simplicity by which the same form of capital punishment was to be meted out to all regardless of class resulted in sweeping totalitarian oppression.

From its inception, when the idea of a decapitating machine was first proposed in the Revolutionary French National Assembly, the guillotine began to exert a profound—and deeply ambivalent—influence on both the popular and artistic consciousness, earning it a notoriety unlike that of any other means of execution. Its hold on the popular imagination has been persistent, as is evident from countless representations of the guillotine in art, literature, and popular culture over the course of nearly two centuries.

To many, the guillotine dramatically exemplifies how revolutionary ideals can quickly become transformed into their exact opposite. It confirms the worst fears of both conservatives and reactionaries by revealing the perverse underside of the human impulse for radical social change. Holding out utopian promises of a new humaneness, the guillotine instead brought about abuses far worse than those the revolutionaries set out to correct. The swift dispenser of justice became a terrible engine of destruction. Consequently, it has most often been depicted as a sinister symbol of the failure of Revolution—an emblem of primeval bloodlust and mob violence.

At the first demonstration of the new invention, Charles-Henri Sanson, the High Executioner of the new Republic, is said to have wondered whether its very efficiency might later prove to be a source of regret. "Facility begat use," as the British historian John Wilson Croker pointed out. This new technology for speeding up executions created a demand for more and more victims, and so it was that the rhythm of the guillotine imposed itself on life, effortlessly transforming it into death. Not surprisingly, histories of the guillotine are for the most part counterrevolutionary in bent, sympathetic to the victims and even the executioners, but not to the awesome machine and its advocates.

In their struggle to eradicate the old society, the French revolutionaries were unable to avoid violence and bloodshed. The guillotine provided a means of ritualizing and channeling the people's long-suppressed desire for vengeance on its oppressors. "The violence that arose out of dark destitution and ancient anger," as the French cultural historian Jean Starobinski put it, found in the geometric guillotine its perfect caliper. "The black heart of the Revolution" and "its fertile chaos" demanded a tool and a point of focus, and the raging mobs found both in the guillotine. This implement of the Age of Reason proved much more than an encapsulation of eighteenth-century technological ingenuity and enlightenment benevolence; it marked the entry of the industrial revolution into the realm of death, ushering in the mechanized ruthlessness of the nineteenth century and leading the way for a return to darkness.

But is it absolutely impermissible to admire the guillotine for the brilliance of its conception? In form it was as beautifully abstract as the revolutionary ideals it was designed to serve. Like the architecture projected for the new revolutionary era, the guillotine's design was monumental and slender, towering and graceful, its symmetry hypnotic.

For all its demonic blackness, the guillotine had style. Its severe lines, bold silhouette, and mathematical simplicity lent it an undeniable elegance. Of perfect proportions, it was a triumph of geometric form—and in the late eighteenth century, geometry was the language of reason. At the same time, the guillotine's design was entirely functional, its utility instantly apparent to the eye. The empty rectangular space between the raised blade and its destination measured the time to annihilation. Only when it was put into practice did horror overpower appreciation of the absolute rigor of the form. This dynamic tension between formal grace and lethal power, high ideals and murderous reality, gave the guillotine its highly charged symbolic resonance.

Immediately following its installation by the revolutionary government as the sanctioned mode of capital punishment in 1792, a guillotine mythos penetrated the recesses of Europe's collective consciousness. The efficient killing machine acquired a folklore and became a part of popular culture; it was acclaimed as an amusing toy, a novel diversion that lent itself to replication, miniaturization, and simulation. Before long, this new decapitating device became a tourist attraction, inspired songs, was reproduced in fashion items (earrings, gowns *en guillotine*), and even appeared as a household appliance, in the form of a bread slicer. The very topography of Paris is marked by sites where the guillotine was erected and by the different routes taken by the wagons that brought its victims to the scaffold.

This book is not a history of the guillotine. A number of excellent studies of this kind have already been written and I have drawn upon them freely. Nor is it a biographical account of the great family dynasties of executioners, such as the Sansons, or a chronicle of the famous criminals who were decapitated—subjects which have likewise been ably and extensively treated. Rather, I propose to consider the guillotine as a cultural artifact and to examine its representation in the arts both high and low—in other words to explore its imaginative metamorphoses over two centuries. But this approach in no way means that I am in favor of regarding the guillotine and its mechanized killing as an aesthetic experience, forgetting all the thousands upon thousands of its real flesh-and-blood victims.

The issue of capital punishment inevitably arouses strong emotions. Throughout its two centuries of active service, the guillotine has left few indifferent. In the face of such an overpowering embodiment of death, one feels compelled to take a stand on the question of the state's taking of human life as retribution. But even the formidable machine's staunchest opponents have not been able to disguise a certain admiration for its power and sinister poetry. Behind the hatred and fear lies irresistible fascination.

We are now in the postguillotine era. It was last used in France in September 1977. Four years later, on the initiative of the new socialist government of François Mitterand, the death penalty was abolished in September 1981 by a vote of both the National Assembly and the Senate. After the Museum of the City of Paris politely declined the offer to house the machine in its retirement, the guillotine at last found its true home in the National Museum of Popular Arts and Traditions in the Bois de Boulogne where, however, it is not on public display. May it rest there forever.

It is only as a museum piece, as part of the repertory of popular arts, that the instrument of death lives on. Left with only a theatrical function, the guillotine has been safely enshrined in popular culture, which has the power to absorb and neutralize all horrors. No longer in the business of decapitation, the sepulchral machine has become a permanent icon of systematic violence.

The historiography that glorifies and sanitizes the French Revolution would prefer not to remember the killing device responsible for such a bloody past. In France's conciliatory celebration of the bicentennial of the Revolution, the guillotine was officially ignored in the festivities intended to bring an end to the centuries-old partisan strife and to promote the ideals of Liberty, Equality, and Fraternity. The falling blade no longer represents the Rights of Man. When in the summer of 1988 members of a television crew filming a series on the Revolution set up a guillotine on the place de la Concorde (formerly the place de la Révolution, where Louis XVI was executed), its removal was ordered by an official from the president's office, who told the producer, "Monsieur, that's not our idea of the Revolution!"

*Guillotine maker on the Seine, July 14, 1989.*

Despite total exclusion from the state-sponsored bicentennial pageantry, on July 14, 1989, an enterprising toy-guillotine maker sporting a red Jacobin bonnet could be found along the banks of the Seine selling his workable models to tourists. At a bicentennial counterdemonstration on August 17, 1989, royalists paraded a twelve-foot guillotine to remind republican Frenchmen of the thousands of innocent Catholics who had been beheaded in a revolution that was an assault on divine authority. Patterned after newspapers of the revolutionary period, *Le Journal des Guillotinés* began to appear on a monthly basis, printing the names of all those who "lost their heads" along with a notice to readers suggesting that perhaps their own ancestors were among the victims of the Terror.

The once-omnipotent machine has become a pariah. But even in the days of its power in the nineteenth century, the guillotine was a social outcast, regarded as shameful and treated with official circumspection. The word *guillotine* never appeared in any government documents. The device was referred to only euphemistically as "the instrument of death" or "timbers of justice" (*bois de justice*), an expression used in the ancien régime for the gallows. Paradoxically, although executions were held publicly because of their supposed deterrent effect, the state did everything it could to prevent public mention of the guillotine and to censor its representation in the mass media.

Neither the executioner nor his machine had any official status. There was no written description specifying the nature of the executioner's duties, no application form or qualifying examination. The executioner occupied his own autonomous realm; he maintained and housed his own machine, and those condemned to die were subcontracted to him by the state. The process of selecting a new executioner, always cloaked in secrecy, invariably resulted in the choice of a member of the reigning family of executioners, as though the office were a privilege of aristocratic lineage—an anachronistic practice jarringly out of keeping with a modern democracy.

It was through literature and the arts, and above all popular culture, that these taboos were broken and the governmentally fostered silence shattered. By focusing on the horrors, guillotinophiles and guillotinophobes alike unmasked the moral hypocrisies of a smug establishment and at least had the honesty to reveal their own—and others'—bloodthirsty obsessions.

Serious issues of capital punishment and societal violence are often trivialized by a proliferation of sensational anecdotes, as indeed happened in the newspapers, magazines, and Grand Guignol performances at the turn of the century, thereby reducing the guillotine to a *fait divers*. In reading about one decapitation after another do we perhaps run the risk of becoming as benumbed as the mob who day after day witnessed the beheadings during the height of the Terror?

Certainly the repertory of guillotine tales and effects is finite, but the philosophical and artistic reflections that it has engendered since its creation are remarkably diverse, given the grim single-mindedness of the machine. Rites and ceremonies require repetition; over the years minor details of the ritual on the scaffold may have changed, but the essentials have remained the same. The relentless monotony of two centuries of guillotinings—both real and imaginary—the repetitious horror, the countless severed heads, creates a vast, obsessive picture, a kind of serial composition or canvas of reduplicated images like Andy Warhol's multiple electric chairs, the mirror image of the endless chain of state-directed killings.

Man's ingenuity in putting his fellow man to death is a subject of irrepressible curiosity in all human societies, whether one's reaction be righteous indignation, horrified revulsion, or spellbound empathy for the victim or executioner. In his nightmarish tale *Melmoth the Wanderer*, the Irish Gothic novelist Charles Robert Maturin acknowledges the fatal attraction of the terrors of capital punishment: "I have heard of men who have traveled into countries where horrible executions were daily witnessed, for the sake of that excitement which the sight of suffering never fails to give. . . . You will call this cruelty, I call it curiosity—that curiosity that brings thousands to witness a tragedy and makes the most delicate female feast on groans and agony."

Throughout history, art has reflected man's fascination with violent death. Classical tragedy is a characteristic high-culture response. Popular culture embraces more sensational forms and has always exploited the primordial horror of ghastly crimes and executions in their most terrifying aspects. But it was only in the eighteenth century that new concepts of the sublime gave rise to a modern aesthetics of terror that transcended neoclassical norms and would find its fullest expression in the age of the guillotine.

The British statesman and philosopher Edmund Burke is best known for his archconservative treatise *Reflections on the Revolution in France* (1790), in which he defended the monarchy and lamented the persecution of the king and queen at the hands of a "band of cruel ruffians and assassins." A confirmed opponent of political terror, Burke nevertheless was a pioneer in developing a theory of terror in literature and the other arts. In his *Philosophical Enquiry into Our Ideas of the Sublime and the Beautiful* (1756), he declared that "terror is in all cases whatsoever, either more openly or latently, the ruling principle of the sublime." Burke maintained that whatever excites "ideas of pain and danger," including terrible objects, is a source of the sublime, producing "the strongest emotion which the mind is capable of."

This theory of the sublime in art paved the way for melodramatic landscape painting, Gothic tales and dramas, and all the various manifestations of the fantastic in literature. The representation of horror soon came into vogue, with emphasis on violent death, decaying corpses, and forbidden erotic subjects, due in no small part to the public imagination having been indelibly altered by the omnipresent guillotine during the Reign of Terror.

But crude and sensational expressions of the aesthetics of terror never gained full critical acceptance. In a scathing review of a lurid melodrama by

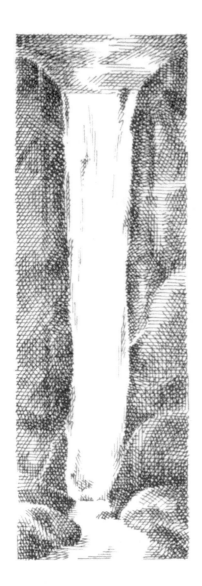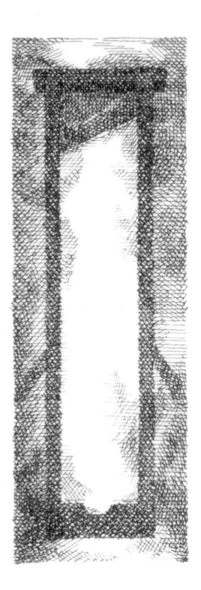

*Ian Hamilton Finlay, with Gary Hincks.* TWO LANDSCAPES OF THE SUBLIME, *1989.*

Maturin, Samuel Taylor Coleridge, himself a poet of the weird and the super-natural, complained that public taste had been utterly depraved by overexpo-sure to the atrocities of the French Revolution. People's feelings had become so callous, Coleridge argued, that only "the grossest and most outrageous stimu-lants" could satisfy the public's cravings for the macabre and repulsive.

These close links between the guillotine, the aesthetics of terror, and the horror genres of both popular culture and high art are a major concern of my study. But I am no less concerned with the guillotine as a source of humor or erotic fantasy. Throughout the text I have let the guillotine serve as a reflection of public taste and as a measure of changes in aesthetic sensibility. My aim is to place artistic representations of the guillotine in the context of culture, past and present, and to follow this haunting icon of disaster and madness through its sin-gular history in the realm of creativity.

**MACHINE PROPOSÉE À L'ASSEMBLÉE NATIONALE,**
**POUR LE SUPPLICE DES CRIMINELLES. PAR M. GUILLOTIN.**

Les exécutions se feront hors de la Ville dans un endroit destiné à cet effet, la Machine sera en—
touronné de Barrieres pour empecher le Peuple d'approcher, l'interieur de ces Barrieres sera—
gardé par des Soldats portant les armes bassées, et le signal de la mort sera donné au Boureau par
le Confesseur dans l'instant de l'absolution, le Boureau detournant les yeux coupera d'un coup de
sabre la corde après la quelle sera suspendu un mouton armé d'une hache.

N: Une semblable Machine a servi au supplice de Titus Manlius romain.

*Anonymous.* M.M.I. ROBESPIERRE, *late eighteenth century.*

# INVENTING THE GUILLOTINE

*There are those who have no luck. Christopher Columbus*
*cannot attach his name to his discovery;*
*Dr. Guillotin cannot detach his from his invention.*
—*Victor Hugo, 1830*

IN A DEBATE on reform of the French penal code in the National Assembly in the fall of 1789, Dr. Joseph-Ignace Guillotin, a deputy from Paris and professor of anatomy at the Faculty of Medicine, argued in favor of uniform punishment for the same crimes regardless of the rank and estate of the guilty. The kindly doctor gave a vivid picture of the cruel tortures of the barbarous feudal past and proposed a single humane mode of capital punishment—decapitation by a simple mechanism yet to be invented.

Describing his proposed beheading device, the gentle doctor grew eloquent. "The mechanism falls like lightning; the head flies off; the blood spurts; the man no longer exists." The assembly listened attentively. But when the professor continued enthusiastically, "Gentlemen, with my machine, I'll take off your head in a flash, and you won't even feel the slightest pain," his words were greeted with uproarious laughter. Although two years were to pass before Dr. Guillotin's machine was to materialize, he became an instant celebrity. The still-imaginary device was christened "guillotine," and typically Parisian jokes, songs, and puns were fashioned on his name.

It was not until June 1791 that the assembly held its next debate on the death penalty. On this occasion many abolitionist voices were raised, and Maximilien Robespierre was among those who argued most passionately against capital punishment. However, the opponents of the scaffold failed in their attempts to do away with the death sentence; to the vast majority, murder and treason still demanded the ultimate sanction. On June 3, 1791, the assembly voted that "all those condemned to death shall have the head cut off," and on September 25 of the same year this provision was included in the new penal code. Progress had been made: the inequality and cruelty of the methods of execution under the ancien régime were forever abolished. The problem now was how to cut off all those heads.

There was a large backlog of prisoners condemned to death; some had been waiting for months to be executed. The executioner Charles-Henri Sanson submitted a memorandum in March 1792, in which he explained the need for a new instrument. His sword grew blunt after each decapitation, and if there were many people to be executed at the same time, the blade had to be ground and sharpened anew. He owned only two swords, accidents were frequent, and numerous executions were bungled and proved cruel and inhumane.

The assembly now had to return to Dr. Guillotin's original proposition for a beheading machine and treat the idea seriously. In these revolutionary times there was only one thing to do next. A committee was formed, and its chairman, Dr. Antoine Louis, secretary of the Academy of Surgery, was asked to issue a report "on the possibility of manufacturing a machine that could be relied on." The Louis Report of March 7, 1792, concluded that decapitation inflicted by the proposed instrument should "be performed in an instant according to the letter and the spirit of the new law" and provided a description of such a machine "already known in England." In fact, the guillotine was nothing new. Human ingenuity in devising ways to kill other human beings has a long history.

## THE PRE-GUILLOTINE: ITS EARLY HISTORY

The beheading machine that was finally constructed and used for the first time in April 1792 was actually a modernized version of an ancient instrument—which some sources place as far back as the times of antiquity. In his *Academy of Armoury* (1678), Randle Holmes cites a family whose coat of arms was a primitive pre-guillotine: "a heading-block fixed between two supporters, and an axe placed therein," with a mallet on the sinister side for driving the axe down. Holmes explains how the mechanism functioned: "This way of decollation was by laying the neck of the malefactor on the block, and then setting the axe

upon it, which lay in a rigget [groove] on
the two sideposts or supporters. The
executioner, with the violence of a blow
on the head of the axe with his heavy
maule [mallet], forced it through the
man's neck into the block. I have seen a
draught [drawing] of the like beheading
instrument, where the weighty axe
(made heavy for that purpose) was raised
up, and fell down in such a riggeted
frame, which being suddenly let to fall,
the weight of it was sufficient to cut off a
man's head at one blow."

*Anonymous.* EVANGELIEN UND
EPISTELN, *1506.*

It is impossible to say whether or not such an instrument was used before
the Renaissance, but some sixteenth-century engravings represent the execution of Titus Manlius in the fourth century B.C. by a machine similar to a guillotine, encased in an ornate frame that would be the pride of any cabinetmaker.
These pictures may in fact be based on a fifteenth-century beheading in Liege.
A decapitating machine—the *Planke*—had certainly been used in Germany and
Flanders for centuries. A Renaissance woodcut shows a Spartan about to be put
to death by another variant of the pre-guillotine. Several illustrations by Lucas
Cranach and others portray the martyrdom of saints and depict a decapitating
machine resembling a pre-guillotine as the death-dealing instrument.

The only surviving example of the pre-guillotine is the Scottish Maiden,
preserved almost intact, and now housed at the Museum of the Society of
Antiquaries in Edinburgh. It is a device introduced in 1561 by the Earl of
Morton, Regent of Scotland, who on one of his journeys had seen its ancestor,
the Halifax Gibbet, and had a similar machine erected at Edinburgh. A traveler to Edinburgh who saw the Scottish Maiden in 1774 gave this account:

> It is in the form of a painter's easel, and about ten feet high; at four feet from the
> bottom is a crossbar, on which the felon places his head, which is kept down by
> another placed above. In the inner edges of the frame are grooves; in these are
> placed a sharp axe, with a vast weight of lead, supported at the very summit by a
> peg; to that peg is fastened a cord, which the executioner cutting [in actual fact, the
> cord was released by a kind of latch], the axe falls, and does the affair effectually.

*Scottish Maiden.*

In Raphael Holinshed's *Chronicles of Ireland* (1577), the Halifax Gibbet, which is said to have been in use in ancient times, is described in the following terms:

> There is and has been a law, or rather a custom, at Halifax, that whosoever doth commit any felony and is taken with the same, or confesses the fact upon examination, if it be valued by four constables to amount to the sume of thirteen-pence-half-penny, he is forthwith beheaded upon one of the next market days, or else upon the same day that he is convicted. The engine wherewith the execution is done is a square block of wood of the length of four-feet-and-a-half, which doth ride up and down in a slot between two pieces of timber that are framed and set upright, of five yards in height. In the nether end of the sliding block is an axe. The block being drawn up to the top of the frame, is there fastened with a wooden pin, unto the middest of which pin there is a rope fastened that cometh down among the people; so that when the offender hath made his confession, and hath laid his neck over the nethermost block, every man there present doth either take hold of the rope or puteth forth his arm so near to the same as he can get it, in token that he is willing to see justice executed, and pulling out the pin in this manner, the head-block wherein the axe is fastened doth fall down with such violence, that if the neck of the transgressor were so big as that of a bull, it should be cut in sunder at a stroke, and roll from the body by a huge distance. If it be so that the offender be apprehended for the stealing of an ox, sheep, kine, horse, or any such cattle, the self beast or other of its kind shall have the end of the rope tied somewhere unto him, so that they, being driven, do draw out the pin, whereby the offender is executed.

The Scottish Maiden was last used in 1710, having had to its credit more than 120 heads, including that of the Earl of Morton himself, who "felt the kiss of its sweet blade" once he had fallen from power and was defeated by his enemies. The machine was called "a sweet maiden whose embrace will waft one's soul into heaven."

## BEATRICE CENCI AND THE ITALIAN *MANNAIA*

There is indisputable written evidence that a pre-guillotine was in widespread use in Renaissance Italy called the *mannaia* or mandara. Fifteenth-century chronicles document actual executions, and several accompanying line drawings, surprisingly modern in spirit, even show the blood-stained *mannaia* with the

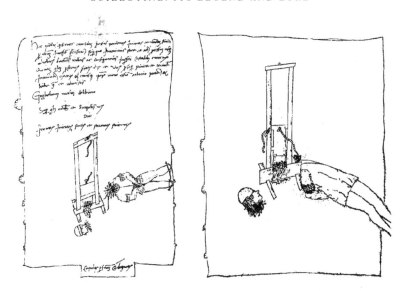

*Late fifteenth-century illustrations of the* mannaia.

bodies of the victims lying on the ground, their hands tied behind their backs and their caps still on their severed heads.

We know from contemporary accounts that the *mannaia* was used for the execution of Beatrice Cenci in Rome on September 11, 1599. Sixteen-year-old Beatrice—with the help of her stepmother, Lucrezia, and her brother Giacomo—arranged the murder of her father, the cruel and sadistic Count Cenci, who had persecuted Beatrice and probably raped her. The tragic story of the beautiful patricide has been the subject of many dramas—by Percy Bysshe Shelley in 1819, the Polish poet Juliusz Slowacki in 1839, Antonin Artaud in 1935, and Alberto Moravia in 1957. Although the *mannaia* does not figure in any of these theatrical versions—perhaps the authors found it inappropriate or impossible to show such a device on stage—an extended description of the execution is given by both Stendhal and Alexandre Dumas *père* in their narratives of Beatrice's life, based directly on Italian chronicles of the period. The more reticent and fastidious Stendhal avoids the gruesome and grotesque details that Dumas particularly relishes, but their accounts are essentially the same.

All night long workmen on the Piazza prepared the scene of the tragedy, setting up a huge scaffold with a block and a *mannaia*. The three prisoners, who had been sleeping peacefully, were delivered the fatal news at six o'clock in the morning. Stendhal reports that Beatrice and her stepmother dressed in special gowns "made like nuns' habits, without ornaments on bosom and shoulders, and gathered only at the wide sleeves." They left the prison at eight o'clock, accompanied by the Company of Misericordia bearing a great crucifix. Each wore a black taffeta veil. Beatrice's youngest brother, Bernado, who had not been implicated in the crime, was compelled to take his place on the scaffold, where he promptly fainted. According to Stendhal, "He was revived with cold water and made to sit opposite the *mannaia*," so that he could not avoid watching his relatives die, although he was pardoned at the last moment.

According to Dumas's description of the *mannaia*, "Above the block was suspended, between two beams, a huge blade, which, sliding between two grooves, came down with the force of all its weight on the block when the spring was released." Even though he claimed not to be seeking gratuitous horror and to have softened the Italian original, Dumas in his *Cenci* (part of his series called *Famous Crimes*) stressed all the sensational aspects of the execution.

Beatrice's stepmother was the first to mount the scaffold. When the executioner tied Lucrezia's hands behind her back and took off her veil, her voluminous breasts became exposed. On seeing the block, she was unable to keep her shoulders from trembling. Unlike the guillotine, the *mannaia*'s plank was stationary and it had no collar. Thus Lucrezia was forced to assume a prone position and stretch out her neck. Dumas described her plight:

> As she was not able, because of her uplifted bosom, to place her neck on the block, it was necessary to add a piece of wood to raise the block; all the while the poor woman was waiting, suffering more from shame than from fear of death. When at last she was properly placed, the executioner released the spring, and the head, detached from the trunk, fell on the scaffold, where it rebounded two or three times causing the crowd to shudder. Finally, the executioner seized it and showed it to the people, then wrapped it in the black taffeta, and placed it with the body in a coffin at the foot of the scaffold.

While the *mannaia* was being prepared for Beatrice, a spectators' stand loaded with onlookers collapsed. Many who had come to watch the Cenci die were killed themselves and still more were maimed and wounded, but the execution proceeded nonetheless. The machine was set up again, the blood washed off, and the executioner went to get Beatrice. She stepped out of her slippers at the foot of the steps, mounted the scaffold, and unaided placed her neck beneath the *mannaia*, so as to avoid being touched by the executioner. But her

*Jacques Wagrez.* EXECUTION OF BEATRICE CENCI.

execution was deliberately delayed in order to allow Pope Clement VII (who was sequestered elsewhere in prayer) to give the doomed girl absolution from a distance. Unnerved by waiting, Beatrice got off the plank and almost stood up. Then she finally had to put her head back on the block. The blade fell. Dumas described the scene.

> A strange effect was seen: while the head bounded to one side, the body drew back, as though walking backwards. Instantly the executioner took the head and showed it to the people, then he wrapped it in the taffeta veil as he had done with the other head. He was going to put Beatrice's body with that of her stepmother, but the Company of Misericordia snatched the body out of his hands, and as one of them tried to lay it in the coffin, the body slipped away from him and dropped from the scaffold onto the ground. In the fall, the entire torso came out of its clothes, so that now being totally covered with dust and blood, a good deal of time had to be spent washing it.

Stendhal points out that "the shades of the Cenci left this world numerously escorted." The sun's heat was so intense that many people in the huge crowd suffered heatstrokes, lost consciousness, and died of fever during the night. As the mob dispersed, others were trampled by horses.

The Italian *mannaia* continued to be used in the early eighteenth century. The anonymous travel book, *Voyage historique et politique de Suisse, d'Italie, et d'Allegmane* (1736–1743), gives the following account of an execution at Milan in 1702:

> A large scaffold was prepared in the great square, and covered with black. In the middle of it was placed a great block, of the height to allow the criminal, when kneeling, to lay his neck on it between a kind of gibbet which supported a hatchet one foot deep and one and a half wide, which was confined by a groove. The hatchet was loaded with an hundred-pounds weight of lead, and was suspended by a rope made fast to the gibbet. After the criminal had confessed himself, the penitents, who are for the most part of noble families, led him up on the scaffold, and, making him kneel before the block, one of the penitents held the head under the hatchet; the priest then reading the prayers usual on such occasions, the executioner had nothing to do but cut the cord that held up the hatchet, which, descending with violence, severed the head, which the penitent still held in his hands, so the executioner never touched it. This mode of executing is so sure that the hatchet entered the block above two inches.

## DESIGNING THE GUILLOTINE: DR. GUILLOTIN, DR. LOUIS, AND THE HARPSICHORD MAKER SCHMIDT

A machine similar to the *mannaia* was on occasion used in France prior to the Revolution, although neither Dr. Guillotin nor Dr. Louis seems to have been aware of the fact. Henri II de Montmorency, Marshall of France, was beheaded at Toulouse in 1632 by means of such an instrument after staging a revolt against Richelieu, as was recorded in *Mémoires de messire Jacques de Chastenet* in 1690:

> In that province they make use of a kind of hatchet (*une doloire*), which runs
> between two pieces of wood; and when the head is placed on the block below, the
> cord is let go, and the hatchet descends and severs the head from the body. When
> he had put his head on the block, his wound [received in the fight in which he was
> taken] hurt him, and he moved his head, but said, "I don't do so from fear, but
> from the soreness of my wound." Father Arnoul was close to him when they let go
> the cord of the hatchet: the head was separated clean from the body. . . .

A similar mechanism is described in a thirteenth-century French poem, *La vengeance de Raguidel*. Some historians of the guillotine push the date back even further. Gustave Lenotre suggested that "decapitation by a machine was a punishment used in France before the Roman conquest." His evidence was the discovery in 1865 of a stone blade weighing well over two hundred pounds, which was called "a Gallic head-cutter, a stone-age guillotine."

Mannaia.

Legend has it that a pre-guillotine like the Scottish Maiden or the *mannaia* existed in Paris just before the Revolution, in miniature form at the marionette theatre. According to the story, Dr. Guillotin took his wife to the fairground where they saw a puppet show of *The Four Sons of Aymon* (based on a famous medieval chivalric romance), by J. F. Arnould Mussot, in which a head is cut off by a tiny decapitating machine. Whether this has any basis in truth or not, certainly it was Guillotin who initially conceived it, Louis who worked out the design, and the German harpsichord maker Tobias Schmidt who constructed the actual machine. Although the Scottish Maiden and the *mannaia* may have provided these "founding fathers of the guillotine" with precedents to follow, crucial conceptual and design differences underscored the originality of their new invention. The guillotine was to be democratically applied to the condemned, regardless of their rank and estate, whereas all the ancestors of the instrument had been used exclusively for nobility. And there were two essential developments in technical design. The early decapitating machines had a horizontal knife which did not cut, but rather chopped, and most of them lacked a lunette (literally, "little moon" in French), the two-part circular collar that held the neck of the victim in a fixed position.

With his knowledge of human anatomy, Dr. Louis was able to introduce improvements that made the guillotine a machine of amazing precision and speed. His detailed plans for the construction and operation of such a machine called for two uprights a foot apart, a convex blade firmly secured in a holder that would slide down in grooves in the uprights, a long rope threaded through a ring, a wooden block on which the neck of the victim, laid face-down, was to be placed within an iron horseshoe-shaped crescent. According to Dr. Louis's instructions, "If everything has been properly arranged, the executioner standing by the machine will be able to hold the two ends of the rope supporting the blade-holder and, on releasing them simultaneously, this instrument falling down from a height will, by its weight and acceleration of speed, separate the head from the body in the twinkling of an eye."

These specifications were given to the carpenter who had previously built scaffolds for the state, but when he submitted an outrageously high estimate of the cost, Dr. Louis's project was entrusted to Tobias Schmidt, a harpsichord maker from Strasbourg and sometime inventor, who had once submitted his own design for a decapitator. For a time the new instrument was known as little Louison or Louisette after its designer, but it soon regained the more popular name of guillotine that was to plague its namesake for the rest of his life and subject the doctor to continual ridicule and opprobrium.

The guillotine was first tested on April 17, 1792, at the famous Bicêtre Hospital just outside of Paris. To the delight of the assembly of dignitaries and officials, Dr. Louis decapitated a bundle of straw, a sheep, and several corpses.

*Fious del Cachet.* THE DEATH OF MARIE-ANTOINETTE, QUEEN OF FRANCE,
16 OCTOBER 1793, *late eighteenth century.*

Accompanied by his two brothers and son, the executioner Sanson supervised
the proceedings. When a corpse with a huge neck was not beheaded after three
tries, Dr. Louis decided to raise the height of the uprights and modify the shape
of the blade. A banquet and celebration followed the demonstration, and toasts
were drunk to the remarkable new machine. Those spectators who had attended
the remarkable event spread the word about Dr. Guillotin's "daughter."
Enthusiastic words praising the new device as "a most distinguished project for
equality" were heard everywhere.

Precisely when the characteristic sloping blade was first introduced is not
known. Dr. Louis's original model called for a convex knife, as can be seen from
a number of engravings and prints from the period. An often-repeated story,
undoubtedly apocryphal, would have us believe that it was the king himself who
proposed the change. According to this account, the mechanically adroit Louis
XVI, whose hobby was locksmithing, heard of the experiments carried out at the
Bicêtre Hospital and asked Dr. Louis to show him the plans for the machine. In
his historical novel *The Drama of 1793* (1851), Alexandre Dumas *père* gives the
popular version of what then happened: "The King examined the drawings

carefully, and when his eye got to the blade: 'The fault is there,' he said, 'the blade should not be crescent-shaped but triangular, and beveled like a scythe.' And, to illustrate his point, Louis XVI took a pen in his hand and drew the instrument as he thought it ought to be. Nine months later, the head of the unhappy Louis XVI would be felled by the very instrument he had drawn." This ironic inversion of roles appealed to the popular imagination and led also to the spurious legend that Dr. Guillotin, who in fact survived the Terror and died at the age of seventy-six in 1812, was beheaded by his own device.

Now the machine was ready to begin its remarkable career which was to last almost two hundred years, during which it underwent only a few minor improvements and transformations. On April 25, 1792, a week after the successful rehearsal at the Bicêtre, the guillotine had its premiere with a live audience and live victim. A thief and assassin, Jacques Nicolas Pelletier, who had been waiting for three months to be executed, could now be done away with in accordance with the ideals of the Revolution.

The sensational news about the of execution spread like wildfire, and Parisians, always eager for novelties, flocked to see the machine. Taller and heavier than the modern guillotine, the instrument took two hours to mount, since all the parts had to be perfectly aligned and the executioner and his assistants lacked experience in such precise work. General Lafayette was in charge of the guard whose duty was to assure that no harm was done to the machine. The throngs at this premiere performance were disappointed—the execution was accomplished so quickly that it seemed nothing at all had happened. And Sanson, who had played such an important and terrifying role before, was unaccustomed to his insignificant part in the proceedings, which consisted simply of releasing a lever.

In the past, executions had derived their drama from the prolonged agony of the victims. Speed now was the keynote. Audiences had to adjust to a totally new kind of spectacle. The establishment of the Revolutionary Tribunals in late 1792 and early 1793 taught spectators how to watch this new style of execution. No longer "an instrument of justice, but the murderous weapon of political factions," the guillotine soon provided the most engrossing theatre in all of Europe.

*Place de la Révolution as depicted in* THE FRENCH REVOLUTION, *1989.*

# THE GUILLOTINE AND
# THE DEATH PENALTY AT THE TIME OF
# THE FRENCH REVOLUTION

*The guillotine decked out in tattered shrouds,*
*Tireless, waved up and down its steely hand,*
*And at each beck, the crowd grew lesser by a head.*
—*Juliusz Slowacki*, Kordian, *1834*

THE FRENCH REVOLUTION was a revolution against death. Its goal was to eliminate famine and starvation and to reduce the causes of dying to the irreducible minimum. If capital punishment could not yet be totally abolished, the revolutionaries argued, it must at least be made simple, quick, democratic, and as painless as possible. And as the embodiment of the people's justice, the guillotine was designed to regenerate society.

The drama of death on the public scaffold—always one of the most impressive state ceremonials—evolved an entirely new stagecraft. In a revolution which was itself highly theatrical and constantly described by both participants and spectators in terms of the stage, the most theatrical of all events were the guillotinings. Of course, the elements of theatrical performance have always been present in public executions. The scaffold is the stage, the executioner and his victim the principal actors (with assistants, confessors, and officials in supporting roles), and the mob is the audience. The inevitable denouement is anticipated from the very beginning in an almost classical form of suspense.

With the introduction of the guillotine, the nature of the ancient spectacle of public executions was entirely transformed. The cast of characters remained the same, but all the relationships were modified. Interest was no longer centered on the prolonged physical suffering of a fellow human; rather, it was the suddenness of death that provided the high drama. With groups of thirty or forty to dispatch at a single performance, quickness and precision in the service of a machine were required of all the participants. Each victim had to be led across the scaffold, placed on the plank, and slid into the neck collar at an accelerated pace, as if in a mechanical ballet.

The mechanization of death under the knife of the revolutionary guillotine, its novel technological artistry and syncopated choreography—these pure performance qualities of the guillotine were accentuated by the fact that the victims themselves were supremely conscious that they were playing a role before an audience. In revolutionary times the victims often sang, danced, and quipped in the face of the guillotine, formulating clever maxims and uttering memorable last words on their way across the scaffold. To reduce their fear of dying a violent, bloody death, these martyrs—whether doomed aristocrats or revolutionaries about to be liquidated by other revolutionaries— "performed" as though they were members of a theatrical troupe. Death became a splendid show.

## AN EYEWITNESS TO THE REIGN OF TERROR

One of the earliest eyewitness accounts of execution by guillotine in the days of the Revolution is that of J. G. Millingen, a British tourist who was in Paris at the height of the Terror in 1794. His description stresses the deft choreography of the event.

> Never can I forget the mournful appearance of these funereal processions to the place of execution. The march was opened by a detachment of mounted gendarmes—the carts followed; they were the same carts as those that are used in Paris for carrying wood; four boards were placed across them for seats, and on each board sat two, and sometimes three victims; their hands were tied behind their backs, and the constant jolting of the cart made them nod their heads up and down, to the great amusement of the spectators. On the front of the cart stood Sanson, the executioner, or one of his sons or assistants; gendarmes on foot marched by the side; there followed a hackney-coach, in which was the *Rapporteur* [reporter] and his clerk, whose duty it was to witness the execution, and then return to Fouquier-Tinville, the *Accusateur Public*, to report the execution of what they called the law.
>
> The process of execution was also a sad and heart-rending spectacle. In

the middle of the Place de la Révolution was erected a guillotine, in front of a colossal statue of Liberty, represented seated on a rock, a Phrygian cap on her head, a spear in her hand, the other reposing on a shield. On one side of the scaffold were drawn a sufficient number of carts, with large baskets painted red, to receive the heads and bodies of the victims. Those bearing the condemned moved on slowly to the foot of the guillotine; the culprits were led out in turn, and, if necessary, supported by two of the executioner's valets, as they were formerly called, but now denominated *élèves de l'exécuteur des hautes oeuvres de la justice* [pupils of the Grand High Executioner]; but their assistance was rarely required. Most of these unfortunates ascended the scaffold with a determined step—many of them looked up firmly on the menacing instrument of death, beholding for the last time the rays of the glorious sun, beaming on the polished axe; and I have seen some young men actually dance a few steps before they went up to be strapped to the perpendicular plane, which was then tilted to a horizontal plane in a moment, and then ran on the grooves until the neck was secured and closed by a moving board, when the head passed through what was called, in derision, *la lunette republicaine;* the weighty knife was then dropped with a heavy fall; and, with incredible dexterity and rapidity, two executioners tossed the body into the basket, while another threw the head after it.

## THE REVOLUTIONARY WAY OF DEATH

Attitudes toward death at the end of the eighteenth century help explain the concept of meeting one's end on the scaffold as a performance that defines character and reveals moral superiority. During the Revolution it was felt by members of all sides of the political spectrum that private life should be subordinate to the welfare of the nation. A public event and social manifestation, death was perpetually on display. All citizens, ready to act upon the slogan "Liberty or death," were potential heroes and martyrs. In both word and gesture, one had to show sovereign contempt for death, following the stoical example of the ancient Greeks and Romans.

"Great men do not die in their beds," declared Louis Antoine de Saint-Just. Willingness to lay down one's own life in defense of revolutionary or royalist ideals was the ultimate test. The omnipresence of the guillotine, ensuring that everyone's neck was at risk, conferred a certain grandeur to all the events of the Revolution.

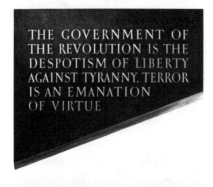

*Ian Hamilton Finlay, with*
*Nicholas Sloane. Detail,*
FOUR GUILLOTINE BLADES, *1987.*

As was the case with executions during the ancien régime, revolutionary guillotinings were national ceremonies which the public was expected to attend. By so doing, one showed approval of the elimination of enemies of the state and took warning from the meting out of swift punishment in these edifying spectacles. The crowds of men, women, and children who gathered around the scaffold came to judge the performances and even to admire the dazzling scaffold/stage presence of certain women such as Charlotte Corday, Lucile Desmoulins, and Madame Roland, even though they had been condemned as counterrevolutionaries.

When, however, the common-born Madame Du Barry grew terrified in the face of death, shrieked in the tumbril (the horse-drawn cart used to transport prisoners to the scaffold), begged the onlookers to save her, and struggled with the executioners on the scaffold, the hysterical former mistress of Louis XV drew attention to the reality of her terror and destroyed the theatrical illusion. Once the stoical rules of the game were broken, spectators began to pity Du Barry and even wished to call off the show planned for the abject victim, however deserving she was of her punishment. The painter Elisabeth Vigée-Lebrun speculates in her memoirs that the mobs might indeed have relented had the victims not played their roles so well.

Madame Du Barry . . . is the only woman, among all the women who perished during the dreadful days, who could not stand the sight of the scaffold. She screamed, she begged mercy of the horrible crowd that stood around the scaffold, she aroused them to such a point that the executioner grew anxious and hastened to complete his task. This convinced me that if the victims of these terrible times had not been so proud, had not met death with such courage, the Terror would have ended much earlier. Men of limited intelligence lack the imagination to be touched by inner suffering, and the populace is more easily stirred by pity than by admiration.

Killing and dying during the Revolution were carried out in the name of a higher principle—in the hope of creating something eternal. A death-defying performance made in defense of an ideal reflected belief in the ultimate authority of the state and its right to execute its enemies—even though in one's own case a terrible injustice had been committed. The appeal was to posterity; at stake was immortality. Those sent to the scaffold were convinced that it was possible to prove the justness of one's cause by dying well. And they performed not only for the spectators and for their oppressors, but for the sake of their fellow prisoners as well. Each word, gesture, and look was designed to give courage to those who would follow, to set an example and serve as a model. Such accomplished performances were neither spontaneous nor improvised; on the contrary, they were carefully rehearsed. Adjutant-General Boisguyon, who was "very much amused by the guillotine," told Sanson as he climbed into the tumbril, "Today's the actual performance: you'll be surprised how well I know my role."

SIMULATIONS: PLAY GUILLOTINE

In prison, the condemned often acted out their own deaths. Other prisoners took the roles of the Revolutionary Tribunal, playing judges, prosecutor, defendants, witnesses, and the executioner and his assistants. The accused always went to the guillotine (represented by a chair or a bed), hands tied behind the back. These guillotine games were meant to reduce fear of death and to insure a good performance on the scaffold. In Alfred de Vigny's *Stello* (1832), a novel about the Terror, these guillotine games are likened to the exercises of the ancient gladiators—the desire to learn to die with grace indicates just how deeply the Roman model was implanted in French culture. In *The French Revolution* (1837), Thomas Carlyle describes these rehearsals. "Recklessness, defiant levity, the Stoicism if not of strength yet of weakness, has possessed all hearts. Weak women and Ci-devants [former aristocrats], their locks not yet made into blond perukes, their skins not yet tanned into breeches, are accustomed to 'act the Guillotine' by way of pastime. In fantastic mummery, with towel-turbans, blanket-ermine, a mock Sanhedrin of Judges, a mock Tinville pleads; a culprit is doomed, is guillotined by the oversetting of two chairs." Carlyle alludes to the selling of the hair and skin of guillotine victims for making wigs and clothes—or so it was alleged in one of the persistent myths of the Revolution, which Carlyle several times refers to as a holocaust.

For young women prisoners, part of the game consisted of mounting the simulated scaffold and lying prone on the simulated plank without letting too much leg be exposed. As in the Gothic fiction of the time and the novels of the Marquis de Sade, death and eroticism were inextricably linked.

## RESURRECTED PRIESTS

A very different kind of guillotine simulation deceptive in nature and propagandistic in intent was practiced by the counterrevolutionary forces during the civil war that raged in La Vendée in 1793 and 1794. To convince the peasants that the royalist cause was divinely supported and to persuade them to fight more eagerly, the leaders produced priests with red lines around their necks whose severed heads, they claimed, had been miraculously replaced after being guillotined.

Of these peasants, Victor Hugo wrote in his novel *93*: "They could be made to believe anything; some priests showed them other priests whose necks they had reddened with a drawn cord, and said to them: 'These are the guillotined brought back to life.'" The reassemblage of separated heads and trunks became a proof of faith and the guillotine an instrument for demonstrating the infinite power of God. But, as we shall later see, it was not only peasants who believed that it might be possible to survive decapitation.

# GUILLOTINOMANIA

*One wore at the buttonhole of one's carmagnole, by way of a flower,*
*a little guillotine in gold, or else a small piece of a*
*guillotined person's heart.*
—*Vicomte François-René de Chateaubriand*, Memoirs, *1849*

FROM 1792 TO 1795 the guillotine reigned supreme in France, permeating every aspect of life and culture. It was a novelty, and the French in the late eighteenth century were enamored of the new. For some it was entertainment, for others a new religion. "Let us go see the red mass celebrated on the altar," said one of the worshipers of the scaffold. The ritual of spurting blood was powerful and hypnotic, a sort of subverted form of Christian liturgy. Indeed, the same fervor surrounded the guillotine as had previously been applied to the cross. The new cult that formed around the guillotine omitted the message of love and forgiveness its predecessor had carried, while retaining its fierce militancy in the extermination of unbelievers and enemies.

Reminiscent of the adoration of the ideal woman in courtly love or Catholic hagiography, those who had adopted the new revolutionary faith addressed their guiding spirit as "Most high and mighty Lady Guillotine" or "Sainte Guillotine." In a strange litany the worshipers implored the instrument of destruction to be their guardian.

*Eighteenth-century medallion*
*containing hair, stamped with*
*the bust of Chalier.*

*Sainte Guillotine, protector of patriots, pray for us!*
*Sainte Guillotine, scourge of aristocrats, protect us!*
*Amiable Machine, take pity on us!*
*Admirable Machine, take pity on us!*
*Sainte Guillotine, protect us from tyrants!*

## COMIC SONGS

From the very start, comic songs were written about the new machine and its supposed inventor. Dr. Guillotin could not go out into the street without hearing satirical couplets set to popular melodies that made light of his humanitarian impulse.

*I've created a machine*
*Tra la la la, la la la, la la, la la la, la la, la la la*
*Which takes heads off.*

Other songs were written as solos for a singer to be accompanied by guillotine, such as the verses for her final appearance in the tumbril written by the Comédie Française actress, Louise Contat (who, in fact, was saved at the last moment by Robespierre's downfall).

*I'm going to climb the scaffold—*
*'Tis only a change of theatres.*

There were also the love songs extolling the machine.

*The sweet guillotine*
*With its seductive way!*

And there was the "Marseillaise of the Guillotine," to be sung to the melody of "Allons, enfants de la Patrie."

*Oh, thou, charming guillotine,*
*You shorten kings and queens;*
*By your influence divine,*

*We have reconquered our rights.*
*Come to aid of the Country*
*And let your superb instrument*
*Become forever permanent*
*To destroy the impious sect.*
*Sharpen your razor for Pitt and his agents*
*Fill your divine sack with heads of tyrants.*

Even at the height of the Terror, reverence for the guillotine was far from universal, and some songwriters treated both the machine and its operator with ironic playfulness.

*Behold Sanson's vast intelligence!*
*With the blade he has killed everyone off.*
*In this frightful fix what will become of him?*
*He guillotines himself!*

A well-known caricature of the period showing Sanson on the plank releasing the guillotine's blade above his own neck illustrated the scene.

A savage song, "The Ambulatory Guillotine" praises the detachments of the revolutionary army that traveled about France with a portable "Widow," enforcing the harsh laws against speculation and price gouging.

*At last order is restored,*
*There's no more resisting;*
*Cursed hoarding cheats,*
*Piss, piss away in fear,*
*Make way for the guillotine.*
*The guillotine will go everywhere,*
*For those who hoard and cheat.*

*The heads will dance the way heads should,*
*Four by four on the scaffold,*
*Sellers of salt and tobacco*
*Find the blow cruel.*
*Make way for the guillotine.*

*Anonymous. Satirical etching of Sanson beheading himself, late eighteenth century.*

Other songs celebrate the vogue of the new machine as a fashionable knick-knack.

> *The guillotine is a jewel*
> *Today so à la mode,*
> *I'd like one in mahogany*
> *To set on my chest of drawers.*

And there were popular rounds of a nonsensical kind.

> *When I've been guillotined*
> *I'll have no further use of a nose!*

Revolutionaries condemned as traitors, profiteers, and collaborators with the English often went to their deaths singing the "Marseillaise" as proof of their dedication to the cause and the injustice of their sentence. Perhaps the most unusual guillotine chorus was a group of sixteen Carmelite nuns from Compiègne, who in July 1794 went to the scaffold singing "Salve Regina" and "Veni Creator." Gertrud von le Fort's treatment of the subject in the German novella *The Song at the Scaffold* (1936) became the basis of a film scenario by Georges Bernanos, *Dialogue of the Carmelites*, which eventually became a play, a film, and most significantly, the libretto of Francis Poulenc's famous opera (1957).

## PLACE DE LA REVOLUTION

In the place de la Révolution vendors hawked their guillotine mementos around the scaffold. There were special pamphlets listing the schedule of those who were to be guillotined—programs of coming events. One of these displayed heads on the cover along with the motto "Go to it, Lady Guillotine, give a close shave to all those enemies of the Country!" Another called itself a "list of the winners in the Sainte Guillotine lottery."

Connoisseurs knew that the best seats for the spectacle at the place de la Révolution were at the end of the Jardin des Tuileries. Some regulars returned every day, and parents often brought their children. An enterprising restaurateur called his establishment the Cabaret de la Guillotine; on the back of the menu each day he listed the "catch of the day" to be served up to the Widow.

*P. A. de Machy and studio. Execution on the*
*place de la Révolution, late eighteenth century.*

The guillotine, instead of the gallows, became a standard prop in the marionette theatres of the Champs-Elysées, and the provocatively titled comedy-
vaudeville *The Guillotine of Love* was a popular favorite. The stylish machine
was used as an emblem on tobacco pouches and seals—even official ones.

Fashionable salons displayed charming miniature guillotines made of
mahogany that were to be brought to the table at mealtimes and used for slicing
bread or fruit. Little dolls resembling one's enemies were sometimes decapitated at dessert; out spilled a red liquid into which the ladies dipped their handkerchiefs—the doll was actually a flask and the "blood" an amber-colored
perfume or liqueur.

Toward the end of the Terror the number of spectators at executions fell
drastically. Audiences grew bored and lost their taste for what began to seem
like the same old thing. Still, the victims often found occasions to display their
wit. The aging Baron Franz von der Trenck—popularly known as the Austrian
Casanova—was a colorful eighteenth-century aristocratic adventurer who made
the mistake of returning to Paris during the Terror and ended up in one of the
last groups to be executed, along with the poet André de Chénier, two days
before the fall of Robespierre. Looking out from the tumbril at the grave expressions of the onlookers on the sidewalk, Trenck called out jovially, "Why look so
grim? We're only performing a hackneyed Robespierrian comedy!"

## GOETHE ORDERS A TOY GUILLOTINE

*von*

In 1793 Johann Wolfgang Goethe, who hated and feared the Revolution, was a guest of the Duke of Brunswick and the Prussian forces engaged in driving out the invading French army. During this campaign the author of *Faust* wrote to his mother in Frankfurt, asking her to buy a toy guillotine for his five-year-old son, August. Standing two feet high, the toys were then all the rage, and dolls, live birds, or mice were the preferred victims in games with these deadly little machines. In Arras, Robespierre's birthplace, an ordinance was passed outlawing the toy on the grounds that it would make children ferocious and bloodthirsty. French prisoners of war made them and sold them to the Prussians; it may be one of these models that Goethe had seen. But his mother, who was caring for the child, indignantly refused. On December 23, 1793, Elisabeth Goethe wrote:

Dear Son,

I'll do anything to please you and do it with great pleasure, but to buy a miniature model of the infamous guillotine as a plaything for the baby—no, I won't do that at any price. If I had a say in the government, the manufacturers of this toy would themselves be put under the guillotine and I would have the machine itself publicly burned. What!—Let children play with anything so revolting and make them think of murder and bloodshed as a game, Oh no, not as far as I am concerned.

A pioneering opponent of toys that teach violence, Goethe's remarkable mother may well have been the first to call for the public burning of the guillotine. No puritanical spoilsport, however, she openly approved of her son's union with August's mother, Christiane Vulpius (whom the poet did not marry for a number of years after August's birth), referring to her as Goethe's "bed treasure." It is not known whether young August ever received his toy guillotine.

## EXTENDING THE REACH OF THE GUILLOTINE

In their desire to have the guillotine "travel everywhere," the fanatical apostles of the new machine, convinced of its beneficial effects, were not content to use it merely in the here and now; they wanted to extend its reach beyond the bounds of time and space, even beyond the confines of this world. To reject the hated past of superstition and tyranny, these zealots guillotined

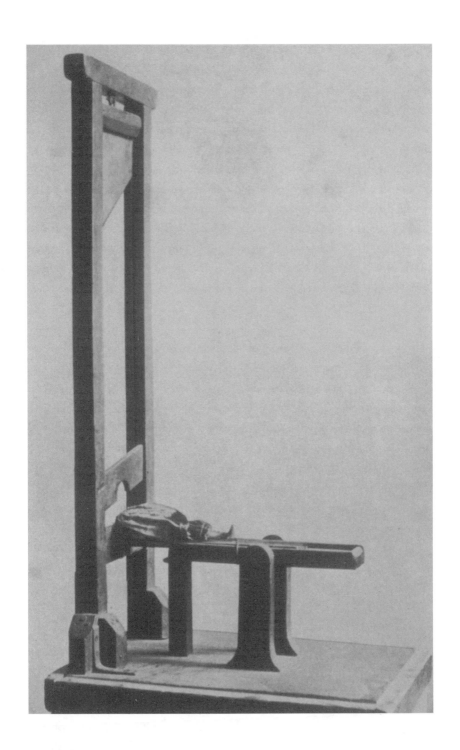

*German toy guillotine, c. 1794.*

wooden figures of cathedral saints, as well as effigies of former monarchs. To get revenge against treacherous aristocrats who had escaped abroad, an incensed schoolteacher built dummies of notorious émigrés and had them decapitated for the edification of his pupils.

The most remarkable instance of the extension of revolutionary justice was the guillotining of the corpses of those who had committed suicide in order to escape being guillotined. Rather than go to the scaffold, the Girondist Charles Valazé plunged a dagger into his heart when he was condemned to die. His dead body was nevertheless propped up on a bench in the tumbril between two other condemned prisoners. Already livid, head hanging down, Valazé's cadaver bounced up and down grotesquely in the journey over the cobblestones. When the tumbril reached the scaffold, his corpse was taken out first, walked up the steps by the assistant executioners, and led to the guillotine, where the lifeless body was beheaded.

Robespierre's loyal follower Philippe Le Bas blew his brains out with a revolver but was guillotined just the same along with his master. This practice continued until at least 1800, when as recounted in Dumas *père*'s historical novel *The Company of Jehu* (1857), four members of a royalist band of outlaws were decapitated, even though three had already committed suicide. To prevent such attempts to cheat the decapitating machine of its live victims, prisoners condemned to die were under constant surveillance, fettered with chains (a practice abandoned only in 1951 after André Cayatte's film *We Are All Murderers*), and throughout most of the nineteenth century, bound in straitjackets that totally immobilized their arms. One such prisoner almost succeeded in cutting her throat, but doctors rushed to the prison and managed to sew up the wound so that the decapitation could proceed. It seemed as though the forfeited life of every condemned prisoner was something sacred; each moment was jealously guarded until the state decided that it was time to exact vengeance.

## EXPORTING THE GUILLOTINE

Ideas of Liberty, Equality, and Fraternity were not the only exports of the Revolution. The guillotine went wherever the revolutionary armies brought French culture and civilization. The new beheading machine was introduced to the West Indies in 1794 and to Belgium in 1796, when parts of that country were annexed by France. Soon the instrument was in use in Northern Italy and in a number of German states, where it continued to be used through the reign of the Third Reich and even shortly after World War II. There is at least one recorded instance of a guillotining in Greece in 1833. In 1859 a guillotine was shipped from Martinique first to Miquelon and then to Saint Pierre, two tiny French islands off Newfoundland.

In the nineteenth-century world market there was profit to be made from the manufacture of French guillotines for overseas sales. A well-crafted Parisian export item, the guillotine enjoyed an international reputation. Guillotines for export were tested on straw men by the famous executioner Louis Deibler, then given his seal of approval. What better guarantee than having been vouched for by "Monsieur de Paris," the official French executioner?

Visiting heads of state and foreign officials came to watch demonstrations and place orders. In 1910 Chinese functionaries ordered a guillotine, which was delivered the next year and apparently put into service. The Shah of Persia witnessed a guillotining that was over so quickly that he asked if it could be done again. According to the aphorist Georg Lichtenberg, Sweden, a country much influenced by French culture, had something similar to a guillotine as early as 1793, and the last Swedish execution to take place was the public guillotining in Stockholm of Alfred Anders on November 23, 1910.

In France itself the guillotine was sent from the capital, where it had been invented and first put into service, to every corner of the country and to all the colonies and territories. Executions by guillotine took place in Algeria and Madagascar through the 1950s until those countries achieved independence.

## THE GUILLOTINE ON PATRIOTIC TOUR

It was not in Paris but in the provinces that the most bizarre events took place during the Terror. Deranged and unsavory characters spawned by the Revolution had the greatest liberty to realize their destructive fantasies in the countryside, where they could operate free of supervision or control. Everywhere the revolutionary army units went, they took the guillotine on "patriotic tour," and special emissaries introduced the fatal machine to small, unsuspecting communities. The arrival of the instrument of justice in a special wagon—dismounted and covered with a canvas—was like the arrival of a macabre circus caravan come to transform the existence of these sleepy provincial towns into a nightmare.

In some cases what happened was so extraordinary that the line between the authentic and the fictional seems impossible to establish. Sober historical narrative becomes a fantastic tale, the real seems hallucinatory. Such is the story of the "Marat of Strasbourg," Euloge Schneider. In this realm of the demented and the diabolic, there is no better guide than Charles Nodier, one of the pioneers of French romanticism and a proponent of Gothic horror who was haunted by fear of the guillotine. He created what he called "the true fantastic story" on the basis of his experience of the Revolution.

In his memoirs, Nodier recounts how in 1794 his father sent him as a precocious fourteen-year-old to study Greek in Strasbourg with Schneider, an eminent German classical scholar who had been professor at the University of Bonn, and formerly a monk, but who had given up the church and come to France because of his passionate devotion to the Revolution. The renegade priest— ugly, stout, roundheaded with enormous bushy eyebrows—became public prosecutor of the Revolutionary Tribunal at Strasbourg where he headed the extreme radical party La Propagande, which considered Robespierre and Saint-Just to be guilty of counterrevolutionary moderation. Schneider greeted the arrival of the decapitating machine in joyful verse: "Oh, Guillotine dear, how welcome you are here!"

The defrocked priest and his "hussars of death"—with crossbones on their shakos, rows of white braid on their jackets resembling ribs, skulls on their pouches—traveled about Alsace with a nomadic scaffold and put to death anyone who during the recent Austrian invasion had had anything to do with the occupiers. These reprisals were called "national vengeance." Parading his guillotine through the streets, the ex-monk all the while conducted innumerable love affairs and lived sybaritically, defying the Spartan rule of Robespierre and Saint-Just.

Nodier recalls his first view of the guillotine, when as a terrified youngster he saw it used on an eighty-year-old woman who had committed the crime of giving bread and water to a hungry Austrian soldier. Immediately thereafter the smartly uniformed members of La Propagande arrived, scattering the petrified crowd of onlookers. The orator of the brigade knelt down before the scaffold, then rose to his feet, and turning toward the spectators, in the name of liberty gave a long panegyric on the guillotine in such elegant and horrifying terms that the boy felt cold sweat running down his face. Nodier was never able to forget the fanatical procession of this new sect, which took the executioner for its pontiff and the guillotine for its altar.

Schneider continued on his forays, levying forced loans, encouraging citizens to denounce their neighbors, exacting heads, and earning the reputation of a ghoul and vampire. Convinced that he must marry to obliterate from public memory his clerical past, the ex-priest selected as his bride Clotilde de Brumpt, the beautiful daughter of the wealthiest aristocrat in Strasbourg. When he came to ask Count de Brumpt for his daughter's hand, Schneider had his guillotine, bedecked with flowers and ribbons, set up outside the window—a rather effective means to persuade his future father-in-law not to withhold his blessing. The choice was simple: the altar for Clotilde or the scaffold for the count.

In the wedding procession, the bridegroom was surrounded by his elite guard brandishing sabers, followed by the portable guillotine and two burly assistant executioners. Pale, thin, and grave, the executioner Maître Nicolas followed in his special carriage.

Learning that Saint-Just was in town, Schneider—arrogant in his triumph—directed the wedding cortege to the house where the representative of the people was staying. Saint-Just, who in fact had come to Strasbourg expressly to discipline Schneider for his violation of orders, listened in astonishment as the bride, suddenly safe in the presence of Saint-Just, unexpectedly denounced her loathsome husband's monstrous abuses of power. Producing a dagger from her bosom, she declared, in obvious imitation of Jean-Paul Marat's assassin, Charlotte Corday, that she would have killed the "Marat of Strasbourg" that night in bed if justice could not be obtained.

When even the executioner testified that Schneider had ordered him to be prepared to kill the father of the *jungfrau* if Clotilde had not agreed to the marriage, Saint-Just instantly ordered the bridegroom sent to the guillotine. Having actually witnessed Schneider's humiliation, Nodier describes how the executioner's two assistants in black blouses, who only a moment before had been devoted henchmen, now seized the ex-priest. The procession to the scaffold was led by the executioner, and two of the hussars of death followed behind, laughing and poking Schneider with their sabers to quicken his pace.

The young boy shuddered as he watched his teacher suffer public abuse, yet he could not avert his gaze. Schneider's small eyes had sunk into their sockets and his pallor was frightful; he kept wiping the sweat off his brow. As the former public prosecutor was forced to mount his own guillotine, the jeering crowd grew livelier. Suddenly, total silence fell. The child Nodier was too small to see what was happening. Fearing that his tutor's head was about to fall, he

*Anonymous.* EULOGE SCHNEIDER, *late eighteenth century.*

looked up to make sure the blade still hung suspended in the instrument of death. Someone explained to the boy that Schneider had been stripped of his cockade, his hat, and his uniform until he stood shivering in the cold rain. A cry rose from the crowd—Schneider had been placed under the knife. But after enduring humiliation before the taunting crowd, he was spared immediate execution because Saint-Just realized that he did not have the power to pass such a summary death sentence.

Sent to Paris, Schneider was thrown into prison, then tried, sentenced, and executed on April 1, 1794, for extortion, abuse of power, and violation of the honor, fortune, and tranquillity of decent families. Robespierre called Schneider a man "whose crazy tyranny renders credible all that is recorded of Caligula or Heliogabalus." But the ex-monk was not without admirers, and reputedly he was mourned by a number of aging ladies of Strasbourg well into the middle of the nineteenth century.

Drawing on the published memoirs of Nodier as well as information provided by him in lengthy private conversations, Alexandre Dumas *père* wrote the story of Euloge Schneider and the young Charles Nodier in his novel *The Whites and the Blues* (1867). Dumas's own dramatization of the novel was performed at the famous Parisian melodrama house le Châtelet in 1869, and adapted and staged by Pierre Lagueunière and the Comédiens de la Conciergerie in 1986.

## THE MARQUIS DE SADE:
### PLAYWRIGHT, NOVELIST, AND GUILLOTINOPHOBE

After he was released from prison in 1790 by the new republican government, the Marquis de Sade became an ardent revolutionary and patriot, delivering passionate speeches demanding power for the people. The notorious libertine hoped thus to divert attention from his suspicious past. When reminded of his noble background, the ex-Marquis replied indignantly that he was the son of poor peasants and had always been known as merely Louis Sade.

As punishment for his offenses against public morality, the ancien régime had kept Sade prisoner in the Bastille for five years (after he had already spent six years imprisoned in the dungeon of Vincennes), but the Marquis's deepest fear and hatred was of the revolutionary totalitarianism maintained by the guillotine. Arrested in 1793 as a former aristocrat and accused of "moderatism," the Marquis saw his name appear on the list of those destined for the guillotine. He was spared the scaffold only by the fall of Robespierre. During his imprisonment under the Reign of Terror, Sade recorded his revulsion at the carnage. Of his incarceration in 1794 in the former convent at Coignart, he wrote: "Paradise on earth; beautiful house, superb garden, exclusive society, wonderful women, when suddenly the execution grounds were placed absolutely under our windows and the cemetery for those guillotined put in the very middle of our garden. We have buried eighteen hundred of these in thirty-five days, a third of them from our unfortunate house." And later he complained, "My detention by the state with the guillotine right before my eyes did me a hundred times more harm than all imaginable Bastilles."

The perverse novels of persecuted virtue and cruel victimization that the Marquis wrote both before and after his release from jail in 1794 became a major—although often unacknowledged—inspiration for the Gothic and macabre tales of the nineteenth century. In 1801 he was arrested for obscenity and confined to the Charenton insane asylum for the rest of his life. The shadow of the guillotine was never to stop haunting the Marquis.

## TWO TALES OF TRANSFORMATION BY THE GUILLOTINE

The twentieth-century Polish author Wlodzimierz Pazniewski recorded the
story of a clown who turned executioner when the Revolution came to the town
of Chinon in central France. According to Henryk Elzenberg, Pazniewski's former professor, the source is to be found in a genuine local chronicle. Like
Nodier's recounting of his experiences of the Revolution, Pazniewski's story
could be said to be a "true fantastic tale."

The Revolutionary emissaries sent from Paris failed to incite the easygoing
inhabitants of Chinon to action in the name of liberty, but the members of a
touring circus then performing in the town rose to the challenge and established a revolutionary tribunal headed by their clown. When the local residents
saw the former clown as the new public prosecutor elegantly dressed in clothes
confiscated from the aristocracy, they laughed derisively, forgetting that revolutionaries are singularly devoid of humor. The laughter stopped when the first
death sentences were passed.

The ex-clown's enthusiasm for carrying out executions was so great that a
second guillotine had to be borrowed from a neighboring town. The most important order of business was the settling of personal accounts, and it hardly came
as a surprise that one of the first heads to roll was that of the circus owner. The
clown-prosecutor became known as the "Flame of Revolution," and before long
the fire burned so intensely that he himself was consumed by it. Within a year of
his ascendence to power, the clown went from being the Flame of Revolution to
a hated enemy of the people and was finally condemned to the guillotine. For
his appearance on the scaffold he was put back into his old clown suit with its
huge floppy boots and comically baggy pants that he had to hold up with one
hand. He was led to the scaffold amidst a crowd of people who seemed to be
having the time of their lives. When the unmistakable clang of the blade
sounded, well-deserved applause rose from the crowd. The clown had never
given a better performance.

A second tale of transformation through the guillotine is unquestionably
historically authentic. Joseph Le Bon, born in Arras (Robespierre's hometown)
in 1765, had begun his career as a village priest when he became inflamed by
revolutionary ideology. He was the first priest to marry and renounce his religious calling for the flamboyant life of an apostle of the guillotine. He was sent
as special emissary to Cambrai in northern France. Wearing a gaudy yellow

*Poirer de Dunckerque.* LES FORMES ACERBES.
*Etching depicting Joseph Le Bon, late eighteenth century.*

outfit and hat crowned with large red, white, and blue plumes, he set up a guillotine in the town square and set to work decapitating victims. His wife Mimie—who was also his cousin—loved to watch executions. She was rumored, in fact, to have been sexually excited by the witnessing of the guillotining of the many pretty young women who had first passed through her husband's bed. The revolutionary tribunal established by the former priest in Arras had as its prominent members his brother-in-law, three uncles, and his wife. After Robespierre's fall, Le Bon was finally arrested for his bloodthirsty exploits and sent to the guillotine himself in 1795.

### HESPEL THE JACKAL, OR THE EXECUTIONER EXECUTED

Yet another variant on the classic ironic tale of the executioner executed comes from the French penal colonies in more recent times. Devil's Island off the coast of French Guiana, the notorious "dry guillotine," or place of harsh exile, had its own decapitating machine and its own court of justice that invariably passed the death sentence for the crime of murder. There a prisoner was made to carry out the executions, and Hespel the Jackal, responsible for cutting off more than thirty heads, was the cruelest executioner ever known in the history of that colony. But for killing a prison guard during an attempted escape, the Jackal was condemned to death.

The night before the sentence was to be carried out, tension ran high in the compound. In the early hours of the morning, the Jackal's former assistant, now the new executioner, was testing the machine by letting the blade fall. One account asserts that the Jackal himself was allowed to set up the machine, as a last tribute to his past services. Reputedly, he turned to his former aide and said, "You see now the executioner becomes executed! My predecessor also at last gave his head to the Widow! Be careful, some day will come your turn!" And after a slight pause, he saluted his executioner and added, "Do it neatly, mon enfant, just like I showed you how the job should be done." And in a moment the Jackal's head fell into the basket that he had so often filled with others' heads.

## DANCING THE GUILLOTINE AWAY: THE VICTIMS' BALLS

The reaction to the fall of Robespierre and the end of the Terror was extreme. As soon as the mass executions ceased, the heavy atmosphere of austerity and repression suddenly lifted. Pleasure and amusement once again became legitimate pursuits, and the French were seized by a mad desire to live life to its fullest. No longer forced to conceal their acquisitiveness, entrepreneurs and profiteers making fortunes from the war against Prussia, England, and Austria displayed their wealth as ostentatiously as possible.

To the celebrated "gilded youth" of these years, life became an extended round of parties. In their *Histoire de la société française pendant le Directoire* (1855), Edmond and Jules Goncourt point out that whereas the Revolution had been marked by spirited singing, during the Thermidorian reaction everyone danced. They danced to forget the bloody past and to avoid thinking about the future. They danced away their tears, and they danced off their garments of mourning. The sons and daughters of executed victims danced with one another, and these orphans danced as well with the sons and daughters of those who had sent their parents to the guillotine.

Paris was one vast indiscriminate orgy of dancing, with a ball on every street corner and over 650 establishments devoted to all-night revelry. At the Bal des

*French model guillotine carved by a prisoner.*

Zephyrs in the former cemetery of Saint Sulpice, couples waltzed on grave-stones—delighting in the erotic new dance imported from Germany. In fashionable society, the most popular of all diversions was the exclusive "victims' ball." To be allowed to attend one had to have lost to the guillotine a close relative: a father or mother, a husband or wife, a brother or sister—a cousin would not do. Eagerness to attend the victims' balls was so great that unqualified Parisians paid to have documents forged to certify their loss of a close relative. Hairstyles and dresses *à la victime* became the latest mode. The women at these galas wore their hair up, exposing their necks, around which was tied a thin red ribbon to simulate the blade mark. Men wore their hair cut close at the nape of the neck, making room for a similar telltale crimson thread. The dancers saluted their partners with an abrupt drop of the head—as though it had been freshly cut off.

A year or two earlier in the revolutionary prisons, their parents—while waiting to be executed—had staged mock ceremonies of the guillotine in anticipation of the real thing; now their children acted out retrospectively the drama of the scaffold. Some viewed the victims' balls as the undignified antics of spoiled young people who, spared the horrors of the previous generation, sought thrills in a garish masquerade that parodied the agonies of the Terror. But perhaps it is just as fair to regard these macabre and erotic rituals as a means for survivors to express and come to terms with their grief over executed relatives, and thus to be symbolically initiated into the ranks of the guillotined. Perhaps the victims' ball was a frenzied dance of appeasement designed to lay to rest the ghosts of a terrifying past.

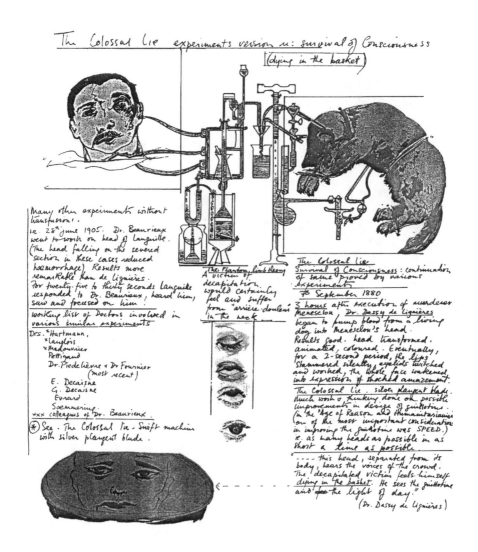

The Colossal Lie experiments version ш: survival of Consciousness
(dying in the basket)

Many other experiments without transfusion.
i.e. 28th June 1905. Dr. Beaurieux went to work on head of Languille. (The head falling on the severed section in these cases reduced haemorrhage). Results more remarkable than de Lignières. For twenty-five to thirty seconds Languille responded to Dr. Beaurieux, heard him, saw and focused on him.

working list of Doctors involved in various similar experiments

Drs. *Hartmann,
*Lauglois
*Medouvier
Pettigand
Dr. Piedelièvre + Dr. Fournier (most recent)
E. Decaisne
G. Decaisne
Evrard
Soemmering.
xxx colleagues of Dr. Beaurieux.

(*) See · The Colossal Lie - Swift machine with silver plangent blade.

The Phantom limb theory
A victim of decapitation would certainly feel and suffer from "arrière-douleur" in the neck

The Colossal lie
Survival of Consciousness: continuation of same proved by various experiments
7th September 1880
3 hours after execution of murderer Menesclou Dr. Dassy de Lignières began to pump blood from a living dog into Menesclou's head. Results good. head transformed. animated, coloured. Eventually, for a 2-second period, the lips stammered silently eyelids twitched and worked, the whole face wakened into expression of shocked amazement.

The Colossal lie · silver plangent blade. Much work & thinking done on possible improvements in design of guillotine. (In the 'Age of Reason and Humanitarianism (one of the most important considerations in improving the guillotine was SPEED.) × as many heads as possible in as short a time as possible.

"---- this head, separated from its body, hears the voices of the crowd. The decapitated victim feels himself dying in the basket. He sees the guillotine and the light of day."
(Dr. Dassy de Lignières)

*Cozette De Charmoy.* THE COLOSSAL LIE—EXPERIMENTS VERSION, *1973.*

# TALKING HEADS
# AND WALKING TRUNKS

*The guillotine is one of the most horrible and*
*most inhumane kinds of death that has ever been invented.*
—*Dr. Séguret, at the time of the Revolution*

VIRTUALLY UPON THE introduction of the guillotine there arose a widespread medical controversy over the question of the survival of feeling and consciousness in the separated heads and bodies of the newly executed. The debate over whether or not the head and trunk of an executed victim instantly cease to live after decapitation goes back at least to the time of Aristotle and has inspired numerous legends and horror stories in the folklore of many nations.

Although a treatise on the subject of the survival of consciousness in severed heads was written by Dr. Pierre Gautier in 1767, the modern scientific controversy did not really begin until the Revolution. Previously, when decapitation had been effected by sword or axe, there had been little concern about the suffering of the victim. But the introduction of a new death machine designed to eliminate pain brought a sense of urgency to the issue. The guillotine was either, as its proponents claimed, the most humane instrument of death, or the most diabolic torture ever devised.

Intense research undertaken by anatomists and physiologists led to strange and often ghoulish experiments and the formulation of bizarre theories, and ultimately these men of science produced a vast amount of "scholarly" literature that is sometimes hardly possible to distinguish from horror literature or science fiction. At first, informal investigations were done on the scaffold during the Terror. Famous among these was the July 17, 1793, incident when the assistant executioner François Le Gros, a pro-Marat carpenter, slapped the cheek of Charlotte Corday as her severed head was held aloft for the crowd to see. Those present asserted that "both cheeks reddened perceptibly" and that the head "showed in its countenance the most unequivocal signs of indignation."

Another anecdote, allegedly from the executioner Sanson, describes a grimly tenacious willpower. It is said that when the severed heads of rival members of the National Assembly who had been executed together were placed in the same sack, one bit the other so fiercely that it was impossible to separate them. Stories abound of winking eyes, blinking eyelids, and headless corpses stumbling across the scaffold.

In 1795 the German anatomist and scholar Samuel-Thomas Sommering maintained that execution by guillotine must be a horrible way to die, since "the personality, the ego remain alive for some time in the head which has been separated from the victim's body." He theorized that the decapitated head would talk if artificial lungs were to be attached to it. Dr. Jean-Joseph Sue (father of the novelist Eugène Sue) went even further, arguing that not only the head suffered, but that sensation remained alive in the arms and legs and inner organs of the body as well. Other medical authorities attempted to rebut all such contentions, accusing their opponents of inciting terror in the public about the new machine, which they considered to be antisocial activity, and claiming that of all forms of capital punishment the guillotine was the most merciful and painless.

Research was conducted internationally, in France, Germany, and England. Dr. Séguret, a professor of anatomy in France, was asked at the time of the Revolution to conduct experiments on the effects of the guillotine. He reported his investigations conducted on corpses sent to his laboratory:

> We exposed two heads to the sun's rays and we opened the eyelids. The eyelids promptly closed, of their own accord, and with an aliveness that was both abrupt and startling. The entire face then assumed an expression of intense suffering. One of these heads had an open mouth from which the tongue protruded. When a student in the surgery decided to prick the tongue with the point of his lancet, it withdrew into the mouth and the facial features grimaced as if in pain. Another of the guillotine's victims, an assassin called Terier, was subjected to similar tests, and more than a quarter hour after decapitation, his eyes turned in the direction of the man who was speaking.

*The heads of Auguste and Abel Pollet, executed January 11, 1909.*

In 1836 the infamous murderer Pierre-François Lacenaire on the eve of his execution made an agreement with Dr. Lelut of the Bicêtre to try to prove the survival of consciousness after decapitation. Lacenaire agreed that after his execution he would close his left eye but leave the right one open. Dr. Lelut observed the severed head of the executed criminal for some time, but he was unable to detect movement of any kind in its features. The experiment failed.

Dr. G. Decaisne and Dr. Evrard witnessed the 1879 execution of a murderer named Théotime Prunier and afterward recorded that "the eyes were closed. If one half-opened the lids, the eyeball was seen to be fixed and sunken. The pupils were equal in size and somewhat dilated. The face was pale, dull, completely bloodless." The doctors next pinched Prunier on the cheek, inserted a brush steeped in ammonia into his nostrils, and held a lighted candle close to his eyes, but not the slightest movement or contraction took place.

A year later the most notorious of all the experiments with guillotined corpses took place. Three hours after the execution of Louis Menesclou, a child rapist and murderer, Dr. Dassy de Lignières had blood pumped from a living dog into his decapitated head. As the blood flowed from the dog into the head, the murderer's face reddened, the lips swelled. "This head is about to speak. . . ." announced Dr. de Lignières. And indeed for a period of two seconds, the lips trembled, the eyelids twitched. The doctor drew grim conclusions about the guillotine. "There is no worse torture than decapitation with the machine invented by that sensitive deputy, Dr. Guillotin. . . . When the knife has done its work, has fallen with that sinister noise which you know, when the head has rolled into the sawdust . . . this head, separated from its body, hears the voices of the crowd. The decapitated victim feels himself dying in the basket. He sees the guillotine and the light of the day."

Menesclou's head returned to its state of rigid immobility without uttering a word; the dog survived unharmed. Dr. Lignières concluded his experiment with the proposal that the executioner immediately shake the head of the victim in the air—as had been done in the public displays during the Revolution—to assure that the blood would flow out and reduce the danger of prolonged suffering.

In 1905, when Dr. Beaurieux addressed the head of a recently executed prisoner by calling his name: "Languille!" the head first responded by opening wide both eyelids and focusing its pupils on the doctor. Beaurieux called his name again, and this time, according to the doctor's report, the head was even more responsive. "The eyelids lifted and undeniably living eyes fixed themselves on mine with perhaps even more penetration than the first time." The head failed to respond, however, to a third try, and "the whole thing lasted twenty-five to thirty seconds."

By the end of the nineteenth century there was an outcry against these nightmarish experiments conducted in the name of science. A critic of these hallucinatory and sinister attempts at revivification argued, "The cruelest of executioners who burns, torments with pincers, and turns on the wheel is a dove in comparison with the scientist who plays with these bloody heads. The law says: no torture may be used on the condemned. No doubt the legislator could not have foreseen that the ingenuity of a physiologist would go as far as torturing a dead person. This decapitated human being has paid his debt. No one has the right to make him pay a second time."

These ghoulish experiments provided later nineteenth-century literature and popular culture with images of learned doctors and scholars examining bloody severed heads, poking them and imploring them to speak or at least wink. Tales by Dumas *père* and Villiers de l'Isle Adam transform such authentically weird instances of medical science into fantastic fiction. The *chansonnier* of the Chat Noir nightclub in Paris, Jules Jouy wrote a song that poses the question of the survival of consciousness, using as his model Pranzini, the celebrated criminal who went to the guillotine in 1887 for murdering two women and a little girl:

*Eh! Pranzini! Tell me now*

*Do you suffer when you've lost your head?*

*Eh! Old pal! Answer me now*

*Do you suffer when you've lost your torso?*

*No, old pal, I won't answer you*

*Your question is really too dumb*

*No! Old pal! All I can say is*

*Have your own head cut off,*

*you'll find out for yourself!*

*Anonymous. Illustration of a scene from*
THE MAN WHO KILLED DEATH
*by René Berton, 1928.*

The theatre of the Grand Guignol embraced these demented doctors and their sinister experiments. In *The Man Who Killed Death* (1928) by René Berton, the celebrated medical scientist Professor Fargus has devised an apparatus to determine whether the severed head retains consciousness. When a bloody head is rushed to him by prison guards immediately after the execution, Fargus places the head on a steel table and attaches electrodes to stimulate brain activity. Then he injects cow's blood into the arteries. The eyes and mouth begin to move. The prosecuting attorney asks whether or not he was guilty of the crime for which he was guillotined. The head replies "No!" The prosecuting attorney goes mad.

As late as 1956 experiments were still being conducted as the battle over capital punishment continued. In a report to the Academy of Medicine, Doctors Piedelièvre and Fournier, on the basis of their examination of guillotined bodies, declared, "Every vital element survives decapitation. The doctor is left with the impression of a horrible experience, of a murderous vivisection, followed by a premature burial." Although the scientific evidence remains inconclusive, the case has long since been decided in the popular imagination—consciousness survives decapitation.

*Guillotining in France, 1902.*

# THE RISE AND FALL OF
# A TRADITION

*Since the invention of the guillotine, my father and I merely supervise.*
*Everything's done by our assistants.*
—*Henri Sanson, son of the Great Sanson*

MANY NINETEENTH-CENTURY Americans on grand tours to Europe tried to take in at least one guillotining during their travels. Henry Wikoff felt himself singularly lucky to be in Paris in January 1836 when the Corsican conspirator Giuseppi Fieschi and his two accomplices were scheduled to be executed for the attempted assassination of Louis Philippe. In the attempt, eighteen people were killed and 142 wounded by an infernal machine, which consisted of a horizontal row of twenty-four rifles, the barrels of which were aimed from low to high, so as to increase the chances of hitting the king when he appeared. Because of the enormity of the crime the twenty-three-year-old American tourist was determined to watch the "odious malefactors" receive their "deserved punishment." Wikoff described the event.

The only means that occurred to me to ascertain when the sentence would be carried out was to employ a man to pass the night at the Barrière St. Jacques, the usual place of execution, to watch when preparations were made for the erection of the scaffold, and then to come to me immediately with the information. After the lapse of several days I was aroused at four o'clock one morning, about the middle of February, and told they were putting up the guillotine.

Accompanied by an American friend, I started off in all haste for the somewhat distant point, and on my arrival could just discern through the misty dawn that the

*Guillotining in France, 1902.*

instrument of death was standing in the middle of the great square, and ready for its victims. It was surrounded by a large body of troops, to prevent any possible attempts at rescue. Already an immense crowd was assembled; and, along with the rest, I pushed my way to the nearest accessible spot, regardless of the repeated orders of the police to fall back. At last a determined charge of cavalry was made, and many of the excited spectators were knocked down, whilst the others were scattered in all directions. To save myself, I dashed headlong into the open door of a small house facing the square, and to my great satisfaction observed a window commanding a complete view of the scene without. By the offer of a liberal sum I obtained possession of this advantageous position, and desired the owner to turn out a motley lot, who in the scamper had sought the same shelter, and would have disputed my monopoly of the sight. The police were called in to clear the house. . . .

It was now seven o'clock and broad daylight. This was the first time I had ever beheld that terrible engine the guillotine, so closely associated with the carnage of the first Revolution. The sight of it at any time would have given me a chill; but now that its glittering axe was so soon to be smeared with the blood of the doomed men, it awakened a feeling of lively horror.

The executioner and his assistants were calmly walking about on the platform, apparently insensible to the dreadful task that would soon devolve upon them. A sombre and impressive silence prevailed among the troops and the multitude beyond, which was only disturbed by the neighing of horses and a low hoarse murmur that revealed the excited emotions at work. Suddenly a startled movement of the crowd indicated the approach of the criminals, and in a moment more three hackney coaches drove up under a strong escort, and stopped directly in front of the guillotine. A suppressed cry, like a groan, was uttered by the harrowed spectators, and then all was silent again. The occupant of the first coach descended. It was Pepin, the grocer. From the second one emerged Morey, the harness-maker; at last appeared the chief assassin, Fieschi, each accompanied by a priest. All three were then led towards the scaffold, and for a few moments each was addressed in a low voice by the confessor, who repeatedly put to their mouths a small crucifix to kiss.

Pepin was the first to mount the fatal platform. He was a short thin man, and his face was ghastly pale, but calm. He turned around, and exclaimed, "I die innocent, I die a victim; farewell to you all." He was then seized by the executioners, who stripped off his coat, pinioned his arms behind, and led him to an upright plank, extending to the top of his breast, to which he was securely strapped. This plank, moving on a pivot, was then placed in a horizontal position, and slid between the two upright bars sustaining the knife, with the back of the culprit's neck directly beneath it. At a signal the cord was loosened, and in an instant the head was severed from the body, and fell into a basket below; the bleeding trunk was then unstrapped, and thrown into another basket on the side. The noise of the knife, which was heavily weighted, had a dull chopping sound, and sent a quiver through all who heard it. The effect on the two wretches whose turn was yet to come must have been agonising.

Morey was the next to ascend the steps of the guillotine. He was an old man, and so enfeebled by illness that he had to be supported. "Assist me," he said; "the spirit is strong, but the body is weak." His countenance, though wan, betrayed no signs of fear. It had a cold austere expression. When a black-silk cap was removed from his head, his gray hair fluttered in the breeze. He showed no desire to speak. As his upper garments were somewhat roughly stripped off by the executioner, he cried out, in an angry tone, "*Pourqoi déchirez-vous mon gilet*" (Why are you tearing my waistcoat?) Strange protest at such an awful juncture! A few moments later he ceased to exist.

The greatest criminal had been purposely reserved to the last, as an aggravation of his punishment. . . . He certainly displayed the utmost intrepidity. When his turn came, he said to his confessor, "How I should like to be able in five minutes from this time to come and tell you how I feel!" and then, with a firm and easy step, he ascended the guillotine. Turning round, and assuming an oratorical attitude, he made a short address, declaring his repentance, and imploring pardon of God for the crime he had committed. Bowing to the right and left, he then advanced with a quick stride, as if to show his readiness to meet death, and delivered himself up to the exe-cutioners. In another minute he joined his guilty associates in eternity.

I gazed fixedly on this terrible tragedy in a sort of stupor. My eyes never wan-dered for an instant, as though spellbound by the hideous scene, and my feelings seemed benumbed with horror. . . . The execution was scarcely over, when the troops began marching rapidly away. I left my place of refuge to retire, but, almost unconsciously, followed a number of people who, seeing the guillotine apparently unguarded, approached, from a morbid curiosity, to inspect it more closely. It was dripping with gore, and the baskets containing the heads and bodies presented a frightful spectacle. The crowd increased every moment, and, to disperse it, a charge of cavalry was suddenly made. My only chance of escape was to leap precipitately on the box of one of the coaches that had conveyed the prisoners. As soon as I could venture to descend I hastened away, and, for some time after, was haunted by the sickening sight I had foolishly resolved to witness.

## THE EXECUTIONER REHABILITATED

The social status, professional position, and importance of the executioner have changed many times and in many ways since 1789. His prestige was highest when his "patients" were aristocrats. As the social station of his victims descended to the level of thieves and common criminals, so did the executioner's standing in the community decline. Prior to the Revolution, Charles-Henri Sanson was an awesome and much-feared person, a representative of the king, who was himself a representative of God. The executioner's was a sacral function. He stood outside the bounds of society; he was set apart from common humankind as someone endowed with special powers, holy but unclean.

The Revolution declared such ostracism to be superstitious and maintained that there was nothing shameful about the executioner's carrying out what was a necessary national duty. The desacralization of social attitudes toward previously suspect professions resulted in the simultaneous elimination of harmful prejudices about both the theatre and the scaffold. In 1789 the Comte de Clermont-Tonnerre made a proposal to the National Assembly for the civic rehabilitation of two groups previously denied citizenship and equal protection under the law: actors and executioners. It was even suggested that one should invite an executioner home for dinner to show one's contempt for old religious biases.

Now the representative of popular sovereignty rather than royal privilege, the executioner was no longer called *bourreau* (always a derogatory term in French) but the "Avenger of the People." The public embraced him. Buoyed by the new liberality, Sanson applied for full rights of citizenship. The stigma had been removed, all legal grounds for discrimination eradicated, and the executioner—as well as the actor—was made a legitimate citizen. Not long after the Revolution, however, the old prejudices reemerged—in the case of executioners, but not of actors.

## PERFECTING THE GUILLOTINE

Although the basic design of the machine remained the same throughout its career, it did undergo significant changes and improvements between the first heavy, massive machine created by the harpsichord maker Schmidt and the modern lightweight precision instrument that was retired in 1981. By the beginning of the nineteenth century, the guillotine's definitive silhouette and dimensions were fixed. It consisted of two uprights four and one-half meters high set thirty-seven centimeters apart and supporting a blade that weighed seven kilos. Attached to the top of the blade by three bolts weighing one kilogram each was a *mouton*, a thirty-kilogram piece of iron that accelerated the blade's descent. Weighing forty kilograms in all, the blade fell two and one-quarter meters in three-quarters of a second before striking the victim's neck and separating the head at the fourth vertebra.

The guillotine during the nineteenth century was the property of the chief executioner, who was responsible for its storage and upkeep. His aim was always to perfect his machine and avoid the frequent mishaps and malfunctions that were so embarrassing for the executioner and distressing to his "patients." Jammed blades and partially severed necks formed the nightmarish obsessions of the servants of the scaffold.

Each executioner added his own refinements to the operating mechanisms of the machine. Henri Sanson, the son of Charles-Henri known as the Great Sanson, improved the method of bolting the blade to the weight. Another important technical development was the replacement of the old cord and pulley that held the blade with an arrow of steel and pincers that were held closed by a spring and released by a lever. Anatole Deibler, a perfectionist in the art of execution, was constantly embellishing the details. By adding to his guillotine four little wheels on the sides of the weight to make the blade's descent faster, he eliminated the crude soaping of the grooves that had been necessary before each use.

## VISIONARY SCHEMES: THE MULTIBLADED GUILLOTINE

The need to kill more victims faster was acutely felt at the height of the Terror, leading to the dream of a multibladed guillotine. According to one widely circulated story, Danton called on Dr. Guillotin to beg him to "design a three-bladed machine to aid the Republic." In 1794 a four-bladed machine was ordered by the military commission at Bordeaux and apparently was actually constructed, although it is unlikely that it ever saw service. An innovative feature was its huge scaffold with trapdoors through which the corpses were to drop down into waiting carts; when filled, these would be driven out through a large door in the side.

In July 1794 a mechanic named Guillot proposed a nine-bladed guillotine and conducted experiments to test the feasibility of his grandiose idea. Guillot's name—a chopped-off version of the now-famous doctor's—did not bode well for the future of his invention. Before his new supermachine could be made, Guillot was arrested for counterfeiting and guillotined with a standard machine—a single blade sufficed to cut off his head.

Paris during the Terror was rife with rumors of monster guillotines. It was reported that a machine with thirty collars was under construction. "The guillotine works too slowly," complained Joseph Fouché, an ex-monk, revolutionary terrorist, and later Napoleon's chief of police and father of the modern police state, on a mission to Lyon in 1793 to liquidate counterrevolutionaries. The American inventor John Fitch, who was in Paris to try to interest the French in his steamboat engine, met with favorable response only from certain revolutionaries who wondered if the steam engine could be attached to the guillotine to speed it up.

In the second half of the nineteenth century there was a proposal to construct an all-metal machine mounted on wheels for greater durability and mobility. But the executioner Jean-François Heidenreich rejected the idea because in order to operate the precision instrument properly the ground beneath it had to be absolutely flat—each installation required clearing the ground by hand and the use of a level. The wheels beneath such a mobile guillotine were sure to throw this delicate balance off.

## SPEED: THE EXECUTIONER AS VIRTUOSO

In 1793 Restif de la Bretonne reported hearing an onlooker at one of the new mechanized beheadings lament that the guillotine would take the sport out of executions because it went so fast that there was nothing to see. In fact, the opposite proved to be true. The importance guillotine aficionados attached to speed and the setting of records in nineteenth-century executions resembles the fanatical obsessions of modern sports fans. The executioner and his team were required to show a remarkable level of coordination in carrying out precise, rapid movements. Newspapers provided a curious public with all the details on debuts, record-setting accomplishments, terrible mishaps, new techniques, and farewell performances.

In the early days of mass executions, staggering records were set. On October 31, 1793, twenty-one Girondins were killed in thirty-eight minutes. Even more phenomenal, in 1804 twenty-six members of the Cadoudal royalist plot against Napoleon were dispatched in twenty-seven minutes—a little over one minute,

*Model of a mobile guillotine.*

two seconds for each victim. By the late nineteenth century, multiple executions were a rare exception and eagerly anticipated by the spectators, who regarded them as a particularly challenging test of the maestro executioner's virtuosity.

Once criticized for being too slow and poorly reviewed for allowing at least ten seconds to elapse before releasing the blade, Louis Deibler protested, "I'd like to see you there, I have no desire to have two or three fingers 'eaten' by the blade." He was referring to the classic guillotine mishap that had occurred in 1829, when an assistant executioner lost three fingers while forcing an unwilling victim's head into the lunette. But a huge crowd turned out for Deibler's farewell performance in 1898, singing and enthusiastically applauding as he dispatched the serial killer Joseph Vacher.

Deibler's son, Anatole (national executioner from 1899 to 1939), far surpassed his father's lifetime record of 169 to become the most famous French guillotiner of the modern era, with over three hundred heads to his credit. At the time of his eagerly awaited debut, Anatole was described in the press as "young, elegant in his redingote, the ideal type of modern executioner," and his accession was warmly acclaimed by the mass media. In 1907 his name was chanted in the streets while President of the Republic Armand Fallières was publicly execrated for pardoning murderers and delaying executions. In 1909 Deibler demonstrated his efficiency, presiding over a quadruple execution carried out in just nine minutes.

## HATS, FLOWERS, AND
## SORROWS OF THE EXECUTIONER

The mannerisms and dress of the executioner were always carefully observed. At one point the Great Sanson's fame was such that it became fashionable to dress à la Sanson: in a tricornered hat, dark green redingote, and striped trousers. In the 1870s Nicolas Roch introduced a major innovation in the style of the executioner's dress by wearing a top hat and frock coat. Louis Deibler was known for his black umbrella, and his son Anatole exchanged the top hat for the derby, enhancing the appeal of the guillotine and its servants for the derby-loving surrealists. Desfourneaux's distinctive trademark was a gray felt hat.

French executioners were especially partial to the wearing of hats during the performance of their official functions, whereas their German counterparts usually wore masks. Undoubtedly the hat served as a sign of professional authority

*Louis Deibler, chief executioner from 1879 to 1898, with his wife.*

and near-royal status; like the king, the executioner was not required to remove his head covering in the presence of others—even as he removed others' heads.

Roger Callois points out that the executioner played the role of a sort of sinister double of the head of state, whose work he carried out. The composite portrait that emerges from memoirs and accounts of visits to the Sanson family from 1792 to 1847 is that of a devoted public servant and a perfect gentleman somewhat in the British style, with impeccable manners. Whether it be Charles-Henri, his son Henri, or his grandson Henri-Clement, everything about the executioner seemed the opposite of his terrible function. He is portrayed as a devoted family man, a good husband and father. He has a sensitive, artistic temperament. A music lover, he plays the violin or cello. In her drama *Olympe and the Executioner* (1989), the American playwright Wendy Kesselman focused on this musical aspect of the executioner's nature by showing the Great Sanson at home playing the cello as a release from the horrors of his day's work.

In various autobiographical works and memoirs for the most part spuriously attributed to the Sansons, the legend is promulgated of the executioner who hates his brutal calling. Thus the Great Sanson is alleged to have written, "The executioner who exercises his profession because he likes it, and who admires his own talents of destruction, is an absurd fiction." Accompanied by his gray parrot, Sanson was happiest working in his tulip garden.

Members of the Sanson dynasty of executioners spoke excellent English—a skill which facilitated their dealings with British tourists. Thomas Paine related that in 1793 he was visited by a man dressed in a Parisian captain's uniform who helped arrange the release from prison of two young Englishmen. "He talked to me about the Revolution, and something about *The Rights of Man*, which he had read in English; and at parting offered me, in a polite and civil manner, his services. And who do you think the man was who offered me his services? It was no other than the public executioner, Sanson, who guillotined the King, and all who were guillotined in Paris, and who lived in the same street with me." The contrast between his awesome function and his personal grace and vulnerability remains a source of wonder.

Various misfortunes rendered the Sansons a family with which the average citizen could sympathize. A terrible tragedy befell the family in 1795 when Sanson's eldest son, assistant, and heir apparent, Gabriel, fell from the scaffold and was killed while displaying a head to the crowd. As a result of the accident—an indication of just how high the platform was in those early days—a railing was built around the scaffold.

The last of the Sansons to hold the position of executioner, Henri-Clement, grandson of the decapitator of Louis XVI, had a singular aversion to his work. Guillotining made him physically sick; ugly red blotches would appear on his body, which would become racked by violent trembling. As a distraction from his horrid profession, Henri-Clement pursued expensive hobbies, indulging in gambling and sexual debauchery and collecting costly paintings and antique furniture.

Guilty of not paying his tradesmen, the extravagant gentleman executioner was arrested immediately after completing an execution and taken to debtor's prison. Once freed, he pawned his guillotine, and when on March 17, 1847, he received orders to conduct a decapitation the next day, Sanson was compelled to disclose the embarrassing truth. The ministry paid 3,800 francs to redeem the machine and promptly dismissed the executioner after the

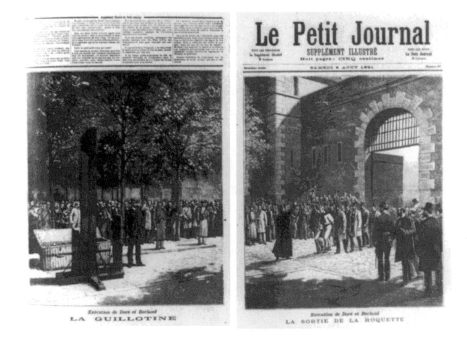

*Exiting la Roquette*, LE PETIT JOURNAL, *1891.*

victim was beheaded, bringing the Sanson dynasty to an end. Destitute, Henri-Clement published the six-volume *Seven Generations of Executioners, 1688–1847* family history in 1862 and 1863; although extensively rewritten by a journalist, it is perhaps based on the original diary kept by his grandfather during the Revolution.

The legend of the kindly melancholy executioner whose brutal profession and personal sorrows are strikingly at odds continued throughout the nineteenth century, reaching its apex with Anatole Deibler. A model civil servant and devoted family man, this executioner cultivated rare roses and made artistic pottery. He was also said to have worked under a pseudonym as a champagne salesman, but his life, like the Great Sanson's, was marked by tragedy. His son died at the age of five due to a pharmacist's error in filling a prescription, and his daughter was unable to marry because of the stigma of his profession. Himself the child of an executioner, Deibler too had suffered this prejudice. In love with the daughter of Heurteloup, a carpenter who supplied guillotines to the whole world, Deibler could not win the approval of the young woman's father, who was loathe to have an executioner for a son-in-law.

## THE "PHOTOGRAPHER" AND THE *TOILETTE DU CONDAMNE*

In the interest of efficiency, the chief executioner assigned special tasks to each of his assistants. It was one team member's job to adjust the victim's head in the lunette to make sure that the neck was properly placed. To accomplish this, the assistant stood facing the guillotine on the side where the head would fall. When the bascule (tilting plank) came down and the victim's head was in the lunette, the assistant would grab the head by the hair, or by the ears if the head happened to be bald. The job of making these last-minute adjustments later earned the assistant the appelation of photographer because he had to find the correct angle for his subject and in effect say, "Hold that pose! Don't move!" The resemblance between being guillotined and having one's picture taken was unnerving; in a sudden flash it was all over.

The executioners claimed that the photographer demonstrated a humanitarian concern, for if the victim were to pull his head back into his shoulders in fear, his jaw or his head would be cut rather than his neck. Because of his position as a "forward," the photographer was often inundated with blood, so a shield was eventually devised to protect him from the blood spurting from the heart which, although the body had become a corpse, continued to pump blood through the arteries of the severed neck.

A sinister ritual of the guillotine was the *toilette du condamné*, or final haircut, in which the executioners functioned as barbers. This simple everyday activity—in this case done to assure unimpeded severing of the neck—seemed particularly ghastly as a prelude to death. The cold steel of the scissors against the bare flesh of the neck became a foretaste of the knife itself. And the *toilette du condamné* was like a parody of sprucing up and getting one's hair trimmed for a rendezvous. But as soon as the collar was cut and removed from the shirt the brutal truth was revealed: the tryst that lay ahead was with the murderous machine.

### BLOODLUST AND RITUAL

Execution by guillotine has always been a primitive ritual. In the days of its proud public display, the guillotine was unabashedly an instrument of vengeance from which immense quantities of blood gushed. Rivulets of gore literally ran in the streets. During the Terror, the guillotine was frequently moved to reduce the menace to sanitation and threat of epidemics that standing pools of blood created.

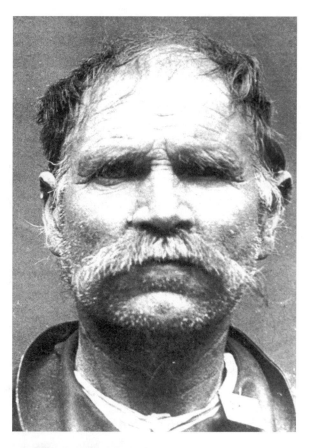

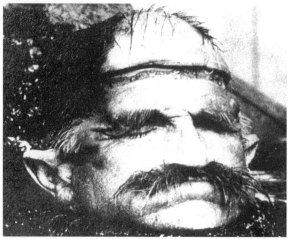

*Louis Lefèvre, arrested May 20, 1915, guillotined April 10, 1916, in Tours, France.*

Guillotines were sometimes erected over open sewers for better drainage. Landlords complained of declining property values in areas near the foul-smelling scaffold.

The philosophical idea of protecting human dignity that had given rise to the guillotine was later used to challenge its very existence. Starting with Victor Hugo and the early movement for the guillotine's abolition in the 1830s and 1840s, the revolutionary concept of freeing man from fear and suffering was quickly wrested away from the machine's advocates and used by the opponents of capital punishment. Another century and a half was to pass, however, before the ideological argument against capital punishment was finally to triumph in France—later than in all the rest of Europe with the exception of Spain—so entrenched was the machine in French culture.

Throughout the period of its greatest sway, the ceremonial traditions of the guillotine evolved less on the basis of ideology than of the reigning aesthetic modalities, which were operatic and theatrical. Nineteenth-century France was an age of great performers and performances. The impressive entrance, the *coup de théâtre*, the startling climax, the sudden denouement were dramatic moments assiduously cultivated in a world of compulsive theatricality.

The cult of the stage and the craze for the histrionic made stars out of executioners and promoted the vogue of public executions as entertainment while the spectacular rituals and paraphernalia surrounding the guillotine gave it an operatic resonance suited to broad gestures, heightened emotions, and memorable final words. These trends found their apotheosis at the end of Umberto Giordano's grand opera *Andrea Chénier* (1869), as the doomed poet Chénier and his beloved Madalena (who has taken the place of a young mother-to-be) mount the scaffold together singing a love duet.

## THE DECLINE OF THE GUILLOTINE

Secularized, the ultimate punishment on the scaffold became pure spectacle, an object of the whims of Parisian fashion. But by the time the guillotine had reached its peak as a star-filled show playing to huge audiences, a strong countermovement had already formed to drain the ceremony of its flamboyant colors, to hide the machine from the public, and finally to take away its audience—in other words, to render the guillotine invisible. First the machine was desacralized. Then it lost its ideological justification. Once it was also detheatricalized what was left? Nothing but the brutal killing.

Around 1870 a number of changes in the tradition of the guillotine began the process of detheatricalization that would eventually result in its final eclipse. On the initiative of Minister of Justice Adolphe Crémieux, the scaffold was eliminated. This major turning point in the history of the guillotine meant the elimination of the famous ascent of the steps, variously reported to be seven, ten, or even as many as twenty-four, and spelled the eventual end of execution as public show.

During Heidenreich's tenure as executioner at about the same time, the frame of the guillotine was painted dark brown, covering the bright red that had once expressed the machine's sanguinary nature. The blade was painted a discreet black so that it no longer gleamed in the first rays of daybreak. By means of these neutral tonalities the once-colorful spectacle was meant to be rendered as inconspicuous as possible. Fitted parts enabled the machine to be erected silently, thereby eliminating the telltale hammering during the night that had previously alerted the prisoner to his approaching fate. Caught unawares, the victim was pounced upon by executioners who stole in upon him in their stocking feet.

There had already been a move toward centralization and consolidation of executioners and machines when in November 1870 it was decreed that there would be a single national executioner for all of France and Algeria, and that he should reside in Paris and have five aides. Nicolas Roch, who served as national executioner from 1872 to 1879, further reduced the theatrics by installing rubber shock absorbers that silenced the horrible double crash of the blade as it fell and rebounded. This "sickening thud" had served as the closing chord in a brief but powerful auditory drama.

Despite these changes and numerous unsuccessful attempts to abolish the death penalty, the popularity of public executions seemed only to grow as the century neared its end. It was considered a great privilege to have an insider's seat at such events. For example, in 1891 the young Russian infantry officer Alexander Winter traveled more than one thousand miles on foot from the Russian-German border to Paris in thirty-nine days, and for this extraordinary feat he was rewarded with a pass to la Roquette to see Michel Eyrand guillotined. In August 1889 during the Paris Universal Exposition, Cook's Travel Agency offered a night tour to the double execution of Joseph Allorto and Jean Baptiste Sellier—the first execution to take place in three years. Three hundred foreign tourists of many nationalities were brought in special oversized wagons, and more than a hundred carriages jammed the surrounding streets.

The event was sold out—every chair, bench, and ladder was filled with spectators and every theatre lorgnette rented, even though now that the guillotine
was at ground level, there was virtually nothing to be seen for all except those
admitted beyond the barricades set up to keep the huge masses at a distance.
The noise, the opportunity to sing, yell, and behave in a disorderly fashion,
the excitement of being there was enough. Once the word was out that an execution was soon to be held, crowds would gather every night before midnight
as early as a week in advance.

In 1898 a motion made by the National Assembly to remove executions from
the public arena was defeated by a compromise. All executions would henceforth take place on the boulevard Arago in front of the wall of the la Santé
prison. The guillotine was being hemmed in; it would no longer be free to roam
through Paris as it had a century earlier. By this time only a pair of guillotines
remained in operation. These two "sisters" were quite different from each
other: the elder was massive and reserved for use in Paris; the younger was
lighter, more streamlined, and suitable for journeys into the provinces. The
smaller machine traveled long distances by train, but its dramatic entrances were
always made by horse-drawn cart. Together they were kept in a hangar known
as the Widow's House.

## OBSOLESCENCE, INFIRMITY, DECEASE

After World War I it was clear that the guillotine and its rituals had grown
antique. No matter how many improvements were made, the aging machine
simply could not adapt to the world of twentieth-century technology. The
horse-drawn wagon and kerosene lanterns, the setting up of the wooden mechanism for each event, the top hats and frock coats, the bran to absorb the blood
in the bucket and the wicker basket, the mounted guards with sabers drawn—
all these once-impressive elements belonged to the pageantry of a dated theatrical scenario. The solemn imagery was well suited to turn-of-the-century
aesthetics and taste, but it was strikingly out of place by the 1930s, the age of
automobiles and airplanes. The criticism now directed against the guillotine
was not rooted in humanitarian concern but was on grounds of style. The guillotine was old-fashioned. In Paris there could be no more damaging judgment
made. Attendance at executions dropped off and interest in the ceremonies of
the scaffold seemed on the wane.

*The execution of Eugène Weidmann, June 16, 1939, Versailles.*

On the day following the June 1939 execution of the serial murderer Eugène Weidmann at Versailles, the newspaper *Paris Soir* published a page of photographs of the event. The government accused the press of catering to the sadistic instincts of its readers and used the episode as justification for finally doing away with public executions. It was said that a large unruly crowd of champagne-drinking merrymakers in evening dress had behaved scandalously during the night and that some of the women had dipped their handkerchiefs in the blood. The newspaper photos, however, show only a small orderly group of spectators.

Henri Desfourneaux, the successor to Anatole Deibler, who had died suddenly at the age of seventy-six from a heart attack in the metro on his way to an execution, went into the record books for having officiated at the last public execution in France. Nervous at his premiere, which was also to be his sole performance before an audience, Desfourneaux—known as a "slow" executioner—did not manage to get Weidmann's neck into the lunette properly until the third try. Due to delays and miscalculations, the decapitation took place in broad daylight rather than at the break of dawn, thereby allowing photographers positioned in a neighboring house to take excellent pictures. Having repeatedly heard the news announced on blaring radios played by revelers during the preceding night, Weidmann had not been at all surprised when the officials came to his cell in the morning. After this execution, even proponents of the machine admitted that its effect on the crowd was not to incite fear and thus deter crime but to provide an invitation for drunken carousing. The clumsy, ill-functioning guillotine and its arcane rites had become an embarrassing and slightly ridiculous anachronism that the government was anxious to keep out of sight.

In the wake of World War II, the atomic bomb, and the Holocaust, the vogue for public executions finally came to an end. The macabre, almost quaint traditions of the guillotine had become a part of history even though such executions still went on occasionally behind prison walls. These events were reported by the major newspapers, but no longer on the front page and only in the sparsest terms. Without an audience, the ceremony lost whatever meaning it had left as ritual. No longer seen by those it was intended to impress, the guillotine lost any possible deterrent value as well.

By 1952 the horse-drawn wagon had been abandoned and the machine was now transported in a small motor van, which occasionally broke down. Long gone were the star performers, the condemned prisoners grandly defying society, the towering personalities as virtuoso guillotiners. The job of executioner had become part-time. Henri Desfourneaux's two assistants also worked as a butcher and a hairdresser—fitting sidelines to their decapitating functions. The last guillotine operator, Marcel Chevalier, incumbent from 1976 to the abolition of capital punishment in 1981, was a full-time printer's assistant and called on only three times in five years to perform his executioner's duty.

The dread machine that had helped to transform a tottering monarchy into a powerful modern nation had long outlived its reason for being. Dropped down to ground level, locked behind prison walls, denied an audience, the guillotine by the time of its abolition was nothing more than a hand-operated mechanical device for the slaughter of pathetic victims, although this was far from apparent to the executioner himself. In his memoir, *The Executioner's Black Book*, the executioner André Obrecht's refuses to let the dignity of the machine's operator be impugned:

> I regret nothing. I am aware of having been a useful citizen. Capital punishment
> has been abolished; that does not mean that it won't be brought back again one
> day. . . . When murderers, having been allowed to live too long, spread their dark-
> ness over our world, the people will reestablish the inexorable light. Not in vain
> am I the representative of many centuries of human order.

# THE MUSEUM, FAIRGROUND, AND THE COLLECTOR'S GUILLOTINE

*The Model of the Guillotine, from the original drawing by*
*Monsieur Sanson, of Paris. This is the first guillotine, the original size,*
*ever seen in England, being exact in every detail as the one in use.*
—*Madame Tussaud and Sons' catalog, 1872*

THE FIRST COMMERCIAL display of heads of the guillotined took place during the French Revolution at the Parisian wax museum where Madame Tussaud served her apprenticeship. For a number of years Dr. Philippe Curtius, a former medical doctor turned wax modeler and showman, had exhibited busts of celebrities and criminals at his Cabinet de Cire on the boulevard du Temple, assisted by Marie Grosholtz, a clever young woman euphemistically referred to as his niece, who made casts and did modeling.

After 1789 growing public curiosity about well-known personalities of the day increased the demand for new displays. A passionate revolutionary and a member of the Jacobin Club, Curtius was on good terms with Danton, Marat, Robespierre, and other leaders; he also knew the executioner Sanson, who provided him with material for exhibitions of criminals. As it was to turn out, some of Curtius's former dinner guests began to appear in his museum as severed heads. They were listed in the catalog as "modeled from the face after death."

Curtius himself—or more often his young assistant—would follow the executioner's wagon to the Madeleine cemetery, where death masks and casts of the freshly severed heads were made. From these the wax busts were then modeled. According to her memoirs, Madame Tussaud went to the graveyard and made death masks of both Louis XVI and, several months later, Marie-Antoinette by order of the Convention. It was no easy assignment. After locating

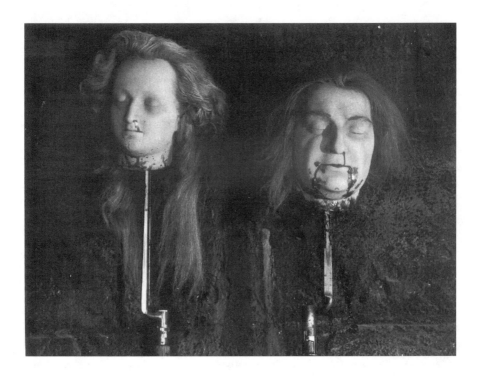

*Wax models of the guillotined heads of Marie-Antoinette and Louis XVI.*
*Madame Tussaud's, London.*

the heads it was necessary to smooth out and oil their features before applying
plaster. All of this had to be done in the dark by the side of the pit that served as
a common grave.

After the death of Curtius and the end of the Revolution, Curtius's former
helper—now Madame Tussaud—took the wax museum with her to England,
where she toured for many years before opening her own permanent exhibition in London in 1834. Included in the collection were the heads of the king
and queen, Robespierre, Fouquier-Tinville, Hébert, and other famous and
infamous figures of the period. The French Revolution, which had been
recorded in wax by Curtius from beginning to end, was the centerpiece of
Madame Tussaud's throughout the nineteenth century.

Most of the historic personalities in the collection consisted of wax heads
and hands attached to bodies made of stuffed leather with carved wooden arms
and legs. The figures from the Terror, however, were displayed as severed
heads. They were housed in a separate room, the Chamber of Horrors, which

was devoted to celebrated criminals and included a model of a guillotine constructed at the scale of three inches to a square foot "accurately measured" from the Parisian guillotine in the place de Grève.

Visitors to Madame Tussaud's were hypnotically drawn to the fatal machine in her Chamber of Horrors. A Victorian gentleman writing in 1860 found such intimacy with the blade almost indecent: "Young ladies who would blush or be indignant at your mentioning of an ankle or a leg, will enter this loathsome den of horror . . . and they will ascend the steps of the guillotine, and feel the edge of the axe, and look at the pailful of sawdust which was placed ready to receive the head; and do all this with a face unmoved."

Almost all of Madame Tussaud's original exhibits were destroyed in a fire in 1925. The guillotine presently on display replicates the nineteenth-century reduced-size simulacrum and was ordered in 1979 from a theatrical prop company. The severed heads are re-creations of the destroyed wax models.

## THE GUILLOTINE AS TOURIST ATTRACTION

As the number of executions by guillotine declined, recreational use of the instrument increased. By 1853 the reductions of regional executioners in France led to the public auctioning of scaffolds and accessories in regions where they could no longer be of service. Often the wood was rotten and the metal rusty. Collectors began buying guillotines, and they began to be shown at fairs as macabre attractions. Some executioners or their widows kept the machines, particularly the blades of supposedly "historic" guillotines, and later sold them to collectors at high prices. A number of blades "certified" to have decapitated Louis XVI were put up for sale over the years.

The executioner became something of a social celebrity and tourist attraction. A constant procession of elegant carriages made its way to the executioner's house. Literary men and foreign visitors were pleased to know such an interesting international star as "Monsieur de Paris," and invitations *chez* Sanson were highly prized. The diplomat Sir John Bowring gave the following account of a visit to Sanson by a group of English gentlemen in the mid-nineteenth century.

> Sanson talked very willingly of the management of the guillotine, which he called
> "la mecanique," of his ancestors, the former *bourreaux* of France—and of his son and
> successor, whom he afterwards introduced to me. He said that the families of the

different executioners in France almost always intermarried, and that there was a
strong clanship among the members of this life-destroying community. He asked
me to his house in order that he might exhibit the operation of "la mecanique," and
I went thither, accompanied by Lord Durham, Mr. Edward Ellice, and Mr. Dawson
Daner. . . . Someone asked Sanson whether after decapitation, he had ever seen any
movement in the head after its separation from the body, as a theory had been put
forward that sensation was not immediately extinguished by the operation, but he
said that he had never observed the slightest movement. He conducted us to a large
outhouse in which the fatal machine was kept. It was painted scarlet. *Un homme de
paille* [a straw man] was prepared, and the usual assistants summoned, in order that
we might witness the whole mode of proceeding. We were struck by the heaviness
and sharpness of the knife, which, falling from a great height, could not but do its
bloody work most effectually. . . . The British character showed itself for what it is,
each man wanted to touch the blade, the baskets, to lie down on the *bascule*.

Visits by British tourists to see the guillotine brought into the open many a
dark desire. En route to the executioner's, Lord Durham had asked whether "it
might be possible to buy a sheep, so as to see the guillotine in action." Such
requests were nothing new. The executioner Sanson of revolutionary days
reported that an Englishman once came to visit with a little dog and "begged me
as a great favor that I would chop off his head so that he could forever boast that
Sanson, the same who had guillotined the King and Queen of France, had also
guillotined his dog."

In his autobiographical *Things Seen*, Victor Hugo recounts the adventure of a
young English girl at the executioner's.

Numbers of English people went to see him. When visitors presented themselves
at M. Sanson's they were introduced into an elegant reception-room on the
ground-floor, furnished entirely with mahogany, in the midst of which there was
an excellent piano, always open and provided with pieces of music. . . .

One day an English family, consisting of the father, the mother, and three
pretty daughters, fair and with rosy cheeks, presented themselves at Sanson's residence. It was in order to see the guillotine. Sanson took them to the carpenter's
and set the instrument at work. The knife fell and rose again several times at the
request of the young ladies. One of them, however, the youngest, was not
satisfied with this. She made the executioner explain to her, in the minutest

details, what is called the *toilet of the condemned*. Still she was not satisfied. At length she turned hesitatingly towards the executioner.

"Monsieur Sanson," she said.

"Mademoiselle," said the executioner.

"What is done when the man is on the scaffold? How is he tied down?"

The executioner explained the dreadful matter to her, and said, "We call that *putting him in the oven.*"

"Well, Monsieur Sanson," said the young lady, "I want you to put me in the oven."

The executioner started. He gave an exclamation of surprise. The young lady insisted. "I fancy," she said, "that I should like to be able to say I have been tied down in it."

Sanson spoke to the father and mother. They replied, "As she has taken a fancy to have it done, do it."

The executioner had to give in. He made the young Miss sit down, tied her legs with a piece of string, and her arms behind her back with a rope, fastened her to the swinging plank, and strapped her on with the leather strap. Here he wanted to stop. "No, no, that is not yet all," she said. Sanson then swung the plank down, placed the head of the young lady in the dreadful neck-piece, and closed it upon her neck. Then she declared she was satisfied.

When he afterwards told the story, Sanson said, "I quite thought she was going to say at last, '*That is not all; make the knife fall.*'"

Nearly all the English visitors ask to see the knife which cut off the head of Louis XVI. This knife was sold for old iron, in the same way as all the other guillotine knives when they are worn out. English people will not believe it and offer to buy it of M. Sanson. If he had cared to trade in them, there would have been as many *knives of Louis XVI* sold as walkingsticks of Voltaire.

*Louis Boulanger. Lithograph depicting a scene from*
THE LAST DAY OF A CONDEMNED MAN *by Victor Hugo (1829).*

# VICTOR HUGO,
# HECTOR BERLIOZ,
# AND THE CONDEMNED MAN

*Berlioz's generation was as much haunted by the guillotine
as we are by the death camps.*
—*Jacques Barzun*, Berlioz and the Romantic Century

THE ROMANTICS of the early nineteenth century—a new generation of artists and writers born after the French Revolution and deeply marked by the subterranean forces that it had let loose—could never forget the nightmare of the Terror and its primal symbol—the guillotine.

Rebelling against the ideals of order and harmony propagated by eighteenth-century neoclassicism, the romantics glorified the weird, the demoniacal, and the frightful. In their embrace of eroticism and cruelty, these bold innovators appealed directly not to human rationality but to our deep-seated fears. Death, sensuality, and the devil were favored subjects of the school known as black romanticism, whose proponents were fascinated with morbidity and self-destructiveness. The macabre was the special realm of this movement. With its predilection for vampires, decaying corpses, and psychic torture, the romantic tale of terror is clearly linked to its precursor the Gothic novel and to the horror film, its present-day descendant.

In 1820, at the age of eighteen, Victor Hugo spoke for his generation when he declared, "For our mothers, the revolution is a guillotine." Guillotine romanticism was launched with Victor Hugo's first novel, *The Last Day of a Condemned Man*, published anonymously in 1829 when the author was twenty-seven years old. For Hugo it marked the beginning of what would be a lifelong obsession with the guillotine and the problem of capital punishment.

One afternoon as Hugo was passing by the place de Grève (now the place de Hôtel de la Ville), he caught sight of the executioner rehearsing for his performance that evening. Having previously avoided the guillotine and never having attended an execution, Hugo unintentionally became a horrified witness as the executioner tested his machine. The blade kept sticking halfway in its descent until the grooves were properly oiled. Once the knife began to fall correctly, the executioner rubbed his hands together joyfully and expressed his satisfaction.

Watching this paid functionary matter-of-factly going about his preparations for killing a fellow human being—all the while talking and joking with curious bystanders—the young poet was overwhelmed by the thought of the terrified victim waiting in his cell, and he began to imagine how the poor wretch must be suffering.

The following day Hugo started *The Last Day of a Condemned Man*, which he completed in three weeks. The story is presented as a manuscript written by a condemned man and left behind in his prison cell when he was finally taken away to the scaffold. In a preface added to the second edition, which appeared in 1832 under his own name, Hugo felt obliged to justify his preoccupation with such a gruesome subject by explaining that the book was an argument for the abolition of the death penalty, an issue then being vigorously debated in the Chamber of Deputies.

To arouse hatred of capital punishment, the novelist imaginatively reconstructed the loathsome preparations for a guillotining. Inviting the complicity of his readers, Hugo asked, "Who has not imagined or dreamed what a condemned man's last day must be?" To gratify the public's morbid curiosity—as well as his own—Hugo offers himself as a surrogate for the victim and experiences vicariously all the condemned man's emotions in this first-person narrative. So that the general reader can identify and empathize with him, the condemned man is made as mundane as possible; he is "any culprit, executed on any day, for any crime."

In his preface to the novel, Hugo describes how he "picked up this fatal idea from where it lay weltering in a sea of blood under the legs of the guillotine," suggesting that the impetus for writing the book was literally a head that had just fallen beneath the blade. Personified and anthropomorphic, Hugo's decapitating machine has legs and two long red arms raised toward the heavens. Where its head should be, it has only a maw—a gaping hole waiting to devour others' heads.

The hallucinatory atmosphere of *The Last Day of a Condemned Man* inspired many visual artists; it is most strikingly captured by Hugo's friend, the poet, painter, and illustrator Louis Boulanger, in a lithograph depicting the condemned man's nightmare exactly as described in the novel. Alone in his cell, the terrified prisoner is confronted by three decapitated ghostly figures, each holding his severed head in the left hand and pointing menacingly at the condemned man with the right. Although not directly influenced by Hugo, Francisco Goya was also impressed by the fatal machine and made two drawings of the guillotine, which he first saw during his exile in France in the late 1820s. And Theodore Gericault and Grandville made numerous studies of decapitated heads.

The overheated imagination of Hugo's fictional prisoner piles horror upon horror; mutilation will follow mutilation. The condemned man knows that once the guillotine has done its work, his body will be taken to the operating theatre

of the medical school to be dissected before a crowd of students. Then his dismembered remains will at last be buried in the notorious Clamart cemetery for criminals and paupers, located not far from the Jardin des Plantes.

The night before his execution, the condemned prisoner dreams feverishly of the return of the thousands who have died under the knife to the place de Grève until the square is tightly packed with corpses. "There will be a guillotine from hell on the square, and on it a devil will execute the executioner." Hugo's satanic dreamscape is reminiscent of satirical revolutionary prints showing Robespierre executing the executioner amidst a virtual forest of guillotines, or the executioner executing himself, and

*Anonymous. Satirical etching depicting Robespierre guillotining the executioner, late eighteenth century.*

*J. J. Grandville. Illustration pour Jérome Paturot.*

of the fantastic visual art of the romantic era. In the grip of these visions of the ghosts of the guillotined returning to the scene of their agony, the condemned man wonders which part of them is really the ghost—the head or the body?

As the hour of the execution draws near, a hateful mob fills the entire place de Grève, howling and laughing as it waits for the victim to arrive. The crowd is largely composed of bloodthirsty criminals, some of whom will later die on the scaffold too, but Hugo portrays the executioners as models of tact and consideration. These kind killers steal upon the condemned man from behind, swiftly and silently as cats. They place him in a horse-drawn wagon facing backwards so that on the journey from the prison to the scaffold he will not see the dreadful machine until the very last moment when he must mount the steps of the scaffold. As they approach the square, the condemned man sees nothing but a sea of heads, hears only the cruel roar of avid spectators. Dealers in human suffering cry out, "Who wants to buy a place?" Heads gawk at him from everywhere—from the windows and doors of houses and shops, even hanging from lantern brackets. The condemned man's mind frantically urges him on to one last attempt at bravado, but the body will not cooperate. Having already experienced death in anticipation, even before leaving his cell, the prisoner has become paralyzed.

Here ends *The Last Day of a Condemned Man*, which Hugo called his "book of the severed head." The writer was unable to take the first-person narrative of the prisoner any further than the foot of the scaffold—at least at this point in his career.

## *A CONDEMNED MAN* REVISITED

In 1853, while in political exile on the island of Jersey in the English Channel, Hugo began to participate in spiritualist seances. He experimented with spirit rapping or table turning as it was called, fashionable at the time as a means of attempting communication with the dead. A small table with a central column ending in a triple clawfoot was set atop a larger table. Two participants placed their hands on the column. When the table mysteriously knocked, someone present called out a letter of the alphabet at each rap, starting with *a*. When the rapping stopped, the last letter that had been named was written down. The process was slow and laborious but the table refused to admit any simplification.

The seances lasted into the early hours of the morning. Hugo himself never took a place at the table but preferred to serve as the scribe, conscientiously noting down every letter. His elder son Charles was an inspired medium, and the rhythm and success of the seances greatly depended on him. There were moments when Hugo doubted; at other times he was a fanatic believer in what seemed to him a new religion confirming the immortality of the soul.

For two years the seances continued. Hugo filled three large notebooks with communications in prose and verse from Molière, Shakespeare, Dante, Racine, Marat, Charlotte Corday, Jesus Christ, Plato, and the prophet Isaiah, as well as from abstractions such as the Novel, Death, and Criticism. Hugo intended to publish these at some point, but their questionable character kept them from appearing in print until the twentieth century. Although these "voices of the dead" have been severely criticized for sounding all too much simply like Hugo, the suppression of conscious control in their composition, akin to surrealist automatic writing, lends them a mysterious authority.

In December 1853 Hugo decided to ask the poet André Chénier, guillotined on July 25, 1794, to complete *The Last Day of a Condemned Man*, as well as to consult other decapitated heads on their postmortem experiences. He initiated these sessions by declaring that the publisher of his novel ought never to have printed "THE END" at the bottom of the last page, which described the prisoner's being led away to the scaffold; only Chénier could bring the book to its conclusion.

On January 2, 1854, Hugo requested Chénier to give him "his impressions during and after his execution." Hugo recorded a transcript of Chénier's response as relayed to him in the seance.

> The man climbs the scaffold. The executioner attaches him to the plank. The half-moon closes on his neck. The soul of those guillotined takes flight through the pillory. The man then has a frightful second. He opens his eyes and sees a basket full of reddish mire, which is the bottom of the sewer for the scaffold, and his head tells him: I'm going to be down there. No, his soul answers. The spectacle has just changed. Instead of mire, he sees an ocean, instead of blood, he sees light. Through this sewer he has entered the heavens. . . . I am alive and yet I no longer bear the burden of life. I receive infinity through all my pores. An invisible mouth covers me with a prolonged kiss in which I detect my mother, in which I recognize my mistress, and which has, one after the other, the perfume of all my loves. A luminous line separates my head from my body. It is a wound tender and exacerbated, which receives a kiss from God. Death appears to me at the same

time on earth and in the heavens, while my body transfigured by the tomb sinks into the beatitudes of eternity. I see, at immense distances beneath me, my other body, which the executioner throws to the worms, my head, which rolls in the gutter, my wound, which bleeds, my guillotine, which is washed, my hair, which hangs at the end of a pike, and I hear my name insulted. Then I hear a voice that says: Glory to Chénier! And I see a halo come down from the heights of the heavens onto my forehead.

Three years later, still in exile but now on the neighboring island of Guernsey, Hugo returned to the theme of the guillotine and severed head, employing another artistic medium in which he excelled: graphics. In sepia and ink Hugo created a visual counterpart of the fantastic visions in *The Last Day of a Condemned Man*. A severed head hurtles through space like a heavenly body above the murky outline of a guillotine, while the hole of the lunette shines in darkness like the moon. Pools of blood have seeped into the cracks between the paving stones, spelling out in bright red letters the disturbing title, *Justitia*, or Justice.

In the same year, Hugo wrote *The Revolution*, a poem that was never published in the author's lifetime. In it he describes a scene for which his picture *Justitia* could be an illustration. The statues of three French kings—Henry IV, Louis XIII, and Louis XIV—step down from their pedestals to seek out their descendants, only to confront in a deserted public square the specter of the guillotine: two black upright posts with a bare and livid triangle suspended above an indistinct aperture, a window opening onto darkness, and two clouds forming the number 93, the year the Terror began. The head of Louis XVI, freshly severed and bleeding, floats by the guillotine, and the blood dripping from his head spells out "that mysterious word, Justice," on the paving stones. Since Hugo believed execution of the king was necessary (indeed he himself would have voted in favor of it), the ultimate justice of the revolutionary deed and its total horror stand in unrelieved tension.

The fatal machine appears throughout Hugo's *Les Miserables*, published in 1862, as an ominous presence. Early in the novel, Christian compassion compels the saintly Bishop Myriel to mount the scaffold with a condemned man and to embrace him shortly before the blade falls. Hugo reflects on the hypnotic power of the awesome structure as he describes how the sight of the guillotine proved a shock from which the Bishop was not to recover for many years.

The scaffold, indeed, when it is prepared and set up, has the effect of a halluci-
nation. We may be indifferent to the death penalty, and may not declare ourselves, yes or no, so long as we have not seen a guillotine with our own eyes. But
when we see one, the shock is violent, and we are compelled to decide and take
part, for or against. . . . He who sees it quakes with the most mysterious trem-
blings. . . . The scaffold is not a mere frame, the scaffold is not a machine, the
scaffold is not an inert piece of mechanism made of wood, of iron, and of ropes. It
seems a sort of being which had some somber origin of which we can have no
idea; one would say that this frame sees, that this machine understands, that this
mechanism comprehends; that this wood, this iron, and these ropes, have a will.
In the fearful reverie into which its presence casts the soul, the awful apparition
of the scaffold confounds itself with its horrid work. The scaffold becomes the
accomplice of the executioner; it devours, it eats flesh, and it drinks blood. The
scaffold is a sort of monster created by the judge and the workman, a specter
which seems to live with a kind of unspeakable life, drawn from all the death
which it has wrought.

Later in the novel Hugo describes children in the streets of Paris who are
among the guillotine's most passionate fans. To initiate the younger boys into
the life of the Parisian gamin, Gavroche promises to take them to the theatre to
see the great actor Frédérick Lemaître and to the opera, where they are allowed
to attend for free as part of the claque. But he saves the best show for last. "And
then we will go see the guillotining," Gavroche explains. "I will show you the
executioner . . . Monsieur Sanson."

The gamins are true connoisseurs, who follow the guillotine with the well-
informed enthusiasm of sportsmen.

To be present at executions is a positive duty. These imps point at the guillotine
and laugh. They give it all kinds of nicknames: "End of the Soup," "Old
Growler," "Sky-Mother," "The Last Mouthful," etc., etc. That they may lose
nothing of the sight, they scale walls, hang on to balconies, climb trees, swing to
gratings, crouch into chimneys. . . . No festival is equal to the execution ground—
la Grève, Sanson and the Abbé Montès are really popular names. They shout to
the victim to encourage him. Sometimes, they admire him. The gamin Lacenaire,
seeing the horrible Dautun die bravely, used an expression which was full of
future: "I was jealous of him!" . . . They have traditions of the last clothes worn

by them all. They know that Tolleron had on a forgeman's cap, and that Avril wore one of otter skin; that Louvel had on a round hat, that old Delaporte was bald and bareheaded, that Castaing was ruddy and good-looking, that Bories had a sweet little beard, that Jean Martin kept on his suspenders, and that Lecouffe and his mother quarreled. "Don't be finding fault now with your basket," shouted a gamin to the latter couple.

## THE SYMPHONY OF THE GUILLOTINE

The hallucinatory and nightmarish sensations experienced by Hugo's condemned man on his last day are expressed musically by Hector Berlioz in the fourth section of his *Symphonie Fantastique,* completed and first performed in 1830. Entitled "The March to the Scaffold," this movement is a graphic portrait in sound of the grim ritual of a beheading as subjectively perceived by the victim of the guillotine. At the symphony's climax the music evokes the falling of the blade, the drop of the head into the basket, and the roaring approval of the crowd.

According to the program for the premiere prepared by Berlioz, the hero, a young musician and tormented lover under the influence of opium, "dreams that he has killed his beloved." He then imagines himself led to execution to the accompaniment of a march "now somber and wild, now brilliant and solemn. . . . At the end, the *idee fixe* [the poet's obsession with his loved one] reappears for an instant, like a last thought interrupted by the fatal stroke." When *Symphonie Fantastique* was in rehearsal, Berlioz declared, "'The March to the Scaffold' is thirty times more frightening than I expected."

Like Hugo, Berlioz became fascinated with the guillotine partly from reading about the execution of the poet André Chénier. For Berlioz, Chénier's destiny as a victim of the Terror was symptomatic of the fate of genius in society, and the composer wished to illustrate this through his alter ego in *Symphonie Fantastique.* According to legend, the doomed poet, who at age thirty-two had scarcely begun to publish, struck his forehead with his palm as he approached the guillotine and exclaimed, "There is something here yet!"

*Pierre-François Lacenaire, c. 1835.*

# THE CRIMINAL-ARTIST OF
# THE GUILLOTINE

*One wants to ask what right the courts have to condemn*
*A murderer so beautiful the day must pale.*
*—Jean Genet, "The Prisoner Condemned to Death"*
*(dedicated to Maurice Piloise, guillotined for killing his lover in 1939)*

During the Revolution, supposed enemies of the people were collectively condemned to death for political reasons, thus becoming heroic martyrs in the eyes of opposition parties. In the nineteenth century, on the other hand, victims of the guillotine were, for the most part, individual malefactors and assassins. They became celebrities of a quite different order, notorious antiheroes of crime. The terrifying confrontation of one man facing death in the total solitude of his existential isolation became the primary focus for both victim and spectator.

The guillotine appealed to the romantic's obsession with death. For the romantic, all of existence was a prelude to dying, and this instrument of mechanical destruction encapsulated the arbitrary suddenness with which a man's life might end. The image of the slant-bladed guillotine began to take the place of the traditional grim reaper with his scythe.

The quick transition between life and death lay in the thin blade of the guillotine. The literature of black romanticism describes severed heads floating through the air and takes the fatal machine as its presiding deity. A poet and author of macabre and fantastic tales, Théophile Gautier called this school a "literature of the mortuary" and the "carcass novel" or "executioner's nightmare." "The century was in favor of the carcass," Gautier asserted, "and the charnel house pleased it better than the boudoir."

## LACENAIRE, THE POET-ASSASSIN, OR SUICIDE BY GUILLOTINE

The most famous of the nineteenth-century romantic criminal antiheroes was Pierre-François Lacenaire. Called the "Manfred of the gutter" by Théophile Gautier, Lacenaire was a dandy and a criminal with literary pretensions. His poetry and posthumously published memoirs—written in prison up to the eve of his execution (and perhaps even afterward by editors)—proved immensely successful. Stendhal, Hugo, Flaubert, Dostoevsky, and other men of letters became fascinated with this cool killer who successfully portrayed himself as an alienated genius at war with society.

As a delinquent sixteen-year-old, Lacenaire was once passing through the town square with his father when suddenly the guillotine stood looming before them. "Look," his father told him, "that is how you will finish up if you don't change your ways."

"Horrible prediction in the mouth of a father!" Lacenaire exclaimed in a paroxysm of voluptuous terror. Conceiving his life in colorful melodramatic terms, the poet-assassin engaged in self-theatricalizations that excited the popular imagination of the period. "From that moment," he wrote, "an invisible bond existed between me and the frightful machine." The poet-assassin knew he had a rendezvous with the triangular blade which one day must be kept, and his life became an ever-intensifying obsession.

"How many times I was guillotined in my dreams!" Lacenaire confessed proudly. "My life was a prolonged suicide; I belonged no longer to myself but to cold steel. Instead of the knife or the razor, I chose the great blade of the guillotine." He never heard the word *guillotine* without a shudder of joy; he referred to the fatal machine as his lovely fiancée, his mistress, his consolation. He is said to have had calling cards printed bearing the inscription "Pierre-François Lacenaire, fiancé of the guillotine."

Arrested for his crimes, which included the murder of a widow and her son, Lacenaire was at last able to indulge his flair for self-dramatization to the full. Wearing a stylish blue coat at his trial, he attacked society as his enemy and professed his hatred of mankind. The condemned man's cell became an ideal theatre for his existential rebellion and also served as a kind of salon where he was visited by authors, doctors, lawyers, phrenologists, society ladies, wealthy English women, and journalists. Excellent food and fine wines were served, which the prisoner much appreciated. To prevent Lacenaire from thwarting justice by committing suicide, a soldier stood guard at his cell night and day. The right-thinking found his "metaphysics of assassination" and the unrepentant flaunting of his crimes reminiscent of the "abominable" Marquis de Sade.

Determined that his execution be as spectacular as possible, Lacenaire was concerned that it be staged properly and worried about its time and place. "It was only in Paris that I wanted to die," the poet-assassin wrote. "I make no secret of it—it would have been very disagreeable to me to have been dispatched by a provincial executioner." That the execution had been set for an unfashionable hour made Lacenaire extremely angry. "I am told they will execute me at seven in the morning, and that I shall be driven in some kind of covered vehicle. I assure you I'm very upset about it. I should have liked it to be in the middle of the day—at two o'clock, for instance—in the place de Grève, or on the Pont Neuf."

Shortly before the execution, a phrenologist visited Lacenaire in his cell to cast a model of his head. Lacenaire recorded his reaction to the procedures. "They really were the preparations for the scaffold, even to shaving my head! . . . Then, lying on my bed, I had to lay my head in a semi-circle of copper, which was fastened round my neck just as it will be on the guillotine. . . . My eyes were closed. At one instant I saw a thousand lights, a vast radiance: they were executing me by torchlight! In another instant I was plunging into a dark, humid gulf and the fiend of a doctor who was torturing my head appeared to me as the Executioner himself!"

Lacenaire conceived of all his experiences preceding his execution in terms of literary and historical antecedents, recalling how prisoners had simulated their own deaths during the Terror. "I too can rehearse the act of my execution. I shall even be more courageous than they, for they were many, and roused each other; they were excited and forgot themselves. . . . I am alone, and my body is completely motionless: I am going to act and witness in my mind; an infinitely more cruel process, since it will allow me to suffer."

Drawing on the models provided by Louis XVI, Marie-Antoinette, Charlotte Corday, and Madame Roland, as well as Victor Hugo's condemned man, Lacenaire recorded the experience of his own execution in advance.

> The carriage is stopping. Horror! Where am I? . . . courage now . . . who am I to
> these people? . . . Lacenaire, the infamous Lacenaire . . . Ah! the blade!
> What . . . is the plank swinging? . . . what a noise above my head, it is the

lucarne [lunette] shutting . . . mercy . . . a spring creaks . . . Oh! . . . my God!

I leave you to imagine the state I was in after this mental performance.

The banality of Lacenaire's imaginings did not diminish the popular appeal of his personality and writings. Lacenaire was a hero to ragpickers and street urchins as well as a social celebrity, and the authorities did all they could to downplay the execution. The time and place were, as usual, unannounced, and the scaffold and guillotine were hastily erected by torchlight during the night at the place Saint-Jacques. The news had somehow spread, and even though it was a cold morning on that day in January 1836, a crowd of five to six hundred had to be held back by municipal guards.

Lacenaire remained unrepentant and nonchalant to the end. His literary ambitions remained uppermost. Shortly before leaving for the scaffold the author recalled, "Monsieur Hugo has written a very beautiful book, *The Last Day of a Condemned Man*. But if I had time, I could have beaten him hollow." In the wagon with Avril, his accomplice, Lacenaire sang a song.

Avril was executed first without a hitch, but when Lacenaire lay on the bascule waiting for the knife, the blade stuck in the grooves of the guillotine after dropping halfway. With great effort, the poet-assassin turned his head in the lunette to look up at the blade. Twenty seconds after the failure of the first attempt, the blade fell all the way. Trying to keep Lacenaire from becoming an object of hero worship and imitation, the ministry of justice felt it necessary to ask the editor of the *Gazette des tribunaux* to publish a false report that the poet-assassin had died a cowardly death. But the lie did not work.

To some extent, Lacenaire succeeded in achieving the fame he had so hungrily sought. Stendhal planned to include him in his unfinished novel *Lamiel*. He appears in Marcel Carnet's film *Children of Paradise* (1944), played by Marcel Herrand, and André Breton included a selection from his poetry in his *Anthology of Black Humor*, an apt resting place for the "fiancé of the guillotine." Three new editions of Lacenaire's memoirs, poetry, and letters have been published in France since 1968. In Francis Girod's recent film *Lacenaire* (1990) Daniel Auteuil gives a romantic portrayal of the poet-assassin's life and death.

# THE SATIRICAL GUILLOTINE

*They cut a man's head off—no matter*
*Though body and head be apart.*
*The latter seems to chatter*
*In a way to make nervous people start.*
*—Barney Maquire's Account of His Visit to*
*Maskelyne and Cook's Entertainment, 1877*

IN 1829, THE SAME YEAR that Hugo wrote *The Last Day of a Condemned Man*, the caricaturist, actor, and writer Henri Monnier portrayed in his dramatic sketch "The Execution" the visit of two Parisian youngsters to the place de Grève to witness a guillotining. A small drawing by the author accompanies the text. In the preface to his *Scenes of Popular Life*, in which "The Execution" appears, Monnier comments, "In the past we have seen very few literary men take up painting and very few painters take up literature. Why not try both mediums, since the studies and observations are the same?"

In "The Execution," Lolo is bringing his inexperienced friend Titi to see his first guillotining. Like hundreds of other gamins, Lolo and Titi have skipped out on their jobs in the workshops where lower-class youths are employed. As they join the streams of people heading toward the scaffold, Lolo remarks that the crowd is so full of the opposite sex because women always find the show more exciting than men. Lolo and Titi are looking forward to the day's events—a quadruple execution of three men and an old woman—although Lolo

*Henri Monnier.*
THE EXECUTION, *1829.*

boasts that during the Revolution his father saw sixty heads fall in a single day.

At the place de Grève, hawkers are selling spaces and mounted police try to keep the regulars from climbing up the streetlamps. From the perch he's secured on a lamppost, Lolo describes to Titi the arrival of the wagon with the prisoners, each of whom is escorted by a "sky pilot," as the priest was called. At first there is only an assistant executioner present on the scaffold. The grand master Sanson does not make his entrance until the last minute, when he arrives dramatically just in time to release the blade.

The first to be guillotined is the youngest of the men; his priest, equally young and even more afraid, weeps openly. After the other two are executed, the old woman is at last decapitated. To the great horror of the crowd, she seems to have no blood. Shaken by all he has seen, Titi turns white as a sheet and cries. He has lost all interest in the planned trip to the graveyard, but Lolo's enthusiasm remains high: "Let's follow the wagon—come on! Let's stick together, we'll see them again when they're dumped out! If we're lucky and the wagon stops, we can climb on. We'll open the baskets, we'll stick our hands in— that's how I got some of the guy's hair last time."

Monnier based this sketch on the actual execution of three men who murdered the concierge of the Hôtel Vaucanson on the rue de Charonne. The terrible "mother" of the convicts was Marie Labouille, owner of the tavern where the trio were carousing all night following their crime. One of the condemned men, Chandelet, refused the consolation of religion, and when he first saw the guillotine he exclaimed, "Ha! So here we are at the Big Machine!" According to the *Courrier des tribunaux*, Chandelet refused the priest and then "rushed forward, climbed the stairs at a single bound, and flung himself like a madman on the plank. . . . The blade fell and the severed head, bouncing across the basket, rolled across the scaffold leaving a long trail of blood! Soon the cart, carrying off the remains, rolled away; it passed back through the vast crowd which had viewed the men and still wished to view the bodies."

## "TALKED INTO BEING GUILLOTINED"

A celebrated example of seemingly inexhaustible French jokes about executions is "Talked into Being Guillotined," a comic sketch in dialogue form written in 1862 by the popular humorist Eugène Chavette. Part of a collection entitled *The Little Comedies of Vice*, the sketch is subtitled "Mistrust."

A provincial town is about to witness its first execution in over fifty years. The executioner has grown old and feeble; his first assistant is long since dead and the second is seriously ill. But excitement runs high in the town. The jury has condemned to death a serial murderer responsible for seventeen homicides. A member of the jury has an apartment overlooking the town square where the execution is to take place. To pay off all his social obligations, the juror invites guests to come for a splendid meal and excellent view of the guillotining.

But just before the execution is scheduled to take place, word comes that the condemned prisoner refuses to participate. The whole party will be spoiled. The twelve guests, including the juror's boss, grow restless. Lamenting that one cannot count on *anything* any more, the distraught host sets off for the prison, determined to persuade the stubborn prisoner that he simply must be guillotined.

Trying every argument at his disposal, the exasperated host reasons, pleads, and cajoles, explaining to the prisoner that people have traveled from all over to see the execution, that the executioner has everything ready, that it will only take a second and won't even cost him anything, and that he really just can't let them all down. Initially sullen and mistrustful, the condemned man finally allows himself to be persuaded when he hears that the Emperor insists. Rather than disappoint so many, the prisoner goes off to be executed. Ten minutes later the boss congratulates his host for bringing a festive occasion to such a successful conclusion.

"Talked into Being Guillotined" reduces the horror of capital punishment to party entertainment, but beneath the lighthearted humor lurks a hidden truth: the victim of the guillotine is required to acquiesce in his own decapitation. Chavette's comically recalcitrant prisoner refusing to be beheaded has a notable precursor in Shakespeare's *Measure for Measure*, where Barnadine tells his executioner, "I swear I will not die today for any man's persuasion." The joke is one of long standing.

## GUILLOTINE TATTOOS

As the example of Lacenaire's life story makes clear, rather than serving as a deterrent to crime, the guillotine often proved a fatal attraction for the criminals who frequented executions. Crooks and thugs often had guillotines and severed heads tattooed on their arms and chests, which were accompanied by inscriptions to the executioner, such as "My Head Goes To Deibler" and

"Promised To Deibler." Sometimes these dark, self-satirical mottoes appeared on their foreheads, as though to stamp the ultimate destination directly onto the goods. Did the criminal thus hope to ward off such an evil destiny? In some instances a dotted line was tattooed around the neck with the directions: CUT ALONG THE DOTTED LINE.

## PORNOGRAPHIC MARIONETTES GO TO THE SCAFFOLD

For its second program on July 8, 1862, the private Parisian marionette theatre Erotikon, which specialized in bawdy farces and irreverent parodies for a select audience of writers and artists, presented "a philosophical drama in three acts," *The Last Day of a Condemned Man*, by the actor Jean-Hippolyte Tisserant. For his satirical puppet show Tisserant invented Coutaudier, an outrageously impertinent and impenitent criminal who makes the inevitable journey from courtroom to scaffold in a broad parody of Hugo's novel.

During the second act, which takes place in la Conciergerie prison (known as "the antechamber of the guillotine"), the executioner Sanson comes to give the prisoner the dreaded haircut that signals impending death. The condemned man peevishly criticizes the barber-executioner for tickling him and cutting his hair too short.

During the final tableau, the condemned man and the chaplain sit in a wagon at the front of the stage, as a ten-foot-long painted panorama is slowly unrolled behind them, representing their progression through the streets of Paris on the way to the place de la Roquette, where executions took place from 1853 to 1899. Once they have mounted the scaffold, the condemned man complains to the Abbé Montès, the famous priest who for many years consoled those about to be guillotined.

> You know what pisses me off, holy Father? . . . To be guillotined with such a hoarse throat. I won't be able to address the people. . . . (*Trying to talk to the crowd.*) Hum! Hum! Fellow Frenchmen! . . . Nation of heroes! Liberty . . . Oh? Look out! (*Enter Sanson.*) See! There you are again, you old queer! Is that bran of yours in the basket clean? You know, I'm going to have to stick my mug in there in a few minutes and I wouldn't like to get pimples or acne! . . . Oh! . . . I've been had! . . . It's sawdust! . . . Fellow Frenchmen, look at how you're being ruled! . . . It's sawdust! . . . I have a right to bran . . . I don't want to die . . . Sanson!

*Erotikon Puppet Theatre, 1862.*

Coutaudier is thrust onto the plank and into the pillory of the fully functioning model guillotine used in the performance. The condemned man's final
words are "Please, pull the cord!" The blade falls and "his soul goes to join that
of the ill-fated Louis XVI," according to the stage direction, which was read
aloud by the author, who spoke all the parts.

The audience roared with laughter. The guillotine has always had the effect
of reducing human beings to puppets, and the sight of a scurrilous gesticulating
marionette on the scaffold seemed irresistibly comic to the witty and cynical
audience of the Erotikon theatre.

Were these artists and intellectuals any less cruel and heartless to take their
elite aesthetic pleasures from a grotesque puppet show than the gamins who
climbed lamp posts to catch a glimpse of the guillotine in action, or the revolutionary *tricoteuses* who cheered raucously as heads fell? Conversely, might we not
argue that gallows humor is the soundest, most human reaction possible to the
horrors of capital punishment? Laughing at the unbearable does not necessarily
imply acceptance of the existing order or a lessening of the will to eliminate evil.

*Antoine Wiertz. Panel one from* THOUGHTS AND VISIONS OF A SEVERED HEAD, *1853.*

# THE GUILLOTINENROMANTIK
## OF GEORG BÜCHNER
## AND ANTOINE WIERTZ

*I am becoming accustomed to the sight of blood.*
*But I'm no guillotine blade.*
—*Georg Büchner, in a letter to his fiancée, Minna Jaegle, 1833*

GEORG BÜCHNER wrote his play *Danton's Death* during a five-week period in 1835 while he was in constant fear of arrest for his revolutionary activities. The twenty-one-year-old German medical student strongly identified with the doomed revolutionary leader Danton, who in his final days stood at the edge of an abyss, attacked by the Convention as an enemy of the people.

Early in the first act of *Danton's Death*, the term "guillotine romanticism" (*Guillotinenromantik*) is used by Danton's friend and disciple, the handsome young journalist Camille Desmoulins, who is to die on the scaffold along with his chief in just a few days. Coined by Büchner, this phrase aptly characterizes the nightmare vision of a terrifying, yet erotic world ruled by the falling blade dispatching its victims into the existential void.

Set at the height of the Terror in the spring of 1794, *Danton's Death* is a long meditation in dramatic form on death, decay, and mortality—like those inspired by midnight visits to the cemetery in the eighteenth-century graveyard school of poetry represented by Thomas Gray's famous *Elegy in a Country Churchyard*. For Büchner and the guillotine romantics, the steps leading up to the scaffold, the blade of the machine, and the severed heads gripped by the hair and held aloft give rise to anguished thoughts on the dissolution of the human personality engulfed by the void. Yet the tone of these reflections was not solemn, but grotesque and sardonic.

For Büchner's hunted and haunted revolutionaries, the guillotine is polymor-
phous, constantly undergoing transformations. In a sick and rotten society the
"Widow" is the best doctor; it provides an effective cure for venereal disease. To
the grief-stricken Lucile Desmoulins, the machine with its tilting plank is a cra-
dle that rocked her husband to sleep. Robespierre's thin fingers, twitching on the
rostrum at the Convention, are called guillotine blades; and the Incorruptible
would have the instrument of punishment be his pulpit or prayer stool.

Above all, the guillotine is theatre. In *Danton's Death*, a gripping play-within-
a-play is repeatedly enacted on the scaffold. As is often the case in the grotesque,
distinctions between the living and dead grow blurred. The executed victims are
obliged to continue contemplating their destiny with a clear gaze. When their
heads are displayed, they stare out at the crowd. Sanson does not close the eyes
of the decapitated. Büchner's characters speculate that the remains of the dead
may well adorn the living: shoes are made from the victims' hides, wigs from
their hair. The guillotine itself is an animate presence; it must keep a straight
face and refrain from laughing lest it cease to frighten people.

Not until the final scenes of *Danton's Death* does the action move to the place
de la Révolution, where the scaffold becomes a communal place of festivity
around which the mob dances and sings. "It's a good thing that dying has been
made public," one woman exclaims.

Disillusioned with the killing and tempted by the oblivion of death, the
flamboyant sensualist Danton must now try to come to terms with the approaching divorce of his head from body, the annihilation of the "I" which has been so
insistent in his life. Previously, "the thighs of Mademoiselle" have been his private guillotine; sexual pleasure provided him a temporary substitute for the
extinction of death. In the final prison scene Danton experiences the existential
terror of approaching nothingness. Even though he no longer wishes to survive
in a world which seems to him no better than primordial chaos, he fears he will
cease to be Danton when his head falls under the knife.

For Danton, the rapid operations of the decapitating machine can only occasion bitter, sardonic laughter at the perversion of revolutionary ideals into senseless slaughter. In the face of sudden, arbitrary death on the scaffold, the only
defense is nihilistic defiance. "To be killed so mechanically," Danton muses, is
an affront to his individuality. But from the point of view of the bloodthirsty citizens eager for revenge, the guillotine works too slowly.

Yet despite the mechanization of killing, the erotic and histrionic Danton triumphs even in death. As one of the executioners pushes him away when he tries to give a farewell embrace to a fellow victim, the revolutionary leader roars out, "You can't prevent our heads from kissing at the bottom of the basket!" Here Büchner uses the historical Danton's actual words; nothing he could invent would better capture the grotesque "playing with heads" that is a defining trait of guillotine romanticism.

## THOUGHTS OF A SEVERED HEAD: ANTOINE WIERTZ AND THE BELGIAN FANTASTIC TRADITION

> For mere supposition sake, if a person could feel conscious for a second or two after decapitation, and be aware of one's mutilated condition, how excessively awkward must be the sensation! One must feel a sort of "divided duty"—a two-fold existence—like a broken series of equations. Yet it must be a moment of refreshing intellectual energy—cut off from the earthy part—the vile body—grand subject for speculation!—Why don't somebody give us "The Reflections of a Decapitated Man?" If it turned out stupid, he might excuse himself for want of a head.

So wrote the Yale graduate Theodore Witmer in *Wild Oats Sown Abroad* (1853), in which he recounts his impressions of seeing his first execution in the mid-1840s. As though he had read Witmer's mind (for it is highly unlikely he could have read his book), in 1853 the Belgian romantic painter Antoine Wiertz, a master of the gruesome, morbid, and garish, created a large triptych, *Thoughts and Visions of a Severed Head*. Intended as a powerful statement against capital punishment, the panels of the picture represent three minutes of the condemned man's experiences of his own decapitation. In images that dissolve and merge, the artist depicts the fatal blow and the moments of anguished consciousness that follow for the guillotined victim as he leaves one world and sets out for another.

The painting has deteriorated badly due to Wiertz's unsuccessful experiments with pigments. Fortunately, the artist provided a description of each of the panels in his own words. The literary text accompanying the canvas is a second-by-second account of the sensations of dying as registered by the severed head.

Wiertz's ornate prose has been much admired by the critic Walter Benjamin, who translated the work into German, and by the Belgian playwright Michel de Ghelderode, who in 1931 had the intention (never realized) of making a radio

play out of the ghastly *Thoughts and Visions*. In contrast to the ecstatic and tran-
scendental revelations given Victor Hugo by the decapitated André Chénier,
Wiertz's lurid depiction of sheer terror experienced by the victim of the guillotine anticipates techniques of horror science fiction.

## THOUGHTS AND VISIONS OF A SEVERED HEAD

FIRST MINUTE. ON THE SCAFFOLD.

Quite recently more heads fell at the foot of the scaffold. This occasion gave the
author of these paintings the idea of undertaking research on this question:

*Does the head that has been separated from the trunk conserve for several seconds the
faculty of thought?*

Here is the narration of an experiment made on this subject. . . .

Accompanied by M—— and by M. D., an expert in mesmeric experiments,
I was placed under the scaffold. There I asked M. D. to the use the new methods
he thought suitable for putting me in contact with the severed head. M. D. agreed.
He made some preparations, and we waited, not without emotion, for the fall of a
human head.

Scarcely had the fatal hour sounded than the horrible blade, having shaken the
entire machine by its fall, caused the head of the executed criminal to roll through
the dreadful red sack.

At that instant our hair stood up on end, but it was too late to back out now.
M. D. took me by the hand (I was under his mesmeric influence), led me toward
the palpitating head, and said to me: "What are you feeling? What do you see?"
Emotion prevented me from answering right away, but soon, in a state of extreme
agitation, I cried out: "Horrors! The head is thinking." I then tried to escape from
all that I was undergoing, but I was nailed there as though beneath the weight of a
frightening nightmare. So the head of the executed man saw, thought, suffered.
And I saw what it saw, understood what it was thinking, appreciated what it was
suffering. How long would it last? Three minutes, I had been told. It must have
seemed three centuries to the condemned man.

What the man who is killed in this way suffers cannot be expressed in any
known language. I shall limit myself here to transcribing the incoherent responses,
often without order, that I made to the questions addressed to me at the moment
when I felt in some way identified with the severed head.

Here are those answers:

A horrible noise is buzzing in his head.

This is the noise of the blade coming down.

The executed prisoner believes that he has been struck by lightning, not by the blade.

Incredible! The head is here, under the scaffold, but it is convinced that it is still up above, a part of the body waiting all the while for the blow that must separate it from the trunk.

A horrible suffocating sensation!

Impossible to go on breathing!

This condition is caused by the appearance of a supernatural gigantic hand, which weighs on the head and neck like a mountain.

The asphyxia becomes more violent.

The monstrous hand presses down harder and harder.

The executed prisoner feels strangled.

A fiery cloud passes before his eyes.

It is red and sparkling.

The pitiless hand succeeds in squeezing the neck still more violently.

The executed prisoner is convinced that he is struggling against the hand; he tries to get free, his hands become attached to this terrible hand, they cling desperately, they twist, they tear . . . all in vain!

What a situation, my God! The sides of the neck are joined together under pressure . . . It's all over . . .

What is this ferocious, inhuman hand? The victim has just recognized it. The purple and the ermine graze his fingers.

Oh! Still more horrible torments are being readied.

SECOND MINUTE. UNDER THE SCAFFOLD.

The pressure has become a gash.

For the first time the executed prisoner is conscious of his position.

He measures with his fiery eyes the distance that separates his head from his body and tells himself, "My head really is cut off."

Now the frenzy redoubles in force and energy.

The executed prisoner imagines that his head is burning and turning on itself, that the universe is collapsing and turning with it, that a phosphorescent fluid is

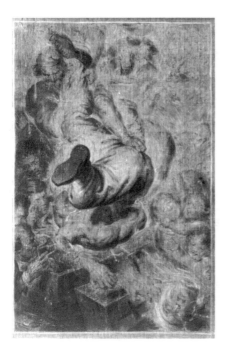 

*Antoine Wiertz. Panels two and three from*
THOUGHTS AND VISIONS OF A SEVERED HEAD, *1853.*

whirling around his skull as it melts down.

In the midst of this horrible fever, a mad, incredible, unheard of idea takes possession of the dying brain.

Would you believe it? This man whose head has been chopped off still conceives of a hope. All the blood that remains bubbles, gushes, and courses with fury through all the canals of life to grasp at this hope.

At this moment the executed prisoner is convinced that he is stretching out his convulsive and rage-filled hands toward his expiring head.

I don't know what this imaginary movement means. Wait . . . I understand . . .
It's horrible!

Oh! My God, what is life that it continues the struggle to the very last drop of blood?

That movement? Well! It's the same instinct of preservation that makes our hands rush toward a gaping wound. That movement! Whose aim, whose dreadful aim is to put back the head on the trunk in order to preserve a little blood still, a bit of life still!

. . . I feel utterly distraught, I want it to end . . .

Now a new type of suffering begins, moral suffering. A myriad of images crowd into the mind of the man killed by the guillotine and suggest the following thoughts:

*I see my coffin, I'm put inside it, thousands of worms are waiting there to eat me.*

*The doctors are all around me and look at my neck, undoubtedly for purposes of study.*

*My judges are further away in a beautiful salon . . . I can see them, peacefully seated at table, talking of indifferent things. Can that be possible?*

*Later today I'll be in the hospital, or at least my head will. Strange experiments will be made; they'll cut into my flesh, and there'll be lots of onlookers. I'll be buried today too, but there won't be any prayers for me. Those who will be present will flee in fear.*

*I see my family: my wife is dead, dead from grief, my children stand around my body and weep.*

*There's no use my telling them to help me a little, to put my head back on my neck, that time is running out, that it will be too late, that the blood keeps flowing—they don't hear me. Now I see them far away, what are they doing there? They are kneeling down in front of people who seem to be laughing and dancing.*

*Oh, my God! They are begging those people for bread.*

*The smallest of my children has stayed close by me. Oh! How I love that one. It's my boy all right; his blond curly hair, his little round rosy cheeks . . . The poor little thing sees me, smiles at me, and wants to kiss me. Three times I pulled him to my chest to cover him with a thousand kisses, three times our heads vainly tried to meet. Alas! One of them was too far away.*

*Now he backs away, crying out in fright. He looks at his little hands, which are stained with blood from my neck.*

. . . The eyes of the condemned prisoner roll in their bloody sockets.

. . . They stare fixedly toward the sky, he thinks he sees the immense canopy of the sky tear in two and the two parts draw apart like huge curtains. In the infinite depths behind, there appears a blazing furnace, where the stars seem engulfed and consumed forever. He has the impression that the air is saturated with a fiery dust, each grain of which encompasses one of his tortures. In the midst of the dazzling brilliance of the heavens, he sees a somber, amorphous object which, at each beat of his heart, draws closer and grows larger; from the breast of this strange phantom there can be heard hateful chucklings which are prolonged and gradually change into sounds of stifled lamentation. Profound darkness is spreading everywhere. The black phantom has touched the feet of the executed prisoner, he feels it stretch out and lie like lead on all his frozen limbs . . . His whole body has turned to granite. Death has come . . . No, not yet.

THIRD MINUTE. IN ETERNITY.

Death still has not come; the head continues to think and suffer.

Pain of fire that burns, pain of dagger that lacerates, pain of poison that benumbs, pain of limbs being sawed off, pain of entrails being pulled out, pain of flesh being hacked and crushed, pain of limbs being cooked in boiling oil on a slow flame, pain of epilepsy, of hydrophobia, of tetanus. All these evils combined cannot begin to describe what the executed man suffers. When will these awful torments ever end?

A gruesome doubt strikes dumb with horror the executed prisoner: could this be death and could this state of suffering be what he must endure forever, perhaps for all of eternity?

Horrible thought! The new phase that he has just entered no longer makes any sense to a living human being. Everything here announces the presence of an unknown world. These clouds in space, these sinister gleams, wavering and transient, ultimately all this chaos, where the elements of life and death are engaged in ceaseless strife, where so many horrible things recur in eternal rotation—could all this be the future abode where our soul after death must roam endlessly?

At this instant, the wretch who suffers is still occupied with things of the earth.

In an obscure corner he see his corpse rot and wither; then, as is given only to spirits of another world to perceive, he sees how the mysteries of transformation are accomplished. All the gases composing his body—the sulfurous, ammoniac, and alkaline substances—he sees emitted as fumes by his putrefied flesh and then watches them serve in the formation of other living beings. Farther off, this man whom the axe has just killed sees the infamous guillotine along with its executioners fall into a fiery abyss.

Is this last apparition one of the effects of the usual foresight with which the dying are gifted? If Dr. Guillotin's dreadful instrument is one day to be destroyed, God be praised!

Now all things human disappear; they seem little by little to dissolve into the darkness of an impenetrable night, a slight haze is still visible, but already it is receding, fading, growing imperceptible . . . Everything goes black . . . The guillotined man is dead.

In these final apparitions, some see eternal punishment meted out to the guilty; others, more human, are convinced that they can discern in the cloud in the center the soul of the executed man receiving from an angel the kiss of peace.

*Julien Deladoès.* L'EXECUTION CAPITALE.

Wiertz was highly esteemed by both the symbolists and the surrealists as a key figure in the Belgian fantastic tradition. *Thoughts and Visions of a Severed Head* still hangs in the artist's vast self-designed studio in Brussels (now the Musée Wiertz) alongside other works on such themes as madness, suicide, cannibalism, and premature burial, creating a chamber of horrors on canvas. Perhaps inspired by Wiertz, his fellow countryman Félicien Rops created a powerful protest against the death penalty with his crayon drawing *Capital Punishment* (1859), showing a despairing woman kneeling on the scaffold by the guillotine above a scattered pile of bleeding heads partially covered with a cloth. A pictorial link between Madame Tussaud's waxworks and the Grand Guignol, Wiertz transgressed all boundaries, including those of "good taste." In his essay "Genius and Insanity in Wiertz's Work" (1897), the Italian doctor and criminologist Cesare Lombroso classified *Thoughts and Visions of a Severed Head* as the hallucinatory outpourings of a paranoiac in a lunatic asylum.

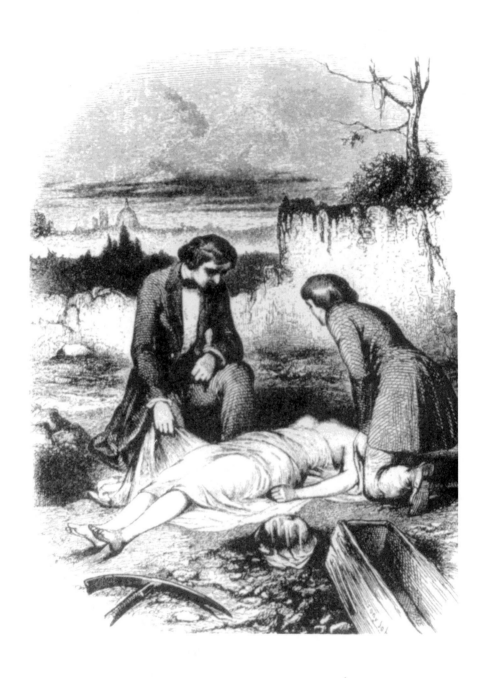

*Tony Johannot. Illustration for*
THE DEAD DONKEY, OR THE GUILLOTINED WOMAN *by Jules Janin (1842).*

# MACABRE TALES:
## IRVING, DUMAS, JANIN, AND SUE

*Shiny domes to the guillotine!*
*—Victor Hugo's young supporters shouting at bald old fogies in the*
*audience during the battle of* Hernani *between romanticists and*
*classicists at the Théâtre-Français, 1830*

ONE OF THE EARLIEST macabre tales of the guillotine, predating even Hugo's *Last Day of a Condemned Man*, is Washington Irving's story "The Adventure of a German Student," which appears in *Tales of a Traveller* (1824). In the first known publication of this oft-told tale, composed during the author's long residence in Europe, the American writer proved himself a master at a delicately ironic treatment of the supernatural, which was immensely popular in continental literature at the time.

"The Adventure of a German Student" tells the story of Gottfried Wolfgang, a melancholy young visionary engaged in lofty speculations on spiritual essences, who comes to Paris to pursue his studies of Swedenborg and mystical philosophy. Oblivious to the Terror that has the city in its grip, Gottfried lives a reclusive life in a solitary garret, his health deteriorating and his imagination diseased. He is convinced that an evil spirit is seeking to ensnare his soul. During the day he frequents the great libraries of Paris, descending into the "catacombs of departed authors" like "a literary ghoul, feeding in the charnel house of decayed literature." At night the student is haunted by the recurring dream of a woman of transcendent beauty who embodies his notion of ideal love.

Returning home late one stormy night, Gottfried passes through the place de Grève. "He shrank back with horror at finding himself close by the guillotine," which stood there "in grim array amidst a silent and sleeping city, waiting for fresh victims." As lightning flashes in the night sky, Gottfried glimpses a female figure dressed in black cowering on the steps of the scaffold, "her long disheveled tresses hanging to the ground, streaming with the rain that fell in torrents."

As he approaches, the German student beholds the very face that has haunted him in his dreams, pale and disconsolate, but ravishingly beautiful. Assuming that she is a "poor mourner whom the dreadful axe had rendered desolate," Gottfried offers his humble dwelling as a shelter to this mysterious stranger, who tells him she has no friend on earth and no home but the grave.

Having escorted her back to his apartment, Gottfried grows intoxicated by her pale face and dazzling whiteness. He notices a broad black band clasped by diamonds around her neck. In the heat of the moment, Gottfried declares his passion, to which the beautiful stranger responds. In accordance with the spirit of the Revolution, when old prejudices and superstitions were being abolished, the German student dispenses with marriage rites and simply pledges eternal love. The two embrace.

In the morning Gottfried leaves his sleeping bride to go out to seek better lodgings. He returns only to find his beautiful new wife lying with her head hanging over the edge of the bed. Her hand is cold, her body cadaverous. A police officer who has been summoned to the scene exclaims, "She was guillotined yesterday!" Gottfried unclasps the black collar around the neck of the corpse, and the head rolls to the floor. Convinced that an evil spirit had reanimated the dead body to trap him, Gottfried loses his mind and dies in a madhouse after relating his tale to an old man there who serves as Irving's narrator.

"The Adventure of a German Student" proved to be one of the most popular guillotine fables in the first half of the nineteenth century and was much imitated. The French author of weird tales, Petrus Borel—who called himself the "Lycanthrope" (werewolf)—translated it into French as "Gottfried Wolfgang" (1843), without acknowledging his source. Taking the idea from Borel, Dumas *père* used it in the plot of his fantastic novel *The Woman with the Velvet Collar* (1849).

Dumas's version is a curiously modern concoction in which historical characters, settings, and events are transposed into a fictional world. *The Woman with the Velvet Collar* is a fantasia on the demonic nature of the artist, with the young German composer and writer, E.T.A. Hoffmann as its hero. In the novel, Hoffmann comes to Paris as a seventeen-year-old in December 1793 to study music (no such visit was ever in fact made by Hoffmann). His friend, the playwright Zacharias Werner, who has preceded him to the French capital, immediately succumbs to gambling and debauchery, but Hoffmann at first resists the temptation because he has promised his sweetheart in Germany he will remain faithful to her and never gamble. He has sworn on her life as his pledge and knows that if he breaks his vow she will die.

Like Irving's Gottfried, Dumas's Hoffmann is also determined to avoid the "popular spectacle" of public executions, even after his landlady tells him that the guillotine is Paris's greatest tourist attraction and the first thing that all foreigners want to see. After all, she boasts, only the French have guillotines. In the beginning, the landlady insists, it was truly entertaining: "It was a fine show, this battle of brave enemies of the nation against death." But the endless procession of old men, women, and children in recent months had been less appealing.

By chance, Hoffmann is one day swept up in the crowd swirling around the tumbril bearing the screaming, writhing Madame Du Barry to the scaffold. The usually scurrilous female spectators watched the execution in hushed silence. In Hoffmann's eyes, Madame Du Barry's cowardly death and the sublime "power of her fear" seem to absolve her; that she did not even know how to die meant that pride had never inherently been part of her nature.

As depicted by Dumas, Paris during the Terror offers a bewildering variety of sensations and the most appalling contrasts. Bejeweled prostitutes at the Palais Egalité (formerly the Palais Royal) solicit foreign customers who can pay with gold coins instead of worthless revolutionary banknotes, while citizen patrols in the same streets round up victims for execution the following day.

Later that evening at the opera, Hoffmann meets a ghoulish doctor whose tobacco pouch is adorned with a death's head, and he falls in love with the leading dancer, Arsene, who wears a velvet collar with a diamond clasp in the shape of a guillotine—a gift from her lover Danton, still at the height of his power. Haunted by Du Barry's death, the hypersensitive Hoffmann imagines that he sees the decapitated ex-mistress of Louis XV dancing on the stage and the opera star pirouetting at the foot of the guillotine into the arms of the executioner.

Convinced that in 1793 "One had to live as one died: quickly," Hoffmann breaks all his promises to his sweetheart back in Germany, goes to a gambling den, and wins a pile of gold coins with which he will buy the love of Arsene, who goes to the highest bidder. Unable to find her, he is drawn to the guillotine by an inexplicable need to touch the scaffold. When he arrives at the empty place de la Révolution, which is dominated by "the silhouette of the hideous machine, whose mouth is moist with blood the night wind had dried and which

*Artist unknown. Illustrations for "The Adventures of a German Student"*
*by Washington Irving (1824).*

slept waiting for its daily column" of victims, the desperate young man discovers Arsene sitting on the lowest step of the scaffold, stiff and cold. He believes that his love can warm her.

After a horrendous night of macabre passion with the dancer in a luxurious private hotel, for which he has paid with his recently acquired gold, Hoffmann awakens the next morning to find a corpse in his arms. Out of nowhere the diabolical doctor appears and explains that Arsene was executed the day before; when Hoffmann removes the diamond clasp and velvet ribbon, his beloved's head rolls to his feet.

Severed heads and the guillotine appear frequently in the fantastic fiction Dumas wrote throughout his career. This is true of his collection of weird tales called *The Thousand and One Phantoms* (1849), which takes as its point of departure a bizarre crime. A stonecutter in a fit of jealousy has cut off his wife's head. He gives himself up to the local authorities, claiming that the decapitated head bit him in the hand and screamed, "You wretch! I was innocent!" A group of distinguished guests gathered on the estate of the mayor discusses the incident, and each tells a story about the survival of consciousness after decapitation in support of the stonecutter's assertion.

One of these stories, also a pseudo-historical tale of revolutionary terror that mixes fact and fiction, is a chilling example of guillotine romanticism. Mayor Ledru, son of Comus, physician to Louis XVI, and a surgeon himself, recounts the experiments that he made during the Revolution on guillotined corpses. A friend of Danton, Desmoulins, and Marat, Ledru attended the execution of Charlotte Corday and witnessed how her severed head blushed when the executioner's assistant Legros slapped her cheek. When Ledru visits Legros in prison, where he is serving a three month-sentence for his breach of scaffold etiquette, the young assistant executioner explains that he had not really been disrespectful to the dead—just because someone has been guillotined does not mean that the person is dead. For proof of that, he argues, all you have to do is to look into the basket into which the heads are tossed—the eyes keep rolling and the teeth grinding. "We have to change the basket every three months, the bottom gets so badly chewed by the teeth." Because of this unsettling experience, Ledru resolves to study the phenomenon and discover the truth about survival of consciousness after decapitation.

Later in the story, the surgeon rescues from a menacing crowd a beautiful young aristocrat masquerading as the daughter of a laundress. To disguise her true identity she pretends to know Ledru, calling him Albert; he takes the cue and claims to recognize her as his old friend Solange. Under these fictitious names they fall in love. Through his connections with Danton, Ledru is able to save the lady and her family. He arranges for her father's safe passage to England, but Solange will not leave her beloved Albert.

Meanwhile, Ledru has obtained official permission to experiment on decapitated heads, convinced that feeling, personality, and a sense of self survive execution: "the head hears, sees, and feels and judges the separation of its being." At first Ledru is revolted by the human debris on which he must experiment, but he soon grows accustomed to the sight, telling himself that his work is for the benefit of society and that he may someday be able to persuade legislators to abolish such cruel punishments.

The Clamart cemetery is put at Ledru's disposal, and a chapel on the grounds is converted into a laboratory, where an electric generator and galvanic excitator are installed. It is the height of the Terror, when thirty or forty victims go to the guillotine each day, and Ledru does not lack for heads on which to experiment. But the situation is growing more and more menacing. On the day of the execution of Marie-Antoinette, both Ledru and Solange are unusually frightened and depressed, dreading the necessary separation of a few days; after a passionate night of love, a tearful farewell leaves the surgeon full of premonition.

The following evening being the time set aside for his research, he returns to his laboratory, where he works by candlelight during a violent storm. The executioner's wagon arrives; Legros the executioner's assistant and a gravedigger bring in a sack full of heads and set it on the altar of the former chapel. The candle sputters in the wind, and the terrified Ledru hears a faint voice from inside the sack crying "Albert." The surgeon reaches into the sack, pulls out the head of his beloved Solange, and places it on the table in front of him. "I let out a terrible cry. This head whose lips seemed warm, whose eyes were half-closed was the head of Solange. I thought I was going mad. I cried out three times: Solange!!! Solange! Solange! On the third time the eyes opened, looked at me, let fall two tears, and giving off a moist flame as if her soul were departing, closed never to open again." Attempting to flee, Ledru falls down and knocks over the table, causing Solange's head to roll across the stone floor. As he lies there petrified and unable to move, the lips of the severed head brush against his lips as it rolls by.

## JULES JANIN AND *THE GUILLOTINED WOMAN*

It is not to the mainstream of the nineteenth-century French realist novel ranging from Balzac to Zola that we must look for extensive portrayals of the guillotine, but rather to popular fiction, the Gothic and the frenetic, the *roman
feuilleton* and the "penny dreadful," horror literature and the fantastic. Not long
after Hugo's *Last Days of a Condemned Man* appeared, the French critic Jules
Janin attacked what he perceived as the many vices of black romanticism. In his
Gothic novel *The Dead Donkey, or The Guillotined Woman* (1830), Janin set out to
parody all the excesses he observed in the new school. He pushed to absurd
extremes the wallowing in horror and preference for moral and physical ugliness
characteristic of the vogue of his day.

Criminals and executioners, horrifying deaths and putrefying corpses
were central to the new aesthetic of black romanticism, and Janin hoped to
counter this trend by deliberately overusing its most blatant devices. But, as
is so often the case in complex parodies, the author ultimately came to relish
what he originally intended to ridicule. Playfully exploiting the conventions
of horror, Janin created an outstanding work of black humor. The seventh
edition of *The Dead Donkey*, published in 1842, is graced with brooding and
ironic engravings by Tony Johannot, one of the leading romantic book illus-
trators of the day.

A compendium of the most bizarre images of guillotine romanticism, *The
Dead Donkey* includes a glimpse into an outdoor workshop where the decapitating machine is under construction, a visit to the executioner at home, and a trip
to the cemetery to see head and trunk reassembled and finally disposed of. The
novel tells the story of the charming and innocent young Henriette and her pet
donkey Charlot, both of whom come to ghastly ends once they abandon the
idyllic countryside for the cruel and depraved life of Paris. The beloved donkey—whose name is also traditionally the nickname of the executioner—is
eaten alive by fierce mastiffs during an animal gladiatorial combat at the slaughterhouse. After having passed through all the moral cesspools of Parisian society
high and low, Henriette is finally condemned to death for murdering the former
lover who first debauched her on her arrival in Paris. When this dissolute rake
had reappeared as her first customer in the cheap brothel where she had been
forced to seek work following a long bout with venereal disease, Henriette
stabbed him in a blind rage.

*Tony Johannot. Illustration for*
THE DEAD DONKEY, OR THE GUILLOTINED WOMAN *by Jules Janin (1842).*

On a stroll through Paris, the voyeuristic narrator of *The Dead Donkey*—a rejected suitor of Henriette's—chances on a happy young carpenter singing merrily as he works on the construction of a strange wooden machine of large dimensions in a delightful pastoral setting. The carpenter's fiancée appears; she is pretty, fresh, and naïve. To satisfy her curiosity about the machine, the workman shows her how to play her role on the stage he has built. He ties her hands behind her back, leads her up the scaffold, and binds her to the plank, which suddenly tilts forward and imprisons her neck in the lunette. The carpenter leaps down to the ground below her, reaching his lips up to the laughing victim who is unable to move or deny him a "guillotine kiss."

The narrator realizes that this guillotine is meant for Henriette and reflects that "this laughing theatre of love will be nothing other than a theatre of murder, the boudoir will become a bloody scaffold." The only kiss on the scaffold will be the one given by the chaplain to the victim about to die.

To try to secure possession of Henriette's remains, the narrator pays a visit to the executioner at his home. The house is surrounded by silence and terror; the street has no name, the building no number—yet everyone knows that it is where the executioner lives. Once inside, the narrator is astonished to notice everywhere the signs of discreet elegance and good taste: flowers, paintings, a piano with a romance opened on the music stand, a clock displaying a mythological Cupid and Psyche set fifteen minutes fast to prevent the executioner from ever arriving late to work.

The paterfamilias, the now-retired Sanson of revolutionary times, is giving a history lesson to his young grandson in an adjoining room. The narrator tries to imagine what kind of lesson could come from a man who "had been the sole God and the sole king of that epoch without authority and without belief, a terrible God, an inviolable king."

Sanson's son, the current executioner, enters. The narrator successfully bargains for Henriette's trunk and head, but he does not beg for her life; he knows that the servant of the guillotine cannot be moved. "Revolution, anarchy, empire, restoration—nothing has touched it; my authority has always remained in place," the reigning Sanson explains."I have been stronger than the law, of which I am the supreme sanction; the law has changed a thousand times, I alone have not changed once: I am as immutable as destiny and strong as moral duty; I have emerged from so many ordeals with a pure heart, bloody hands, and a spotless conscience."

Janin's portrait of the executioner is similar to that painted by the Catholic counterrevolutionary philosopher Joseph de Maistre, who in his *Saint Petersburg Dialogues* (1821) provides an apologia for the hangman.

> He is an extraordinary being, and for him to exist in the human family a particular decree, a FIAT of the creative power is necessary. He is a species to himself. . . . Scarcely have the authorities fixed his dwelling place, scarcely has he taken possession of it, than the other houses seem to shrink back until they no longer overlook his. . . . And yet all grandeur, all power, all subordination rests on the executioner: he is the horror and the bond of human association. Remove this incomprehensible agent from the world, and at that very moment order gives way to chaos, thrones topple, and society disappears.

Henriette manages to delay her execution by yielding to the lust of her hideously deformed jailer. Pregnant, she gains a nine-month reprieve, but almost as soon as the baby is born the executioner's assistants come to claim their victim, and the nursing child is taken off to the foundling home where it will grow up to a life of crime and infamy.

Henriette's date with the machine can no longer be deferred. A huge mob throngs to see the execution, including the carpenter and his fiancée; even Henriette's aged parents come, not realizing that the victim is their child. "Paris is constructed that way: virtue or vice, innocence or crime, the populace bothers little about the victim, provided there will be a death! A minute of agony on the place de Grève—now of all the free shows offered in Paris, that is the most enjoyable!"

The narrator rushes to the cemetery with a fresh, clean sheet to recover the corpse of his love. He bribes the gravedigger to keep the body from being sent directly for dissection in the medical amphitheatre located nearby. The executioner's assistants soon arrive with the corpse and present the narrator with a detailed and padded bill including such grisly items as charges for sharpening the blade, greasing the grooves, bran for the sack, and three brandies for drinking to the health of the deceased.

The distraught admirer then makes an inventory of the red basket. "The assistant opened it; he first removed a head drained of blood, the hair cut and trimmed as though by a razor; the mouth was horribly contracted; the eye was dull, and yet it still seemed to look at you; the convulsion had been so strong that the jaws were no longer parallel; with the result that this mouth, so full of smiles and a thousand charms, was closed on one side and hideously open on the other."

The narrator removes Henriette's remains for burial, dressing the trunk in a silk chemise, which he ties at the neck, and placing the head in a pillow case. At the graveside milk oozes from her breasts while blood flows from her neck. In the coffin the body parts are reassembled and the sheared hair replaced on the head. He has paid the gravedigger extra to dig the hole deep and pack the dirt tightly, but when the narrator returns the next day, the grave has been robbed. The old crones who haunt the cemetery have stolen the silk chemise and sold the torso and head to the medical students. Of Henriette nothing remains but a gaping hole in the earth.

Janin's narrator has proof, even beyond his darkest dreams of catastrophe, of the total corruption of human life. *The Dead Donkey, or the Guillotined Woman* is a deeply ambivalent tribute to the emerging sensibility and taste for romantic horrors—the new poetics of the cadaver.

## BALZAC AND STENDHAL: REALISTS SLIGHT THE GUILLOTINE

Serious realist authors such as Balzac and Stendhal did not exclude executions from their novels, but at the key moment they always elected to avert their narrators' eyes from anything as sensational and hallucinatory as the guillotine. In Balzac's *Country Parson* (1839), the execution of Tascheron for murder is described tersely: "He met his death like a Christian, penitent and forgiven. The poor curé of Montégnac was taken away unconscious from the foot of the scaffold, though he had not so much as set eyes on the fatal machine." In *An Episode under the Terror* (1830), Balzac presents the executioner Sanson as deeply aggrieved at having had to behead Louis XVI, for the repose of whose soul he arranges to have a secret mass said, but nowhere does the novelist dramatize the ritual of the scaffold.

*Honoré de Balzac.*

At the end of *The Red and the Black*

(1831), Stendhal's novel based on a criminal *fait divers* from the *Gazette des tribunaux*, the hero Julien Sorel is imprisoned and waiting to be executed for the attempted murder of his mistress. In chapter seventy-four, called "In the Shadow of the Guillotine," Julien confesses to himself his inner fears and cowardice but resolves to play the role required in the eyes of the public; on the scaffold he will feign courage. Duty dictates that he be strong and resolute. But all the events of the day of execution, from the *toilette du condamné* to the march to the scaffold and the functioning of the engine of death, are passed over in discreet silence, as if in fulfillment of Julien's wish to avoid public spectacle. "Everything passed simply, decorously, and without affection on his part" is all that Stendhal reveals.

Only after Julien is executed does Stendhal partake of the guillotine romanticism of the period and its erotic and metaphysical interest in the survival of consciousness after decapitation. Julien's mistress Mathilde de la Môle recovers Julien's head from the executioner, in emulation of Marguerite de Navarre, queen of France, who in 1574 had taken the severed head of her executed lover Boniface de la Mole (Mathilde's distant ancestor) and buried it herself. Once she has taken it back to her home, Mathilde lights candles and places Julien's head upon a little marble table in front of her. She repeatedly kisses the forehead, but not the lips, of her lover. Later in her carriage, the curtains tightly drawn, Mathilde rides with Julien's head upon her knees and finally buries it with her own hands. Stendhal gives no indication that Julien's severed head ever showed any sign of life.

## EUGENE SUE AND THE SERIALIZED NOVEL:
### THE MYSTERIES OF PARIS

Unlike Balzac and Stendhal, popular French serial writers of the time addressing a vast public never hesitated to dwell on the horrors of the guillotine. On the contrary, scenes dealing with the scaffold were consciously elaborated to thrill the mass audience.

The most successful of all the nineteenth-century French serialized novels was *The Mysteries of Paris* (1842). Its author, the humanitarian socialist Eugène Sue, presents vignettes of poor working-class prisoners awaiting execution. The author's father, Jean-Joseph Sue, was a doctor and professor of anatomy who in 1797 published the results of his scientific research on the suffering of the guil-

lotined, concluding that both the
head and the body continued to
experience sensations of pain after
decapitation. Eugène Sue's gruesome
descriptions of the hideous rituals of
the guillotine were undoubtedly
influenced by his father's theories.

*The Mysteries of Paris* introduces us
to the Lion's Den of la Force prison,
where the most dangerous prisoners
are kept. One of the condemned,
nicknamed Skeleton, jokes about his
coming appointment with Père Sanson. " 'There's a sharp blade, and

*Eugène Sue.*

they put a head under it, and that's all. And now that I know my road, and must
stay at the abbey of *Mont-à-Regret* [guillotine], I would rather go there today than
tomorrow,' said the Skeleton, with savage excitement. 'I wish I was there now,
my blood comes into my mouth when I think what a crowd there'll be to see me;
there'll be, at least, I should say, from four to five thousand who will push and
squeeze to get good places, and they'll hire seats and windows, as if for a grand
procession. I hear 'em now crying, "Seats to let! Seats to let!" And then there'll
be troops of soldiers, cavalry and infantry, and all for me—for the Skeleton!' "

In another installment of the serial, the hardened widow Martial and her
terrified daughter Calabash await execution in the cell of the condemned at
Bicêtre prison. Dressed in black with a large cravat, the executioner appears
accompanied by two assistants and the governor of the prison. He presents an
official paper signifying his having received two females for the purpose of
guillotining them.

> The almost expiring Calabash having been supported to a chair by the two
> assistants, one sustained her all but inanimate form, while the other tied her
> hands behind with fine but excessively strong whipcord, knotted into the most
> inextricable meshes, while with a cord of the same description he secured her
> feet, allowing her just so much liberty as would enable her to proceed slowly to
> her last destination. The widow having borne a similar pinioning with the most
> imperturbable composure, the executioner, drawing from his pocket a pair of

huge scissors, said to her with considerable civility:

"Be good enough to stoop your head, madame."

Yielding immediate obedience to the request, the widow said: "We have been good customers to you; you have had my husband in your hands, and now you have his wife and daughter!"

Without making any reply, the executioner began to cut the long gray hairs of the prisoner very close, especially at the nape of the neck.

Refusing the consolation of a priest, the widow thanks the executioner for his services, recommending her son Nicholas to him: "You will cut his hair some day." When offered a glass of strong drink, she declines.

"No, I thank you; this evening I shall take a mouthful of earth." After this remark the widow rose firmly. Her hands were tied behind her back, and a rope was also attached to each ankle, allowing her sufficient liberty to walk. Although her step was firm and resolute, the executioner and his assistant offered to support her; but she turned to them disdainfully, and said, "Do not touch me, I have a steady eye and a firm foot, and they will hear on the scaffold whether or not I have a good voice." Calabash was carried away in a dying state.

After having traversed the long corridor, the funereal cortege ascended a stone staircase, which led to an exterior court, where was a picquet *gens-d'armes*, a hackney-coach, and a long, narrow carriage with a yellow body, drawn by three posthorses, who were neighing loudly.

A vast mob—"the foul and fetid scum" of Paris, comprised of thieves and abandoned women—howls with "savage delight at the idea that, after a night of filthy orgies, they should see two women executed on the scaffold." Dancing *La Chahut*, a frantic and obscene dance, the crowd follows the wagon to the Barrière St. Jacques, where the scaffold stands waiting.

As a reformer and socialist, the author of *The Mysteries of Paris* fought for the relief of the social misery afflicting the "virtuous poor" worthy of rehabilitation. But Eugène Sue had no doubt that the vile mob of convicts and degenerates who danced around the guillotine were beyond redemption and deserved only to be punished themselves.

# LITERARY EYEWITNESSES

*I went with a magistrate friend of mine to the execution of the Bonnot gang. . . .*
*First prisoner. Two steps forward. Plank tilts. Click. Corpse disappears.*
*Three buckets of water. All over. Second prisoner: same business.*
*Third prisoner: same business.*
*An American reporter who had consulted his watch during the triple execution*
*said to my friend: "You know, monsieur le procureur, how long*
*the whole thing lasted? Forty seconds exactly: it's the new record!"*
*—Gabriel Astruc, impresario who presented*
*Sergei Diaghilev and the Ballets Russes in Paris, 1929*

AUDIENCES AT nineteenth-century executions included representatives of all classes and professions, but it is the famous artists and writers who have left us the most vivid accounts of the drama enacted on the scaffold.

Wherever Napoleon's armies went they brought the guillotine with them. Thus it was that the new French instrument for decapitation was introduced into northern Italy, and in 1817 Byron wrote to his friend John Murray, describing an execution that he had witnessed and expressing his admiration for the style of the machine.

*Lord Byron.*

The day before I left Rome I saw three robbers guillotined—the ceremony—including the *masqued* priests—the half-naked executioners—the bandaged criminals—the black Christ & his banner—the scaffold—the soldiery—the slow procession—& the quick rattle and heavy fall of the axe—the splash of the blood—& the ghastliness of the exposed heads—is altogether more impressive than the vulgar and ungentlemanly dirty "new drop" & dog-like agony of infliction upon the sufferers of the English sentence. Two of these men—behaved calmly enough—but the first of the three—died with great terror and reluctance—which was very horrible—he would not lie down—then his neck was too large for the aperture—and the priest was obliged to drown his exclamations by still louder exhortations—the head was off before the eye could trace the blow—but from an attempt to draw back the head—notwithstanding it was held forward by the hair—the first head was cut off close to the ears—the other two were taken off more cleanly;—it is better than the Oriental way—& (I should think) than the axe of our ancestors.—The pain seems little—& yet the effect to the spectator—& the preparation to the criminal—is very striking & chilling.—The first turned me quite hot and thirsty—& made me shake so that I could hardly hold the opera-glass (I was close—but was determined to see—as one should see everything once—with attention) the second and third (which shows how dreadfully soon things grow indifferent) I am ashamed to say had no effect on me—as a horror—though I would have saved them if I could.

## CHARLES DICKENS

An avid follower of crime and punishment, Charles Dickens had the opportunity to see an execution by guillotine when he was in Rome in 1845. The religious ritual, as he noted, seemed to have changed little since the time of Beatrice Cenci.

On one Saturday morning [the eighth of March], a man was beheaded here. Nine or ten months before, he had waylaid a Bavarian countess, travelling as a pilgrim to Rome . . . robbed her; and beat her to death with her own pilgrim staff. . . .

There are no fixed times for the administration of justice, or its execution, in this unaccountable country; and he had been in prison ever since. On the Friday, as he was dining with other prisoners, they came and told him he was to be beheaded next morning, and took him away. It is very unusual to execute in Lent; but his crime being a very bad one, it was deemed advisable to make an example of him at that time, when great numbers of pilgrims were coming towards Rome, from all parts, for the Holy Week. I heard this on the Friday evening, and saw the bills up at the churches, calling on the people to pray for the criminal's soul. So, I determined to go, and see him executed.

The beheading was appointed for fourteen and a-half o'clock, Roman time: or a quarter before nine in the forenoon. I had two friends with me; as we did not know but that crowd might be very great, we were on the spot by half-past seven. The place of execution was near the church of San Giovanni decolláto (a doubtful compliment to Saint John the Baptist) in one of the impassable back streets without any footway, of which a great part of Rome is composed—a street of rotten houses, which do not seem to belong to anybody. . . . Opposite to one of these, a white house, the scaffold was built.

*Charles Dickens.*

An untidy, unpainted, uncouth, crazy-looking thing of course: some seven feet high, perhaps: with a tall, gallows-shaped frame rising above it, in which was the knife, charged with a ponderous mass of iron, all ready to descend, and glittering brightly in the morning sun. . . .

There were not many people lingering about; and these were kept at a considerable distance from the scaffold, by parties of the Pope's dragoons. Two or three foot-soldiers were under arms, standing at ease in clusters here and there; and the officers were walking up and down in twos and threes, chatting together, and smoking cigars. . . .

Nine o'clock struck, and ten o'clock struck, and nothing happened. All the bells of all churches rang as usual. . . . A pastry-merchant divided his attention between the scaffold and his customers. Boys tried to climb up walls, and tumbled down again. Priests and monks elbowed a passage for themselves among the people, and stood on tiptoes for a sight of the knife: then went away. Artists, in inconceivable hats of the middle-ages, and beards (thank Heaven!) of no age at all, flashed picturesque scowls about them from their stations in the throng. . . .

Eleven o'clock struck; and still nothing happened. A rumour got about, among the crowd, that the criminal would not confess; in which case, the priests would keep him until the Ave Maria (sunset); for it is their merciful custom never finally to turn the crucifix away from a man at that pass, as one refusing to be shriven, and consequently a sinner abandoned of the Saviour, until then. People began to drop off. . . .

Suddenly there was a noise of trumpets. "Attention!" was among the foot-soldiers instantly. They were marched up to the scaffold and formed round it. The dragoons galloped to their near stations too. The guillotine became the centre of a wood of bristling bayonets and shining sabres. The people closed round near, on the flank of the soldiery. A long straggling stream of men and boys, who had accompanied the procession from the prison, came pouring into the open space. . . . The cigar and pastry-merchants resigned all thoughts of business, for the moment, and abandoning themselves wholly to pleasure, got good situations in the crowd. The perspective ended, now, in a troop of dragoons. And the corpulent officer, sword in hand, looked hard at a church close to him, which he could see, but we, the crowd, could not.

After a short delay, some monks were seen approaching to the scaffold from this church; and above their heads, coming on slowly and gloomily, the effigy of Christ upon the cross, canopied with black. This was carried round the foot of the scaffold, to the front, and turned towards the criminal, that he might see it to the last. It was hardly in its place, when he appeared on the platform, bare-footed; his hands bound; and with the collar and neck of his shirt cut away, almost to the shoulder. A young man—six-and-twenty—vigorously made, and well-shaped. Face pale; small dark moustache; and dark brown hair. . . .

He immediately kneeled down, below the knife. His neck fitting into a hole, made for the purpose, in a cross plank, was shut down, by another plank above; exactly like a pillory. Immediately below him was a leathern bag. And into it his head rolled instantly.

The executioner was holding it by the hair, and walking with it round the scaffold, showing it to the people, before one quite knew that the knife had fallen heavily, and with a rattling sound.

When it had travelled round the four sides of the scaffold, it was set upon a pole in front—a little patch of black and white, for the long street to stare at, and the flies to settle on. The eyes were turned upward, as if he had avoided the sight of the leathern bag, and looked to the crucifix. Every tinge and hue of life had left it in that instant. It was dull, cold, livid, wax. The body also.

There was a great deal of blood. When we left the window, and went up close to the scaffold, it was very dirty; one of the two men who were throwing water over it, turning to help the other to lift the body into a shell, picked his way as through mire. A strange appearance was the apparent annihilation of the neck. The head was taken off so close, that it seemed as if the knife had narrowly escaped crushing the jaw, or shaving off the ear; and the body looked as if there were nothing left above the shoulder.

Nobody cared, or was at all affected. There was no manifestation of disgust, or pity, or indignation, or sorrow. My empty pockets were tried, several times, in the crowd immediately below the scaffold, as the corpse was being put into its coffin. It was an ugly, filthy, careless, sickening spectacle; meaning nothing but butchery beyond the momentary interest, to the one wretched actor. Yes! Such a sight has one meaning and one warning. Let me not forget it. The speculators in the lottery station themselves at favourable points for counting the gouts of blood that spirt out, here and there; and buy that number. It is pretty sure to have a run upon it.

The body was carted away in due time, the knife cleansed, the scaffold taken down, and the hideous apparatus removed. The executioner: an outlaw *ex officio* (what a satire on the Punishment!) who dare not, for his life, cross the Bridge of St. Angelo but to do his work: retreated to his lair, and the show was over.

## LEO TOLSTOY

During his first visit in 1857 to western Europe, the twenty-nine year-old Leo Tolstoy, acting against his better judgment, went to see the guillotining in Paris of François Richeux, condemned for robbery and homicide. The Russian author's reaction was that of a stern moralist, outraged at the arrogance of the state for taking upon itself the role of God, and filled with a personal sense of guilt and horror at the bloodthirsty mob, estimated at twelve thousand. He described his feelings in a letter to his friend Vasily Petrovich Botkin.

*Leo Tolstoy.*

I was stupid and callous enough to go and see an execution this morning. Apart from the fact that the weather has been dreadful here for the last fortnight and that I'm very out of sorts, I was in a vile state of nerves, and the spectacle made such an impression on me that I shan't get over it for a long time. I've seen many horrible things in war and in the

Caucasus, but if a man had been torn to pieces before my eyes it wouldn't have been so revolting as this ingenious and elegant machine by means of which a strong, hale and hearty man was killed in an instant. In war it's not a question of the rational will, but of human feelings of passion; but in this case it's cold, refined calculation and a convenient way of murder, and there's nothing grand about it. It's the insolent, arrogant desire to carry out justice and the law of God—justice, which is determined by lawyers taking their stand on honour, religion and truth, and all contradicting each other. With just the same formalities they killed the king, and Chénier and the republicans and the aristocrats and the man (I forget his name) who, a couple of years ago, was declared innocent of the murder for which he was killed. Then the repulsive crowd, the father explaining to his daughter the convenient and ingenious mechanism that does it etc. . . . . The law of man—what nonsense! The truth is that the state is a conspiracy designed not only to exploit, but above all to corrupt its citizens.

After witnessing the execution, Tolstoy changed his initially favorable impression of Paris and left hurriedly for Switzerland. Twenty years later Tolstoy was still haunted by the guillotine and returned to the horrible spectacle on the scaffold when he wrote his autobiographical *Confession* in 1887.

When I saw the head part from the body and how it thumped separately into the box, I understood, not with my mind, but with my whole being that no theory of the reasonableness of our present progress could justify this deed, and that though everyone from the creation of the world, on whatever theory, had held it to be necessary, I knew it would be unnecessary and bad; and therefore the arbiter of what is good and evil is not what people say and do, nor is it progress, but is my heart and I.

## IVAN TURGENEV

By the latter third of the nineteenth century, executions had become a major social event in Paris. Newspapers seeking to expand their readership devoted column after column to the spectacle and sent their best reporters. Specialized criticism developed in which the guillotine reviewer commented on the attitude of the condemned, praising displays of courage and reprimanding signs of weakness, clocking the time from departing the prison to the fall of the blade, and evaluating the speed of the executioner and his skill in dispatching his patient. The critic gave good or bad reviews as if he were writing about actors in a play.

The trial and execution in 1870 of the twenty-one-year-old Jean-Baptiste Troppmann, who murdered a family of eight, attracted an unusual amount of attention. For months every class of Parisian society eagerly awaited details of the trial. "Penny-dreadful" accounts of the murder were sold in the streets; the prison cell in which Troppmann had been confined was besieged by visitors, including men of science, ambassadors, society ladies, and writers. To satisfy the mounting curiosity, the authorities placed a life-size portrait of the assassin in the hall of the prison, and row after row of pictures of him were exhibited in the windows of photographers, stationery shops, and souvenir kiosks.

The execution, which took place at seven o'clock in the morning on January 19, 1870, at the place de la Roquette, was attended by a huge mob waiting in the cold to get a glimpse of the celebrities as they arrived. Leading Parisian personalities (including Maxime du Camp and Victorien Sardou) had been invited by the governor of the prison and were issued special guest passes allowing them to go through police lines. These privileged guests spent the night preceding the execution in the governor's lodgings, were served a buffet consisting of sandwiches, *pâté de foie gras*, cold chicken, punch, and wine, and then were permitted to study the machine at close quarters. The distinguished-looking executioner, Jean-François Heidenreich, wearing a frock coat with velvet collar and eyeglasses on a black silk cord, demonstrated the workings of the mechanism. Sardou, in a playful mood, asked to be put in the place of the condemned. The executioner went along with the game and secured the playwright to the plank. A bale of straw, always used to test the guillotine before each execution, went into the collar where Sardou's neck would have been, and the blade came down, not far from the head of the famous practitioner of the well-made play, who was delighted with the smooth operation of the well-made machine.

Ivan Turgenev, who was then living in Paris, was among the celebrities invited. The Russian novelist, who commented that only the horses who drew the guillotine were innocent, recorded a chilling account of the entire horrifying spectacle.

When the invited guests arrived at the place de la Roquette, Turgenev reported, "a squad of soldiers was drawn up four deep across the square, and about two hundred feet from it, another squad was also drawn up four deep." The tall, gray Russian author was at first mistaken for the tall, gray executioner

*Jean-Baptiste Troppmann.*

by a group of excited urchins. The celebrities were allowed into the prison "with immense precautions," and following detailed questioning, they were led to the governor's lodgings on the second floor and given a report on Troppmann's condition—he was sound asleep. After a while they were informed that the guillotine had arrived, whereupon "we all rushed out into the street—just as though we were glad of the news!"

> Before the prison gates stood a huge, closed van, drawn by three horses, harnessed one behind the other; another two-wheeled van, a small and low one, which looked like an oblong box and was drawn by one horse, had stopped a little further off. (That one, as we learned later, was to convey the body of the executed man to the cemetery immediately after the execution.) A few women in short blouses were to be seen around the vans, and a tall man in a round hat, white necktie and a light overcoat thrown over his shoulders, was giving orders in an undertone. . . . That was the executioner.

Turgenev noted "the respectful familiarity" with which the executioner was treated by all, the remarkable whiteness and the beauty of his hands, and described the erection of the guillotine by the workmen (within fifteen feet of the prison gates), the confused din of voices, and the great number of people milling about. The time now was fifteen minutes past midnight. Back in the governor's apartment they were treated to mulled wine and shown a huge mound of letters addressed to Troppmann (which he had left unopened).

"Most of them seemed to be full of silly jokes, but there were also some that were serious. . . . One Methodist clergyman sent a whole theological thesis on twenty pages; there were also small notes from ladies, who even enclosed flowers—marguerites and immortelles." A lazy conversation dragged on, touching lightly on "politics and theatre." At three o'clock the distant noise of the crowd was growing louder and louder; more than twenty thousand people had already gathered outside.

> The noise struck me by its resemblance to the distant roar of the sea: the same sort of unending Wagnerian *crescendo*, not rising continuously, but with huge intervals between ebb and flow; the shrill notes of women's and children's voices rose in the air like thin spray over this enormous rumbling noise; there was the brutal power of some elemental force discernible in it. . . . And what, I could not

help asking myself, did this noise signify? Impatience, joy, malice? No! It did not serve as an echo of any separate, any human feeling. . . . It was simply the rumble and the roar of some elemental force.

Turgenev ventured out into the street again.

The guillotine was ready. Its two beams, separated by about two feet, with the slanting line of the connecting blade, stood out dimly and strangely rather than terribly against the dark sky. For some reason I imagined that those beams ought to be more distant from each other; their proximity lent the whole machine a sort of sinister shapeliness, the shapeliness of a long, carefully stretched out swan's neck. The large, dark-red wicker basket, looking like a suitcase, aroused a feeling of disgust in me.

Large contingents of mounted police arrived, cutting back and forth across the square to hold the crowd back. Turgenev drew closer and ". . . gazed for a long time at the people; their shouting actually was elemental, that is, senseless." The piercing cries of hawkers selling leaflets about Troppmann, describing his execution and even relating his "last words," could be heard, sometimes accompanied by "a hideous burst of laughter." At one point Turgenev was able to make out the "Marseillaise" haltingly sung by a small group of men. "The Marseillaise," Turgenev observed, "becomes significant only when thousands are singing it. . . . A heavy, rank breath of alcoholic fumes came from the crowd; a great deal of wine had been drunk by all those bodies."

On the way back to the governor's apartment, Turgenev passed the guillotine and saw the executioner "surrounded by a small crowd of inquisitive people." He was carrying out a "rehearsal" for them; he "threw down the hinged plank . . . let fall the knife, which ran down heavily and smoothly with a rapid, hollow roar, and so on."

As the hour of execution drew near, the invited guests went to Troppmann's cell, accompanied by a priest and the prison officials. Troppmann to the very last refused to name his accomplices and, "with a slight bow," politely declined an offer of wine. Then his *camisole de force* (prison straitjacket) was taken off by the warders and he was given a new, clean shirt. Troppmann put it on and "carefully buttoned the neckband." Turgenev observed: "Nothing in him disclosed, I won't say, fear, but even agitation or anxiety." Next he put on his boots "cheerfully and without any sign of constraint—almost gaily, just as though he had been invited to go for a walk." One of those present later remarked that "he had kept imagining that it was not 1870 but 1794, that we were not ordinary citizens but Jacobins, and that we were taking to his execution not a common murderer but a *marquis-legitimist, un ci-devant, un talon rouge, monsieur!*"

The procession through the prison was almost like a flight.

Troppmann walked in front of us with quick, resilient, almost bounding steps; he was in a hurry, and we all hurried after him. Some of us, anxious to have a look at his face once more, even ran ahead to the right and the left of him. So we rushed across the corridor and ran down the other staircase, Troppmann jumping two steps at a time, ran across another corridor, jumped over a few steps, and, at last, found ourselves in the tall room . . . with the stool on which 'the toilet of the condemned man' was to be completed. We entered through one door, and from the other door there appeared, walking importantly, in a white necktie and a black 'suit,' the executioner, looking for all the world like a diplomat or a protestant pastor. He was followed by a short, fat old man in a black coat, his first assistant, the hangman of Beauvais. The old man held a small leather bag in his hand.

Two assistants began tying rawhide straps around Troppmann's entire body while the priest mumbled some prayers, and monsieur de Beauvais painfully tried to bore holes in the straps used to hobble the prisoner's legs, which had turned out to be too large. "The man who made the holes had a fatter man in mind." Further delay occurred in the next step of the ritual when Troppmann's hair and the collar of his shirt were cut off with "none too sharp blades." The chief executioner supervised, indicating at every point how much more hair he wanted to have cut off. Meanwhile, "Troppmann kept bending his head in the same obedient manner; the priest dragged out the words even more slowly." At last all the preliminaries were over. Troppmann shook his head and "the executioner grasped his elbow." It was time to appear before the public.

The roar of the crowd encompassed us by an unbroken, ear-splitting, thunderous wave as soon as we stepped over the threshold. . . . Troppmann minced along nimbly—his shackles interfered with his walk. . . . Suddenly the two halves of the gates, like some immense mouth of an animal, opened slowly before us—and all at once, as though to the accompaniment of the great roar of the overjoyed crowd which at last caught sight of what it had been waiting for, the monster of the guillotine stared at us with its two narrow black beams and its suspended axe. . . .

I saw the executioner rise suddenly like a black tower on the left side of the guillotine platform; I saw Troppmann, separated from the huddle below, scrambling up the steps (there were ten of them—as many as ten!); I saw him stopping and turning around; . . . I saw him appear above two men pouncing on him from the right and the left, like spiders on a fly; I saw him falling forward suddenly and his legs kicking. . . .

But here I turned away and began to wait, the ground slowly rising and falling under my feet. . . . And it seemed to me that I was waiting a terribly long time (as a matter of fact, only *twenty* seconds passed between the time Troppmann put his foot on the first step of the guillotine and the moment when his dead body was flung into the prepared basket). I managed to notice that at Troppmann's appearance the roar of the crowd seemed suddenly to roll up into a ball and—a breathless hush fell over everything. . . . At last I heard a light knocking of wood on wood—that was the sound made by the top part of the yoke with the slit for the passage of knife as it fell round the murderer's head and kept it immobile. . . . Then something suddenly descended with a hollow growl and stopped with an abrupt thud. . . . Just as though a huge animal had retched. . . . I cannot think of any better comparison. I felt dizzy. Everything swam before my eyes.

Turgenev stood too great a distance from the guillotine to see how Troppmann, in a final gesture of revolt, managed to draw back his head from the collar. He was grabbed by the hair and pulled into position by one of the assistants. Stretching his neck "obligingly forward," Troppmann managed to sink his teeth deep into the assistant executioner's index finger, biting it almost clean through. When the blade had fallen and the body been thrown into the cart, which was rapidly driven away, two men forced their way through the lines of soldiers and, "crawling under the guillotine, began wetting their handkerchiefs in the blood that had dripped through the chink of the plank."

Later, Turgenev related a discussion of the execution with his friend Maxime du Camp, an authority on life in Paris who had written learnedly about the guillotine.

A whole stream of human beings, men, women and children, rolled past us in disorderly and untidy waves. . . . And what drunken, glum sleepy faces! What an expression of boredom, fatigue, dissatisfaction, disappointment, dull, purposeless disappointment! . . .

We talked of the unnecessary, senseless barbarism of all that medieval procedure, thanks to which the criminal's agony went on for half an hour, of the hideousness of all those undressings, dressings, hair-cutting, those journeys along corridors and up and down staircases. . . . By what right was all that done? How could such a shocking routine be allowed? And capital punishment itself—could it possibly be justified? . . .

But I am not going to indulge in arguments; they would lead me too far. And, anyway, who is not aware of the fact that the question of capital punishment is one of the most urgent questions that humanity has to solve at this moment? I will be content and excuse my own misplaced curiosity if my account supplies a few arguments to those who are in favor of the abolition of capital punishment or, at least, the abolition of public executions.

## ALEXANDRE DUMAS *FILS*

At about the same time that Turgenev recorded his witnessing of the guillotine, Dumas *fils* (whose father had written so luridly of the guillotine) recounted how he had long wanted to watch an execution but felt ashamed of his curiosity to see the "sinister spectacle." Several times he had been able to learn the day and hour in advance (always a deeply guarded secret), but the sensitive author of

*Camille* had always backed out. "My courage failed me in the face of the night and the manner in which I imagined this terrible spectacle."

Dumas *fils* decided that what he needed was a criminal guilty of such horrible crimes that only the death penalty would be fit punishment. Then the playwright could go to see justice served as an interested member of society, which had a right to exact retribution. He did not have to wait long. Dumas *fils* learned of the impending execution of a certain Bixner, who had

*Alexandre Dumas* fils.

raped and then murdered his own daughter. Here was a criminal who deserved to be executed if anyone ever did. Now the author would be able to watch a guillotining with a clean conscience.

> The execution was to take place at eight o'clock, I woke up at six quite spontaneously.
>
> It was strange, at six o'clock I knew this man was to die even before he knew it, and I woke up to witness his death, at the hour when it had just been announced to him.
>
> I made this association as I opened my eyes; because my mind concentrated on this thought and this thought alone, through the gloom of the night, isolating me in the action that I was about to commit, everything else disappeared, and I saw nothing but him and me. . . .
>
> The weather was terrible. The sky was churning with swollen clouds, the color of slate and transparent as mourning gauze, which were whipped by the West wind. It had rained. The pavement was covered with mud. It was cold and somber. As you can see, the stage setting couldn't have been better.

Dumas *fils* was able to find a carriage in front of the fashionable all-night restaurant la Maison dorée (which also figures in Villiers's guillotine tale, "The Eleventh-Hour Guest"), and the driver set off for the Barrière St. Jacques.

As they traveled along, "the streets were deserted. In approaching the dismal neighborhood, we met groups of policemen going in the same direction." Ashamed, the writer had the driver stop several blocks from his destination. He completed the journey by foot in the total darkness of the early morning. The square itself was poorly lighted, but Dumas *fils* could see bayonets gleaming and "a vague, formless mass rising up in the middle of the square." He drew near, his heart beating faster.

> It is something to be taken seriously, I guarantee you; this inert object which holds eternity suspended by a thread, this inanimate monster, whose maw is bottomless, and which at a single blow sends a soul up to God. There it was, fully upright, ready, gaping. When I reminded myself that a being was still living, who, in an hour at most, was going to be forced to stick his head in that strange collar and to die of its embrace; when I reminded myself that I had come to see that, all I wanted to do was to get out of there.

I had never seen a guillotine, either from afar or close up. I drew near it. Everyone knows the form of the instrument. Placed upright on a platform, it resembles a ladder without rungs, with a wooden collar below and a triangular knife above. It's horribly simple: alongside the ladder, there's the box where the body is thrown; underneath, the basket where the head falls; from the very tip of the ladder, in the corner of the balustrade, the cord that only has to be pulled; the whole thing painted red and seen at night.

There were scarcely twenty people, not counting the gendarmes on foot. Since it was early, the audience was allowed to roam about and have a look at the theatre before the play.

And the unfortunate actor? What was he doing, what was he saying, what was he suffering at this moment?

Little by little the spectators became more numerous. Wan daylight made the sky open wider and wider and revealed more precisely the silhouette of the machine.

A star, a solitary star, shone directly above.

From time to time, a lumbering butcher's wagon, with its load of bloody meat, lighted by a red lantern, passed through the square.

The day light grew brighter and brighter, small groups gathered, and strange conversations indicated which were the habitués, the old-hands, even those who had more than their fill.

"You're not staying?" a voice cried out to a departing shade.

"No, *not today*, I've got things to do."

It was no longer possible to get near the machine. A company of dragoons had taken up positions in front of the scaffold; then there were the gendarmes, all around the guillotine, between the horses and the public, in the rear.

The star disappeared, and with it the night. The day grew distinct, everything was bathed in light; you could see from a distance.

Moment by moment the throng grew larger. These were no longer individual spectators coming with their loaf of bread under one arm and a pipe in their mouth; these were bunches of curiosity seekers, running like people who are afraid of being late, pouring in from all the streets that led into the square.

I had looked so intently at the machine that I had grown accustomed to it. I too began to wait with a certain impatience.

Two young people ran up beside me.

"Where are you going?" one asked the other.

"I'm going to the head side."

And he went to where the head would fall.

The windows began to open and fill up with people. At one of them I saw a woman nursing her baby. How could she have been so sure that what she was going to see wouldn't curdle her milk?

"Mamma doesn't want to miss any of it," said a gamin who must have been fifteen years old. And at the same time he threw a stone at the shutters of still-closed window, in order to wake his mother up in time.

Women and children were in the majority.

There was a little brat four years old who was crying because it was cold.

"If you keep crying, I'll take you home," his mother threatened.

The child kept quiet.

Quite a few jokes were told about the instrument and about the poor fellow who was soon to arrive. But I didn't believe in the sincerity of these jokes. For me they were proof of a shaky courage, which feels the need to hold on to something or to convince itself by its very exaggeration. . . .

The moment was approaching. Even if everyone had not said so, the general hubbub would have announced it.

Shall I go to the head side or the body side?

I stayed on the body side; the head side was too much for a first time. . . .

An excited murmur ran through the crowd, then there was total silence. Two carriages, preceded by gendarmes, came in at a spirited trot along the boulevard to the right side of the scaffold.

In the first, a closed cabriolet, was the priest.

In the second, a vehicle with grilled sidings, sat a soldier, who represented the law, the executioner, who represented justice, and the condemned man, who represented crime.

The second carriage stopped, turning its back to the red staircase, and vomited the fodder for the beast!

All looks were fixed on the patient. I said to myself: "So there is a thing that lives, a being that stirs, a creature that thinks. Everything is still operating in this human machine, and nature this morning has given him, for the entire day and for many years to come, the daily élan of life. This machine is the admirable work of God; not one of his organs, not one of his fibers, not one of the least of his vessels that is not a marvel, that is not a miracle. This being is a being like us, made like us, who has been born, who has lived, who has loved, who has suffered like us. Well, in a second that inert knife which is suspended in the air is going to fall between the shoulder and the neck of that man, set in motion by the hand of a man to whom he has done nothing, in the midst of men who have nothing for which to reproach him, except for a crime that they have not suffered because of; and that will be the end of it; and this admirable human contraption will be nothing but a heap without strength, without equilibrium, without thought; and life, which was running its ordinary course within this body, will have been forced to come to a stop in astonishment in the face of this sudden and implacable death."

Death lays hands on all of us at some point along the road, a point so unknown that we sing while waiting; but death awaits him at the last step of that staircase which has only eight. That is certain, that is inevitable, whatever he says, whatever he does, whatever he wants to have happen, were he to repent, were he to be innocent.

And yet this man has calmly climbed those steps to eternity. All his life has been nothing more than the courage to face death.

And who wants it to be this way? Society. And why has it condemned this man to death? . . .

Now, is it because the scaffold will inspire fear in criminals and consequently restrain them when they are about to commit a crime? Is it because it will serve as an example to others?

I don't believe it, and the proof is that there is always just as much crime, despite these examples, not counting the large number of criminals who have mounted the scaffold as though it were a rostrum, who have used it to insult the justice of God and the justice of men, with the same gesture and the same word, and who die sneering at the society that kills them.

To whom is this example of any value? The guillotine has raised vice in triumph, it has served as a pedestal for crime.

As for its effect on the masses, let the magistrates go judge for themselves as I have done this morning, and they will see that it is virtually nonexistent.

"How fast it went," the people said in disappointment; for them the excitement of the denouement is less than the excitement of the anticipation.

And the people are right.

Death on the guillotine is only a bit of sleight-of-hand that makes life vanish: a trick with a goblet in which there's a head displayed. It is either too much or too little.

After his neck was divested of hair (this neck, which had no further purpose but to be cut, is sinister to see, especially from where I saw it—from behind), Bixner said a few words very low to his confessor, then, sustained by the holy man, he made his entrance, walking quite calmly across the stage to the scaffold. No time was wasted. The assistant to the executioner pushed him down onto the plank. At the same time that his head was caught in the circle, the knife fell with a dull thud, a strange sound similar to the sound that death would make knocking on the door of eternity. The assistant threw the corpse, now stiff as a mannequin, into an open coffin, and did it with a marvelous adroitness; the head had fallen all by itself into the basket that was instantly covered again, and the blade, red as a tiger's tongue, shut the jaws of the satisfied monster.

A universal tremor, which might be called the electricity of death, ran through the crowd; each spectator looked at his neighbor as if astonished to have seen what he just saw, as if in need of an accomplice, and the crowd began to ebb away.

"Oh! The scoundrel died well," said a young boy who passed by me on the arm of an old woman, undoubtedly his mother.

Dumas *fils*'s analysis of the dramaturgy of an execution made a powerful statement against capital punishment by showing how the guillotine served not as a deterrent but rather to glorify criminals and their courage in facing death.

# DOSTOEVSKY'S "IDIOT"

*About instincts and Lacenaire . . .*
—*Fyodor Dostoevsky*, Notebooks, *August 1864*

*Fyodor Dostoevsky.*

NLIKE HIS TWO contemporaries Turgenev and Tolstoy, Fyodor Dostoevsky never witnessed a guillotining. He was, however, sentenced to death in 1849 for radical political activity, and after eight months in a dungeon, he was tied, blindfolded, and led out to be shot and reprieved only at the last moment in what had been from the very start a cruel mock execution. It is not surprising that in *The Idiot* (1869) Dostoevsky was able to give such an authentic description of the condemned man's final moments that it was long taken to be an eyewitness account. Dostoevsky advances the view that the deepest suffering of those condemned to be guillotined is spiritual, since they are denied even the possibility of redemption through physical pain. In *Problems of Doestoevsky's Poetics* Mikhail Bahktin identifies the "final moments of consciousness" of a man condemned to death as "time on the threshold," a central conception in the Russian novelist's work.

*Execution scene.*

Dostoevsky was inspired by Hugo's *Last Day of a Condemned Man*, which he considered to be Hugo's masterpiece and which played an important role in his own life and work. Dostoevsky first read Hugo's novel in French, and witnesses reported that he spoke about it while he was waiting to be executed. In a letter written shortly after, he cited a phrase in French from the book, and motifs from it appear in *Crime and Punishment* and *The Devils*. Dostoevsky's brother Mikhail published a new Russian-language version of Hugo's novel in 1860, a time when pending legal reform gave the issue of capital punishment new urgency.

At the beginning of *The Idiot*, Prince Myshkin, the saintly epileptic hero of the novel, pays a visit to General Yepanchin's family. In conversation with a servant who is hesitant to announce the arrival of such a shabby-looking guest, the overemotional prince embarks on the subject of capital punishment and tells of an execution he saw in Lyon. The servant is astonished to learn that in France they don't hang people but instead cut off their heads.

"What did the fellow do—yell?" asked the servant.

"Oh no—it's the work of an instant. They put a man inside a frame and a sort of broad knife falls by machinery—they call the thing a guillotine—it falls with fearful force and weight—the head springs off so quickly that you can't wink your eye in between. But all the preparations are so dreadful. When they announce the sentence, you know, and prepare the criminal and tie his hands, and cart him off to the scaffold—that's the fearful part of the business. . . .

"The criminal was a fine intelligent fearless man; Le Gros was his name; and I may tell you—believe it or not, as you like—that when that man stepped upon the scaffold he cried, he did indeed, he was as white as a bit of paper. Isn't it a dreadful idea that he should have cried—cried! Who ever heard of a grown man crying from fear—not a child, but a man who never had cried before—a grown man of forty-five years. Imagine what must have been going on in that man's mind at such a moment; what dreadful convulsions his whole spirit must have endured; it is an outrage on the soul, that's what it is. Because it is said 'thou shalt not kill,' is he to be killed because he murdered someone else? No—it is not right—it's an impossible theory. I assure you, I saw the sight a month ago and it's dancing before my eyes to this moment. I dream of it often."

The prince explains that the guillotine was designed with the purpose of avoiding pain, but that the whole idea may well have been a bad plan after all.

The rack and other tortures caused such terrible physical pain before death that there was no time for the victim to suffer spiritual anguish.

> "I should imagine the most terrible part of the whole punishment is, not the
> bodily pain at all—but the certain knowledge that in an hour—then in ten
> minutes, then in half a minute, then now—this very instant—your soul must quit
> your body and that you will no longer be a man—and that this is certain, certain!
> That's the point—the certainty of it. Just that instant when you place your head
> on the block and hear the iron grate over your head—then—that quarter of a
> second is the most awful of all."

Unable to get rid of the terrible picture that still looms before his eyes, the prince once again narrates the story of the execution he saw in Lyon to his hosts, Mrs. Yepanchin and her three marriageable daughters. Instinctively understanding the intense pleasure that can be derived from displays of cruel suffering, Aglaya, one of the daughters, asks if he liked the execution very much and if he found it very edifying or instructive. Myshkin replies that it made him ill, but he admits that his eyes were drawn to the sight and that he "could not tear them away."

The prince tells Adelaida, another of the daughters who had asked him to suggest a subject for a picture, that she should draw the face of a condemned criminal "one minute before the fall of the guillotine, while the wretched man is still standing on the scaffold, preparatory to placing his neck on the block." Watching the execution, Myshkin had thought "at the time what a picture it would make," and he remembers seeing a painting of just that sort in Basel. Dostoevsky probably had in mind a sixteenth-century picture of the beheading of John the Baptist by the Swiss artist Hans Fries, showing the sword poised above the victim's neck.

Carried away by his recollection, the prince forgets everything around him and again describes in detail what he saw in Lyon and how he imagined the victim to have felt. This time, Myshkin identifies with him from the very instant he caught a glimpse of the prisoner's eyes as the prisoner had set foot on the scaffold, and he relives all his experiences.

> "The three or four hours went by, of course, in necessary preparations—the
> priest, breakfast, (coffee, meat, and some wine they gave him; doesn't it seem

ridiculous?). And yet I believe these people give them a good breakfast out of
pure kindness of heart, and believe that they are doing a good action. Then he is
dressed, and then begins the procession through the town to the scaffold. I think
he, too, must feel that he has an age to live still while they cart him along.
Probably he thought, on the way, 'Oh, I have a long, long time yet. Three streets
of life yet! When we've passed this street there'll be that other one; and then that
one where the baker's shop is on the right; and when shall we get there? It's ages,
ages!' Around him are crowds shouting, yelling—ten thousand faces, twenty thousand eyes. All this has to be endured, and especially the thought: 'Here are ten
thousand men, and not one of the is going to be executed, and yet I am to die.'

"At last he began to mount the steps; his legs were tied, so that he had to take
very small steps. The priest, who seemed to be a wise man, had stopped talking
now, and only held the cross for the wretched fellow to kiss. At the foot of the
ladder he had been pale enough; but when he set foot on the scaffold at the top,
his face suddenly became the color of paper, positively like white note paper. His
legs must have become suddenly feeble and helpless, and he felt a choking in
his throat.

"When this terrible feeling came over him, the priest had quickly pressed the
cross to his lips, without a word—a little silver cross it was—and he kept pressing
it to the man's lips every second. And whenever the cross touched his lips, the
eyes would open for a moment, and the legs moved once, and he kissed the cross
greedily—hurriedly—just as though he were anxious to catch hold of something.

"How strange that criminals seldom swoon at such a moment! On the contrary, the brain is especially active, and works incessantly—probably hard, hard,
hard—like an engine at full pressure. I imagine that various thoughts must beat
loud and fast through his head—all unfinished ones, and strange, funny thoughts,
very likely!—like this for instance: 'That man is looking at me, and he has a wart
on his forehead! and the executioner has burst one of his buttons, and the lowest
one is all rusty!' And meanwhile he notices and remembers everything. There is
one point that cannot be forgotten, round which everything else dances and turns
about; and because of this point he cannot faint, and this lasts until the very final
quarter of a second, when the wretched neck is on the block and the victim listens
and waits and knows—that's the point, he knows that he is just now about to die,
and listens for the rasp of the iron over his head. If I lay there, I should certainly
listen for that grating sound, and hear it, too! There would probably be but the
tenth part of an instant left to hear it in, but one would certainly hear it. And

imagine, some people declare that when the head flies off it is conscious of having flown off! Just imagine what a thing to realize! Fancy if any consciousness were to last for even five seconds! Draw the scaffold so that only the top step of the ladder comes in clearly. The criminal must be just stepping on to it, his face as white as note-paper. The priest is holding the cross to his blue lips, and the criminal kisses it, and knows and sees and understands everything. The cross and the head—there's your picture; the priest and the executioner, with his two assistants, and a few heads and eyes below. Those might come in as subordinate accessories—a sort of mist. There's a picture for you!"

A year after completing *The Idiot*, Dostoevsky read "The Execution of Troppmann" by his literary rival Turgenev and reacted negatively to what seemed to him a dubious pose as horrified spectator. He complained that Turgenev had been squeamish and hypocritical when he turned his head away and refused to witness the last stages of the execution. For Dostoevsky, Turgenev's pretended argument for the abolition of capital punishment was only an egotistical expression of concern for his own comfort and peace of mind. "Why is he so coy and why does he keep on saying that he had no right to be there? Of course, if he had admitted that he had merely gone to be present at a public show, then one could understand it." Dostoevsky demanded the honest avowal of one's own secret impulses.

# NOVELS OF THE FRENCH REVOLUTION

*"The knife of the guillotine strikes you in this place,"* she said, *rapidly passing the nail of her little finger round the young man's neck and then drawing it away. "The scar is quite a thin one, like a red thread. . . . But only at the first blow. When many people are executed at the same time the blade soon becomes blunt. Teeth are formed on it. . . . If you are executed try to be one of the first."*
—*Mark Aldanov*, The Ninth Thermidor, *1923*

Charles Dickens's version of continental guillotine romanticism appears in *A Tale of Two Cities* (1859) as the decidedly Victorian idea of self-sacrifice and substitution. Taking another's place on the scaffold becomes an occasion for moral improvement. Dickens's cautionary novel, warning the British of the dangers of popular grievances that could lead to mob violence, decisively shaped all subsequent Anglo-Saxon responses to the French Revolution and its decapitating machine. However, Dickens could not conceal his fascination for the guillotine and the macabre and grotesque humor to which it gave rise. In *A Tale of Two Cities* he cataloged some of the best known jokes, using Carlyle's *French Revolution* as his primary source and inspiration.

One hideous figure grew as familiar as if it had been before the general gaze from the foundations of the world—the figure of the sharp female called La Guillotine.

It was the popular theme for jests; it was the best cure for headaches, it infallibly prevented the hair from turning gray, it imparted a peculiar delicacy to the complexion, it was the National Razor which shaved close: who kissed La Guillotine looked through the window and sneezed into the sack. It was the sign of the regeneration of the human race. It superceded the Cross.

*Dirk Bogarde in* A TALE OF TWO CITIES, *1958.*

The climax of the novel occurs on the scaffold as the noble-hearted ne'er-do-well Sydney Carton takes the place of his friend Charles Darnay, the one-time Marquis d'Evremonde. More original and unruly than British respectability would permit, Carton has a weakness for the bottle and guilt and regret over his unworthiness. A profligate outsider living on the fringes of society, he must expiate his otherness by becoming a scapegoat, a willing surrogate under the blade in order to save Darnay, the husband of his beloved Lucy. Like the Christ he emulates, Carton is a sacrificial victim suffering in silence while awaiting resurrection.

These tight-lipped British scaffold heroics are in sharp contrast to the rowdy, boisterous, histrionic displays of Danton with his jesting, singing fellow revolutionaries! *A Tale of Two Cities* concludes with Carton's pious thoughts and bracing words to the little French seamstress he met in prison who must also die. These innocent victims and martyrs neither "look through the window" nor "sneeze into the sack"; instead of taking the downward view as seen from the plank, the perspective is literally uplifting, rising toward eternity and the open heavens.

In dramatic versions and offshoots of *A Tale of Two Cities*, however, the final stage image is of the towering arms of Sainte Guillotine and its gleaming knife as Carton goes to meet his destiny on the scaffold.

The many British and American films that have been based on Dickens's novel have followed the stage versions, making the guillotine the focus of the sacrificial substitution. The most famous of them, MGM's *Tale of Two Cities* (1935), directed by Jack Conway and starring Ronald Colman, shows the falling blade of the giant machine ironically mirrored in miniaturized versions. A vendor hawking toy models at the Revolutionary Tribunal cries, "Buy a guillotine!" At Madame Defarge's wine shop, an old crone *tricoteuse* (one of the vengeful furies who knit while counting guillotined heads) shows Lucy's young daughter a toy guillotine; next little Lucy is shown playing with the tiny machine until her horrified mother snatches it away. For the finale of the Ridiculous Theatrical Company's 1988 version, a comical two-dimensional guillotine slid out onto the empty stage all by itself (pulled by wires), and the blade fell to end the play.

## FRATRICIDAL STRIFE

French writers have repeatedly explored the guillotine's deadly role during the civil war ignited by the Revolution. In his historical novel *The Chouans and the Blues* (1879), the prolific *roman-feuilletonist* Paul Féval depicts the royalist and Catholic insurrection in western France. The promonarchist peasant insurgents known as "Chouans"—a corruption of the French for screech owl—were given this nickname because it sounded like the secret call their leader Jean Cottereau used to rally his troops.

One installment of the story, "Doctor Bousseau" (first published in 1876), illustrates the barbarity of the internecine strife. In their attempt to suppress the revolt, the Jacobin Blues have executed many civilians with their traveling guillotine, but they have not been able to finish off the valiant Chouan Doctor Bousseau. When the liberating counterrevolutionary forces arrive, they find the doctor near death.

> The light of the lantern falling on the scaffolding disclosed a guillotine, whose bloody triangle was stuck in the neck of the unfortunate doctor. Pinned to the apparatus, he was forced to remain motionless, and he rolled his bright, serene eyes back and forth.

Hearing Bousseau's name, Jacques bounded forward; he was about to lift his hand up to the triangular blade.

"My young friend, you are going to kill me," said the doctor. "That piece of steel must be raised with the utmost caution."

Once freed, the doctor got up; streams of blood were flowing from his wound.

"As you can see," he said to Jacques, "They don't guillotine any better than they shoot."

## A NIHILISTIC KNIFE

The most extreme and violent of all the nineteenth-century guillotine novels that take place during the French Revolution is *Under the Knife*, written in 1876 by the twenty-four-year-old Elémir Bourges, who later became one of the fin-de-siècle masters of symbolist prose and esoteric philosophy. A reader of Dumas *père* and Féval, Bourges knew how to tell a fast-paced story. But unlike Féval and other popular serial writers who adopted a conservative antirevolutionary stance, Bourges—a mystical recluse and friend of Stéphane Mallarmé—highlighted the heroic exaltation and sublime fanaticism and cruelty of both revolutionaries and counterrevolutionaries. First published as a serial novel in 1883, *Under the Knife* is an apotheosis of the guillotine. The fatal machine becomes a symbol not only of the Revolution, but also of the characters' desperate quest for absolute nothingness and annihilation.

The young republican officer Gérard, the hero of the book, considers it an evil omen that it is he who must guard the traveling guillotine that his unit carries with it to execute civilian enemies of the Revolution. In this bloody and brutal civil war, prisoners are tortured and crucified by superstitiously religious peasants who have formed counterrevolutionary brigand armies; on the other side, mass reprisals are quickly carried out by the Jacobin troops.

The "sinister machine," which joined the regiment as a "virgin," creates so many orphans that it becomes known as the "Voracious Lady." Gérard has a vision: "the all-crimson guillotine seemed to rise up and move towards him; a sea of blood sparkled before his eyes, the blood of those killed by the Voracious Lady; he heard his name called by voices, thousands of voices whispering his name." He knows that one day he too must mount the scaffold.

When the republican forces set up the guillotine in the square of a provincial village in La Vendée, the Voracious Lady becomes a primordial, hallucinatory presence whose effect is hypnotic. To the village idiot, "this all-crimson giant, with its two arms stained in blood and its blade for cutting off heads, appeared as a devouring Moloch." Overwhelmed by "the grandeur of this God, to whom the flesh and blood of men belonged," the feeble-minded peasant rushes at the scaffold, impelled to touch the knife and kiss the bloodsoaked posts. From that moment on, wherever the Voracious Lady goes, the large, ungainly idiot follows, helping the executioner's assistants take the boards from the wagon and assemble the machine.

Gérard becomes romantically involved with Rose-Manon, a beautiful adventuress who is fighting on the side of the promonarchist brigands and who has been condemned to die on the guillotine but remains in the custody of her lover. Passing by the scaffold he contemplates his nemesis.

> The two posts were silhouetted against the clear sky (one of them was even wearing a revolutionary red cap);—but the horizontal beam where the blade is attached hadn't yet been put in place. . . . The basket for the heads was open; the gaping aperture seemed ready to receive its prey: and low, massive, thickset—because in the haste of departure, the carpenter had erroneously made his stairs only of eight steps, instead of the regulation ten—the Voracious Lady looked like the frightful altar of a bloodthirsty divinity. The young man studied the guillotine, fascinated despite his revulsion.

Gérard notices a triangular red wooden case in a pile of boards and workmen's tools, opens the cover, and discovers the guillotine blade. He cannot resist the temptation to save his love by stealing the box. When he shows the half-opened case containing the knife to Rose-Manon, she runs her finger tenderly along the edge of the blade, leaving behind a faint, moist line. "Examining it, the lovers savored the voluptuousness of terror, mysterious and abominable, such as the priests guarding ancient idols must have experienced in surreptitiously lifting the veils that brought about dying. . . . The knife burned their hands; they had to turn their eyes away." To dispose of this piece of iron that seems to be darkly flaming (as mythical as King Arthur's magical sword, Excalibur), the lovers go out in a small boat to the middle of a murky pond overgrown with reeds, where they silently bury the triangular case. On their way back they are apprehended by revolutionary forces, and Gérard is sentenced to death for stealing the guillotine blade, but for that very reason it is impossible to execute him!

Thus the hunt for the knife is urgently pursued. Possessed by the devil, the idiot is taken out in a skiff to demonstrate his magical powers. Moaning excitedly, he senses where the water has been transformed into blood, leaving behind the taste of death, and he fishes the knife case up from the muddy depths with a hook on a pole. The revolutionary commander in charge of the mission returns to the town with the precious box just as the Blues enter into decisive battle with the peasant brigands.

> He drew the guillotine blade from the case, and arms spread, standing up in his stirrups, he brandished the knife, striking up the anthem: "Allons, enfants de la patrie." Turning their heads, the Blues looked at him, and by the light of the torches saw the blade. It waved above the soldiers as the symbol of the Revolution, its principle become a mighty sword—and this apparition caused the men to shudder. The goddess of the Terror was electrifying, hurling their masses forward. The "Marseillaise" rose in the sky with a beating of ardent wings. The Blues closed ranks, resisted the influx of the brigands, and the battle was joined.

When the officer brandishing this talisman of death is shot, the idiot grabs the blade and installs it between the uprights on the scaffold. Having taken the place of the mortally wounded executioner, the feeble-minded giant gleefully goes about his business of guillotining the remaining twenty prisoners (mostly women), one after the other, groaning with delight as the palpitating heads fall into the basket. This slaughter takes place against an apocalyptic landscape of raging combat and a burning village.

Gérard, the last of the condemned, places his head under the knife, no longer resisting the death for which he was fated. The novel ends with a Wagnerian love-death on the scaffold. The warring Rose-Manon reaches the scene a moment too late, finding the idiot standing on the platform, his hands dripping with blood and nostrils dilated. "He had finally satisfied his abominable desire, his rage for extermination, and hideously sated with murder, he calmly looked at the blade as the red drops trickled from it." The young woman dismounts and, with one of the two pistols in her belt, puts a bullet through his forehead.

> Then she climbed the steps one by one, quickly moved across the scaffold, and looked into the bottom of the basket. . . . She knelt down, took the head of her lover in her hands, and piously kissed him on the lips, let out a deep sigh, and

without trembling, with a steady hand, blew her brains out.

And now, raising her two triumphant arms bathed in blood, brightly illumined by the light of the conflagration, the Voracious Lady stood alone on this fatal Esplanade where her servitors had fallen.

So ends Elémir Bourges's celebration of the guillotine and of the nihilistic heroics of its worshipers. The final scene of a burning landscape and mounds of corpses recalls the devastation and slaughter of the last days of the Paris Commune and forecasts the horrors to come in the twentieth century. Despite its outstanding artistic merits, there can be little wonder that this bleak novel of the French Revolution has never won a place in French literary history.

## A SUPERNATURAL TALE OF THE GUILLOTINE

The revolutionary guillotine during the height of the Terror also appears in a work of popular fiction dealing with the transmigration of the soul. In *The Man Who Was Born Again* (*Die Wiedergeburt des Melchior Dronte*, 1921) by Paul Busson, an Austrian journalist and author of weird tales, the guillotine plays the role of liberator of the soul from the body on its passage from one existence to another. In the tradition of E.T.A. Hoffmann, *The Man Who Was Born Again* is a fantastic historical narrative that is set in eighteenth-century Germany and France and can be read as either a popular thriller or an expressionistic novel of the occult. Beneath the story's Gothic surface, it is a mystical story of reincarnation told in the first person.

His journey through earthly trials and supernatural encounters on the way to spiritual redemption takes the hero Melchior Dronte to Paris during the Terror. Condemned as a spy by the Revolutionary Tribunal, the German traveler is sentenced to be "hugged by Sanson's coquette."

Awaiting execution, Melchior feels his soul becoming detached from his body even before the guillotine has done its work. The condemned prisoner has achieved such an acute consciousness of being outside himself that even his own hands seem strange to him.

The prisoners are slowly driven in tumbrils through streets swarming with an expectant mob. Along the way Melchior experiences a number of epiphanies as he notices the brass basin of a barber's shop, a black dog, a steel blue fly, and a flight of sparrows.

*Jacket illustration for* THE MAN WHO WAS BORN AGAIN *by Paul Busson (1921).*

When the wagons arrive, Melchior sees "the lean, brownish-red engine of destruction that towered above all the heads in its awful simplicity." At just the same instant "the clouds were torn asunder and a pale ray of sunlight fell with a dull glitter on the slanting knife that hung, up above, under the crossbeam." Thick blood runs down the scaffold in a sluggish stream. Before Melchior, the Marquis Carmignar ascends the short, slippery ladder and is placed on the guillotine.

> Swish!—boom—grr—boom. . . . A wheezing sound came from his beheaded neck. The feet, well bred even in death, beat the boards gently; the body moved in the straps, as if it were trying to find a more convenient position, and was still. The soaked straps were unfastened and they turned him on one side; the gold snuff-box rolled on the boards, the little lid opened and the brown snuff scattered. A hand quickly grabbed at the glistening thing.
>
> I was the next. I ascended the steps. A hand gently propped me up as I slipped, saving me from a fall. I saw a serious, fine-cut face. It was Sanson, the executioner. He invited me forward with a polite gesture. Behind him stood the red-bristled monster, his chief assistant. . . .

A strong hand took me by the arm. Faces glided past me. I stood against the board. The warm smell of blood rose tickling and nauseating in my nose. Thin straps of leather tied down my shoulders and legs. I fell forward. I heard a creaking sound; my throat descended painfully, striking a wooden crescent.

I thought: Now the knife will cut through my neck, sawdust will fly into my eyes, my mouth, my nostrils. . . . Wet wood descended on the back of my neck. . . .

I opened my mouth. I felt dry wooden splinters, moist sawdust. . . .

Then it was night—a rush of air—the noise of wind—a painful rending asunder—a thread cut in twain. . . .

Busson then gives a visionary rendering of the new existence of the soul after the condemned man has been guillotined, including its eventual reentry into life. Hugo and Wiertz also attempted such an evocation of disembodied consciousness, but Busson, working within the context of a supernatural tale of reincarnation, takes the wandering spirit on a longer journey culminating in rebirth.

I was outside my body.

My corpse lay on the guillotine in its tattered brown coat, the shirt-collar soaked in blood. In spite of the tight straps it was stretching itself violently. Fountains of blood spurted from the neck. The head lay in the basket, the eyes were wide open. The face bore a smile.

The people gathered round the scaffold looked on in silence. The boards were emptied, and prepared for a new victim. . . . For now I was rising on the air, gliding over a crowd of heads. Without making any effort or meeting any resistance I floated through wall and windowpanes, propelled by an unknown force.

Somehow I had eyes and saw everything. I heard but I did not feel. Nor did I think. I was consciousness, sheer and simple.

Now a spirit, he is driven to find a new human body to dwell in. "The will for reincarnation was the one impulse that dominated me." Hovering above mating humans, Melchior's consciousness finally finds its way to reenter the course of existence on earth. "My own quest ended in a flash of lightning. At last the coition of two cellae made me once more alive." After sleeping in the womb, he is born again as Sennon Vorauf, who from the beginning of the novel has been telling the story of Melchior Dronte, knowing him to be his earlier incarnation. The circle is complete.

*Artist unknown. Political cartoon depicting Voltaire's statue*
*applauding the burning of the guillotine by the commundards on the*
*place de la Révolution, late nineteenth century.*

# THE GUILLOTINE BURNED
# AND THE GUILLOTINE NOSTALGIA
# OF VILLIERS DE L'ISLE-ADAM

*Since the condemned man will henceforth have to be decapitated in the prison,*
*the experimenters' surgical table, loaded down with instruments and electrical*
*apparatus, will be placed next to the guillotine. The men of Science will at last*
*receive, with hardly any lapse of time and in keeping with their oft-expressed*
*wish, the still-warm head directly from the hands of the executioner.*
*—Count Philippe Auguste Mathias de Villiers de l'Isle-Adam,*
*"The Moment of God"*

VICTOR HUGO OBSERVED that the scaffold is the only structure which revolutions do not demolish, because revolutionaries of all persuasions wish to use the death penalty to prune and trim society. The one exception to this rule was the Paris Commune of 1871, a proletarian revolution that sought to create a humane, nonviolent society. The Communards were indignant that the salary of the Paris executioner was more than ten times higher than that of a worker and more than five times greater than that of a teacher. Upon learning that their adversary, the reactionary Versailles government, had commissioned the manufacture of improved guillotines and was accelerating their production, a local committee decided to demonstrate its opposition to the death penalty by publicly burning a newly built guillotine.

Citizens: We have been informed of the construction of a new type of guillotine that was commissioned by the odious government—one that is easier to transport and speedier.

The Sub-Committee of the 11th Arrondissement has ordered the seizure of these servile instruments of monarchist domination and has voted that they be destroyed once and forever.

They will therefore be burned at ten o'clock on 6 April 1871, on the place de la Mairie for the purification of the Arrondissement and the consecration of our new freedom.

*Artist unknown. Political cartoon, late nineteenth century.*

At nine in the morning on April 6, the guillotine itself was publicly executed not far from the rue de la Roquette, where previously the state had performed its decapitations. To the applause of an immense crowd, the fatal machine was broken to pieces and then burned at the foot of Voltaire's statue, suffering the prolonged tortures used before 1789.

By mid-May, as the Commune entered its final phase, some militants were suggesting that the guillotine should be brought back to execute traitors, as in 1793. The futility of the symbolic guillotine burning became clear when the Versailles forces entered Paris on May 21, crushed the uprising, and during Bloody Week executed twenty thousand prisoners: men, women, and children. The reprisal killings were done by firing squads, not by the guillotine, which was too slow and old-fashioned and no longer the instrument of choice for mass political extermination.

In Bertolt Brecht's play *The Days of the Commune* (written 1948, performed 1956), soft-hearted, idealistic, and impractical Communards boast of renouncing terror for the sake of human dignity, declaring, "The generosity of the Commune will bear fruit" and "Let them say of the Commune: they burned the guillotine," while the shrewd chief of police Rigault pleads for the use of terror to fight terror.

Claude Prin's *Ceremonial for a Combat*, a radio drama about the women of the Commune, conceived in the aftermath of the almost-successful student and worker revolution of 1968, presented the burning of the guillotine in a much more positive light than Brecht's work did. Written and performed in 1971 for the one hundredth anniversary of the Commune, Prin's play shows the female Communards defending themselves and their actions before the Versailles tribunal, which is trying them for their lives. In one scene the women reenact their destruction of "the nonperson of the guillotine," which they first insult and kick, calling it "gaping mug with one front tooth," "eye of Cyclops unfeeling as their God," and "cuttlefish without tentacles."

Asking the guillotine how many murders it has on its conscience, the female Communards condemn to death the hated instrument of death. They tip over the basket, pour out the bran, and chop down the towering structure with an axe as though felling a tree. The working men and women together, as brothers and sisters, dance festively around the burning remains of *la guillotine*, thereby momentarily gaining control of their destiny. But this freedom is short-lived. After the ruthless suppression of the Commune, the guillotine went back to work for its new master, the Third Republic.

## VILLIERS DE L'ISLE-ADAM AND GUILLOTINE NOSTALGIA
## OF THE LATE NINETEENTH CENTURY

The greatest of all the nineteenth-century guillotinophiles was the impover-ished nobleman Villiers de l'Isle-Adam, author of the visionary Wagnerian drama *Axel*, the science fiction novel *The Future Eve*, and a large number of macabre and ironic stories—which he called "cruel tales"—much admired by André Breton for their black humor.

Unlike Hugo, Villiers was no opponent of the death penalty. On the con-trary, he wanted to retain the full ritual of the scaffold and objected to the detheatricalization that resulted from lowering the guillotine to street level rather than keeping it on its traditional raised platform. Villiers's imagination was deeply stirred by the guillotine. He studied medical literature on the sub-ject and was regarded by professional executioners as a knowledgeable amateur. The aristocratic novelist and playwright attended many public executions, and he liked to play the part of the condemned man under the knife. "His hands crossed, his legs as though tied, he mimes the death of Pranzini, whom he saw executed the day before yesterday," recalled Gustave Guiches, a friend of Villiers. In his "nostalgia for the guillotine," Villiers, an apt pupil of the Marquis de Sade, masks neither his nor our complicity in the cruel spectacle.

Villiers's "Eleventh-Hour Guest" (1874) introduces a guillotine enthusiast who pays to perform the executioner's role. Effecting this last-minute substi-tution on the scaffold for perverse pleasure is the moral inversion of the surro-gacy practiced by Dickens's self-sacrificing hero.

On leaving the opera ball late one evening, a group of fashionable revelers—the narrator (Villiers himself), a poet, and three masked actresses—meet an ele-gant but mysterious "guest" and take him with them to la Maison dorée, a sumptuous restaurant where they spend the night eating, drinking, and talking. The enigmatic guest with impeccable manners turns out to be an immensely rich German nobleman known as the Baron Saturn. His deathly pallor and cryp-tic remarks about being required to leave at dawn for unspecified duties in a place not far distant create a mood of apprehension. As the Baron slips away like a specter at daybreak, one of the ladies recalls that there is to be a guillotining that morning at the place de Grève.

A doctor approaches the spirited party and explains that the Baron is a mad-man suffering from an obsession with executions. He travels the world to witness gruesome modes of capital punishment, paying large sums to be allowed to mount the scaffold and assist the executioner. According to the doctor, Saturn's delusion is that the ceremony on the scaffold is a work of art and the guillotine an object of pure contemplation. He is an aesthete of the machine and sees the profession of executioner as an "artistic branch of civilization."

As the clock tower tolls six o'clock, a lurid light comes through the window, and all present shudder, knowing that the blade has fallen. Staring at the ornamental demon's head that holds together the scarlet curtains, the narrator comments that they are all accomplices in the Baron's madness. "Are we not at this very moment implicitly sharing in a barbarity nearly as sinister as his own?"

Another of Villiers's guillotine tales, "The Secret of the Scaffold" (1883), tells the story of a real murderer, Dr. Couty de la Pommerais, who had recently poisoned both his wife and mother-in-law. At the time Villiers wrote this story, there was renewed interest in executions and in medical experiments on decapitated heads. The abolition of the death penalty was being debated. Its opponents had once again raised the argument that the guillotine may be an instrument of atrocious posthumous torture.

The great surgeon Dr. Velpeau, an historical character Villiers included in his story, is sent by the medical faculty to visit Dr. de la Pommerais in his cell to arrange a postmortem. Assuring Pommerais that the guillotine is a perfect instrument which will cause him no suffering, Dr. Velpeau offers the condemned man the opportunity to participate in a grand experiment whereby his name will go down in the annals of science, erasing the social disgrace of his conviction as a criminal. Together the two doctors can determine whether the head retains consciousness after decapitation. All that Pommerais must do is exchange a simple sign of intelligence with Dr. Velpeau, who immediately after the execution will get possession of the head. Pommerais is to wink his right eye three times when Dr. Velpeau asks him the agreed-upon question.

Everything proceeds as planned. The self-possessed victim sees Velpeau in front of the scaffold. "Suddenly, the plank tilted, the wooden collar came down, the lever was pulled, the blade flashed by. A terrible shock shook the platform; the horses reared at the magnetic smell, and the echo of the noise kept vibrating as the bloody head of the victim already palpitated in the calm hands of the famous surgeon, bloodying his fingers, his cuffs, and his clothes." Dr. Velpeau looked intently at the head and demanded that it respond to his inquiry about survival. The right eye closed while the left eye looked directly at the questioner. Despite the surgeon's entreaties, the lid would not go up again, and the entire face went rigid. Dr. Velpeau handed the head to the executioner Heidenreich, who placed it in the basket between the victim's legs.

Villiers leaves the riddle unsolved. He rejects the purely physiological explanations that would insist that consciousness is totally dependent on the body, but he also finds inadequate the evidence for the idealist and symbolist position that maintained that the spirit triumphs over the flesh. Villiers took his stand in ambiguity, the province of the fantastic.

Villiers's "Astonishing Moutonnet Couple" (1888) emphasizes the dichotomy between head and trunk in the life of the imagination. The story takes place in 1793 during the Terror when everyone had constant cause to envisage his own death or that of someone close.

The hero of the tale, Thermidor Moutonnet, calls on his former schoolmate Fouquier-Tinville, now the dreaded public prosecutor, to denounce his own young and attractive wife Lucrèce as a traitor and ask that he have her sent to the guillotine. Out of consideration for their longstanding friendship, the public prosecutor overlooks the charges and denies his apparently deranged friend's inexplicable request, but having gone this far with his plan, Thermidor is now able to fantasize freely that he has had his wife decapitated. And these fantasies prove to be a source of boundless sexual excitement.

Thirty years later the Moutonnets remain a truly happy couple, enjoying a life of passionate sensuality. Thermidor has clung to the perpetually arousing secret image of his wife, believing that she has no inkling of his fantasy, but all the while Lucrèce's secret source of pleasure lies in knowing that her husband imagines her decapitated but never letting him know. Headlessness is the uncommunicated fantasy that unites them in their most intimate moments.

"The Phantasms of Monsieur Redoux" (1888) is Villiers's classic tale of a visit to the wax museum in search of vicarious thrills. In London on business, the usually sober and pragmatic Redoux, haunted by strange dreams of the guillotine and slightly tipsy from a bottle of wine drunk at dinner, drops in at Madame Tussaud's and hides in the Chamber of Horrors at closing time. Alone for the night in the museum, the nineteenth-century bourgeois Frenchman climbs the ancient scaffold and lies down on the plank to experience the terror that Louis XVI must have felt. Suddenly the neck collar snaps down. Redoux is trapped, afraid to make the slightest movement lest he release the blade. After a long, excruciating night, he is rescued the next morning by the guards, who explain that there had been no danger whatsoever since the blade had been removed for cleaning and repairs. Yet Monsieur Redoux has aged ten years and his hair and beard have gone totally white, as was often said to happen to prisoners during the *toilette du condamné*.

In addition to cruel tales, Villiers wrote several theoretical pieces about the guillotine. In an essay he called "Realism in Capital Punishment" (1885), occasioned by recent proposals to move executions behind closed doors, Villiers opposes any change in the traditional guillotine ritual. Above all, the author laments the elimination of the scaffold with its awesome seven steps, which had taken place fifteen years earlier for reasons of economy and convenience. Villiers accuses the legislators of being pragmatists with no concern for the theatrical who hide their moral hypocrisy behind a false philanthropy. He argues that if the execution is not treated as a sublime and sacred ceremony reaffirming the eternal solemnity of death, then society is guilty of outright butchery and the state is nothing but a killer no better than the criminal it murders. By doing away with the scaffold and steps, society had removed the divine sanction that made capital punishment something absolute and had reduced the guillotine to a sordid mechanical killer. The ground-level, courtyard guillotine deprives the victim of the entire meaning of his execution. A complacent bourgeois society, Villiers proclaimed, does not want anything that will upset its illusory sense of material well-being, and therefore the terrifying and soul-searching mise-en-scène of the scaffold and steps had been suppressed in the name of a bogus concept of progress.

To make his point, Villiers went on to give a dramatic account of an execution that he had witnessed as a journalist.

But what is this? I find myself near an isolated object that is illuminated from above by the moon and from below by two lanterns placed on the ground.

It is reddish brown: it makes one think of a prayerstool from the Middle Ages. It is placed at ground level. Between the uprights of this holy chair I can distinguish, attached to the top, a cast-iron suspension, blackened and rectangular like a soldier's knapsack—and under which there is embedded, in the center, the wan, sloping blade of a cleaver.

It is the "Louisette."

What? No more scaffold? . . . No. The seven steps have been abolished. A sign of the times. A progressive guillotine. . . .

*Pierre Lagueunière.* Le prie-dieu-guillotine, *1987.*

While I watch the fluttering shadows of the leaves of surrounding trees reflected on the large blade, it suddenly disappears. I hear a shock, dry and dull, deadened by springs—comparable to that of a rammer breaking a paving stone. I understand. It is a test. The deadly plank was put down on its rest, like a table leaf, to become a kind of classic Procrustean bed. There is nothing new under the sun! So they are having a rehearsal of the drama, on the spot, to try out the stage properties. Oh! Suddenly I notice next to me is the *metteur en scene* himself, who exchanges an oblique glance with his two assistant directors. In front of the instrument stands someone (the chief of security, I believe) for whose benefit the tragic mechanism has been set in motion. He silently signals his approval with a nod of the head, then he pulls out his watch and tries to make out the hour.

Having sized up the tool in one look, he heads for the threshold of the prison to receive his final orders, because the coming dawn is gradually whitening space, objects, silhouettes; the lanterns and streetlamps are turning yellow. The moment is drawing near.

Everyone wonders: "Is he sleeping?"

The chief jailer, who is passing by, confirms, "Yes, he is sleeping, and soundly."

At the entrance, near a wagon, I see a black shape, a priest: it is the chaplain. I go to him. His voice is highly emotional, his eyes are full of tears; he is trembling. He is quite young, tall and blond. This is his first head. But the priest is being called in a low voice. It is time to wake the sleeper. The chaplain goes in, followed by the five or six witnesses, as specified in the regulations. The executioner and his seconds bring up the rear.

Their reappearance, with the addition of a third character, will take place in the near future, within thirty to thirty-five minutes at the most.

So I move away and walk in one of the paths, in the direction of the far-off crowd. The stars are growing dim: it is becoming possible to recognize other human beings.

Villiers maintained that once one link was removed, the entire chain of symbols was called into question. The scaffold must be raised above the level of human heads because it represents and renders material the superior realm of the Law. The guillotine is merely a perfected block, whose whole reason for existence depends on the scaffold. Villiers argued that the guillotine should be restored to its rightful place in all its salutary and sacred horror or relegated to the

*A priest and prisoner approach the guillotine.*

slaughterhouse posthaste. The obviously perverse and cruel aspects of Villiers's attachment to the rituals of the scaffold mask his profound distaste for the senselessness of executions in a secular, modern world.

Examining the psychology of the crowd, Villiers asked why the masses pass the night waiting in the cold and the dark. What was it they were waiting for? It wasn't simply death. What the crowd came to do was to "commune morally and from as close as possible with the horror of a man who, alone among human beings, *has been told in advance of the instant of his death.*"

At half past four o'clock, the doors of the prison open.

At this signal, seen from afar, on all sides everyone grows quiet; hearts contract; I hear the rustling of the sabers; I take my hat off.

The executioner appears—he is first this time!—then a man in shirt sleeves, his hands tied behind his back—next to him, the priest. Behind them the assistants, the chief of public security, and the prison warden. That is all.

"Oh! The poor wretch!" Yes, *there* is a truly terrifying face. Head held high, face pale, neck sheared bare, eye sockets enlarged, his gaze passes over us for a second, then fixes upon what he sees in front of him. Very short tufts of black hair unequal in length stick up on this wild and resolute head. His step, slowed by fetters, is firm because he *will* not waver. The poor priest, as white as he is, raises the crucifix in trembling hands to hide the knife from the prisoner's sight and to show him the eternity of the sky.

Halfway there the ill-fated man looks the mechanism over:

"*So that's it? That's where?*" he asks in an unforgettable voice.

He notices the big gaping basket in trelliswork, the cover held open by a pickaxe. But the priest interposes his body and, with permission granted by the one about to die, gives him the last embrace of Humanity. . . .

Now he stands in front of the plank.

Suddenly, as he casts an almost furtive glance at the knife, a push by the assistant tips him over onto the bridgeway to the abyss; the other half of the pillory comes down; the executioner pulls the catch. A flash in the air . . . Splash! Ugh! What a splattering! Two or three thick red drops fly past me. But the trunk already lies in the funeral basket into which it was propelled. Very quickly bending down, the executioner takes *something* out of a kind of child's bathtub placed *out front*, beneath the guillotine. . . .

The head, which the headsman of France now holds by the left ear—and which he shows us—is immobile, very pale—and the eyes are tightly closed.

Averting my gaze toward the ground, what do I see a few inches from the sole of my shoe!

The point of the Knife-sword of our National Justice piteously dipping into the blood-soaked mud of morning!

As if to bear out Villiers's contention that the ground-level decapitating machine was an insult to the victim's humanity, Michel Campi on the day of his execution, May 1, 1884, expressed his disappointment at the guillotine's insignificance. He had expected a high and imposing scaffold; instead he saw before him a small red machine attached by four sockets to the paving stones of the place de la Roquette. "That's all it is?" he exclaimed contemptuously—and was promptly guillotined.

## FREUD'S "READYMADES": GUILLOTINE DREAMS
## IN A COLLAPSING BED

Not only nineteenth-century novelists such as Villiers or criminals such as Lacenaire were haunted by guillotine dreams. The French archivist, ethnographer, and historian of superstition and magic Louis Ferdinand Alfred Maury, who made pioneering experiments on dreaming and recorded them in his book *Sleep and Dreams* (1861), had a guillotine dream that has become famous through Sigmund Freud's analysis of it.

Freud's *Interpretation of Dreams* (1900) recounts Maury's dream of his own guillotining, "which was like a full-length story set in the days of the French Revolution," although it actually took place in a matter of seconds.

[Maury] was ill and lying in his room in bed, with his mother sitting beside him, and dreamt that it was during the Reign of Terror. After witnessing a number of frightful scenes of murder, he was finally himself brought before the revolutionary tribunal. There he saw Robespierre, Marat, Fouquier-Tinville and the rest of the grim heroes of those terrible days. He was questioned by them, and, after a number of incidents which were not retained in his memory, was condemned, and led to the place of execution surrounded by an immense mob. He climbed the scaffold and was bound to the plank by the executioner. It was tipped up. The blade of the guillotine fell. He felt his head being separated from his body, woke up in extreme anxiety—found that the top of the bed had fallen down and had struck his cervical vertebrae just in the way in which the blade of the guillotine would actually have struck them.

Freud noted that this long dream, the subject of heated debate among psychologists, showed that much material could be compressed into the very brief period of time between the rousing stimulus and the waking moment. Freud asserted that Maury was able to dream such a coherent story because it was "a fantasy which had been stored up ready-made in his memory for many years." The dreamer merely chanced upon it in his sleep (much as the surrealists would later come across "readymades" or found objects for their art). The fantasy had been aroused or alluded to by the piece of wood that struck the back of Maury's neck. Thus "the dreamwork made use of the impinging stimulus in order rapidly to produce a wish-fulfilment." The dream-story, or wishful fantasy, was constructed by the young man under the influence of powerful, exciting impressions.

> Who—least of all what Frenchman or student of the history of civilization—could fail to be gripped by narratives of the Reign of Terror, when the men and women of the aristocracy, the flower of the nation, showed that they could die with a cheerful mind and could retain the liveliness of their wit and the elegance of their manners till the very moment of the fatal summons? How tempting for a young man to plunge into all this in his imagination—to picture himself bidding a lady farewell— kissing her hand and mounting the scaffold unafraid! Or, if ambition were the prime motive of the fantasy, how tempting for him to take the place of one of those formidable figures who, by the power alone of their thoughts and flaming eloquence, ruled the city in which the heart of humanity beat convulsively in those days—who were led by their convictions to send thousands to their death and who prepared the way for the transformation of Europe, while all the time their own heads were insecure and destined to fall one day beneath the knife of the guillotine—how tempting to picture himself as one of the Girondists, perhaps, or as the heroic Danton!

Freud pinpoints the essential composition of guillotine stories as dreamwork based on fear and longing, love and death, and substitution as a sacrificial victim. *The Interpretation of Dreams* provides the final word on guillotine romanticism. The heroic dream of the nineteenth century ends in a collapsing bed.

*Aristide Bruant. "A la Roquette," illustrated by Théophile Steinlen.*

# CABARET, GRAND GUIGNOL, AND BROADWAY

*At the break of day, guillotine some human wretch half-dead with fright*
*and there won't be enough soldiers, their bayonets fixed, to hold back the*
*pushing throng of those who want to watch.*
—André de Lorde, *"Fear in Literature,"* 1927

P OPULAR CULTURE of fin-de-siècle
Montmartre brought a radically new
perspective to the guillotine—that of the poor and downtrodden. By the early
1890s themes of low life gained wide currency in the graphic arts through the
poster and lithograph as well as in popular song. Composed in racy street
slang, the *chanson réaliste* (realistic song) painted a sympathetic picture of
bums, pimps, prostitutes, and petty thieves. In the cabarets, metaphysical anxiety about death joined social protest about the wretched plight of the dispossessed, and the guillotine starred as Fate in this new genre of the proletarian
tragic drama.

The most famous writer of songs celebrating the picturesque but squalid
working-class districts of Paris was Aristide Bruant. He first appeared at outdoor
*cafés-concerts* (music hall or variety shows) before a working-class public and
later at literary cabarets, such as the Chat Noir and the Mirliton, for an elite
audience of artists, intellectuals, and society notables who particularly relished
his biting delivery and insults hurled at the well-to-do. With his trademark felt
hat, cape, and red scarf (familiar to us still from Henri Toulouse-Lautrec's
posters), the singer quickly became a popular figure in Parisian folklore.

Bruant published his earliest songs and ballads in two volumes called *In the
Street* (1889 and 1895), with illustrations by the radical Swiss artist Théophile
Steinlen. Throughout each volume, the guillotine is evoked in both word and

image. Bruant's truculent but vulnerable heroes frequently came to violent ends, often under the executioner's knife. No longer joyful revolutionary paeans to the machine, the ballads of the 1880s were elegies and lamentations for France's blighted urban youth.

"A la Villette" is the song of a poor working girl who sings of her only love, the handsome Toto Laripette, not yet twenty and sent to his death in the notorious square opposite la Roquette prison where the guillotine reigned throughout the Belle Epoque.

> *The last time that I saw him*
> *His chest was stripped bare*
> *And his neck held fast in the lunette*
> *At la Roquette.*

Another song, "A la Roquette" goes on to give a grisly first-person account of the condemned man's ordeal during his last few hours. Like Hugo and Dostoevsky, Bruant focused on the inhuman suffering of waiting before the drama on the scaffold unfolded. The prisoner imagines over and over the horror of putting his head into the lunette and hearing the rush of the falling blade. The president of the Republic has refused to grant him a pardon, and the sun has already begun to light the morning sky. Gentlemen in black suits will be coming for the victim soon; the wild mob outside is howling already. Face to face with the Widow, he must show the boys from the neighborhood that he knows how to die.

> *Don't want them saying I had stage-fright*
> *At the lunette*
> *Before I sneeze into the sack*
> *At la Roquette.*

Bruant used the freedom of the cabaret to treat the guillotine in ways censored elsewhere by the government. In 1887 the authorities had forbidden public performances of the one-act play *At Home* by Bruant's friend Oscar Méténier, in which a pimp recounts in lurid detail the execution of a criminal friend. The future founder of the Grand Guignol, Méténier was able to stage the play only at a late-night private showing at André Antoine's Théâtre Libre.

Another important cabaret artist working in the realist style established by
Bruant was Yvette Guilbert, who enjoyed
great success at the Moulin Rouge.
Included in her repertory of tragic songs
dealing with social outcasts was a terrifying and moving guillotine number. "My
Head" tells the story of a young *apache*
who knows that sooner or later his life of
crime will bring him face to face with the
fatal machine. A spellbinding climax is
reached when, in hushed tones, the victim
foresees his own decapitation.

*Yvette Guilbert.*

> *I'll have to wait, pale and dead beat,*
> *For the supreme moment of the guillotine,*
> *When one fine day they'll say to me:*
> *It's going to be this morning, ready yourself;*
> *I'll go out and the crowd will cheer*
> *My head!*

Of all the Chat Noir artists commemorating the guillotine, the decadent
poet, actor, and musician Maurice Rollinat had the greatest effect on audiences.
A poetic sensation for a few years in the early 1880s Rollinat, who was George
Sand's godson, was admired by Victor Hugo, Jules Massenet, Oscar Wilde, and
Sarah Bernhardt, among others.

When he stepped out in front of the curtain at the Chat Noir, the poet-
musician seemed a phantom, a specter of neurosis, a demon of metaphysical
anxiety. A disciple of Poe and of Baudelaire, for whose poems he composed
musical settings, Rollinat was able to unnerve audiences with his hallucinatory
gestures and demented voice, by twisting his mouth into a hideous grin and
convulsing his face in horror. His nightmarish evocations of madness, evil, and
death sent spectators into paroxysms of fright and made their spines tingle with
horrified delight. Putrefying corpses, vampires, suicide, diabolism, and inex-
pressible anguish—these delirious products of his own sick brain he daringly
revealed on stage.

*Maurice Rollinat.*

*Alfred le Petit.* MAURICE ROLLINAT, *in* LE CHARIVARI, *January 6, 1883.*

Accompanying himself on the piano, he acted out and sang his bitterly ironic poems of terror and heartbreaking lunacy. "Troppmann's Soliloquy" is Rollinat's re-creation in gruesome detail of the satanic state of mind of the celebrated criminal who murdered a family of eight. In preparation for the piece, Rollinat visited the actual scene of the murders at Pantin in order to enter into the mind of the criminal. Adopting the persona of the remorseless killer, Rollinat described becoming splattered with scraps of flesh and blood and feeling his shoes sink into the soft muck as he hacked to pieces the bodies of the six children. Feeling traitorously abandoned by his infernal confederate Satan, Rollinat's alter ego Troppmann must go alone to the guillotine at la Roquette.

> *In twenty-four hours I shall be buried*
> *With my head between my legs.*
>
> *Well, so be it! For the red Widow*
> *My neck will soon be a banquet;*
>
> *My blood will flow like a river,*
> *Into the repulsive bucket;*
>
> *What does it matter! Right up to their machine*
> *Boldly I'll go—without a cart;*
>
> *But before I bend my spine*
> *I'll bite the executioner's hand!*
>
> *And now, shades, make way!*
> *Sneering, Troppmann claims*
>
> *That among all celebrated killers*
> *He alone possesses cursed grandeur!*

Rollinat's "Monomaniacal Executioner" is based on the supposedly true perverse and macabre tale of a retired master of the scaffold who spends his miserable old age dreaming of the triangular blade, consumed by desire to guillotine just one more victim.

*Everywhere, in stillness as in storm,*

*He conjures up the blade; with a mad eye he seeks out*

*The grimace of a neckless head*

*And the horrible stream of blood spurting from a headless neck!*

Yvette Guilbert remembered Rollinat as being like a "character out of the tales of Hoffmann" and a "Paginini of the vocal chords." According to Gustave Guiches's contemporary eyewitness account, on the small, darkened stage of the Chat Noir cabaret, Rollinat's head, illumined by a single spotlight, appeared to have been cut off at the neck and placed on a bare table. His livid head, hairy and open-mouthed, was like a John the Baptist of human madness who had decapitated himself.

To a bourgeois audience frightened and fascinated by the "dangerous classes," the cabaret songs of the guillotine were an opportunity to experience vicariously the life of criminal excitement led by those at the bottom of society. The climax of these excursions into the world of the "other" Paris was violent death by decapitation simulated in the safety of a fashionable cabaret that offered the spectators a glimpse of their own secret desires.

## JULES JOUY AND THE FEMME FATALE

Severed male heads and decapitated bodies play a prominent role in the decadent art and literature of the late nineteenth century, particularly in the many treatments of the biblical stories of Judith and Salome. Flaubert, Huysmans, Laforgue, and Wilde in literature, and Moreau, Klimt, Beardsley, and Munch in painting are the best known of a whole host of male fin-de-siècle artists obsessed by visions of vengeful, headhunting "demonic" women.

The macabre, erotic thrills provided by portrayals of these biblical vampires in "high" art parallel those of the popular culture of the guillotine. The severed head is held up, caressed, kissed. After all, the *machine fatale*—invariably considered feminine, referred to as a devourer of men, and called a "virgin" until she had drunk her first blood—is a version of the femme fatale. Being placed on a virgin guillotine, which was all of white wood, was called "mounting Mademoiselle," while lying with the deflowered Widow, painted red, was referred to as "mounting Madame."

According to the popular mythology created by men, the most fanatical votaries of *la Sainte Guillotine* have always been portrayed as bloodthirsty furies. In Carlyle's *French Revolution*, the militant women of Paris are likened to ten thousand Judiths, and the Marquis de Sade observes in a note to his novel *Justine* (1791), "Whenever there is a legal assassination, do we not find our public squares totally filled? What is most singular is that almost always women are in the majority; they are more inclined to cruelty than we are, and that is because they have a more delicate nervous system."

A former apprentice butcher, blind in one eye, the *chansonnier* Jules Jouy (who died insane at forty-two) was a pioneer of the new "realist" songs and a principal creator of the famous shadow shows at the Chat Noir. His noted cabaret song "The Widow" (1887) explicitly develops the image of the guillotine as a femme fatale, who like the praying mantis, devours her lover in the act of coitus. The Widow lives in a somber shed and only leaves her lair when a criminal is to die.

> *The witnesses, the priest, and the law,*
> *You see, all are ready for the nuptials,*
> *Every object has its use;*
> *The black van serves as coach,*
> *All the properties are there,*
> *The two horses for the journey,*
> *And the two baskets full of oats*
> *The wedding presents.*
>
> *Then, reaching out her long russet arms,*
> *Smartened up, having turned over a new leaf,*
> *She awaits a new spouse,*
> *The Widow*
>
> *Here comes her suitor*
> *Beneath the portal of la Roquette,*
> *Calling the expected male,*
> *The Widow offers herself to him coquettishly,*
> *While the crowd around them*
> *Looks on, shuddering and pale: In a hideous copulation*
> *The man gasps out his last death rattle.*

*Adolphe Willette. Untitled, 1887.*

*Because her lovers boasting of their strength*
*Are killed at the first ordeal*
*They sleep but one time with*
*The Widow*

*Cynical, under the eye of the idler,*
*Like a prostitute in her boudoir,*
*The Widow undresses, washes in lots of water,*
*And takes her makeup off.*
*Impassive amidst the screams,*
*She returns to her hovel.*
*For her innumerable lovers*
*She mourns in red.*

*Climbing up into her carriage,*
*Horrible jade, whose thirst is slaked by man,*
*She goes home to sleep off the blood she's drunk*
*The Widow . . .*

During the 1920s and 1930s Jouy's "The Widow" became closely identified with the music hall artist Damia (Marie-Louise Damien), who presented the song theatrically in her appearances at the Folies-Bergères. One of the first to use modern lights and projectors on stage, Damia held her long, bare arms aloft in a red spotlight to evoke the uprights of the guillotine.

In addition to "The Widow," Jules Jouy created a number of other guillotine songs. Reminiscent of Villiers de l'Isle-Adam, Jouy's "Two Scaffolds" ironically contrasts the traditional machine raised aloft for all to see with the modern guillotine shamefully hidden away from sight.

*Formerly, the scaffold, minister*
*Of grandiose punishment,*
*Boldly displayed its sinister shape*
*On the bright horizon.*

*But today the scaffold trembles,*
*Lurking in some forsaken spot.*

*It fears open spaces*
*And decapitates low to the ground*
*Between two prison doors*

*Well! Gentlemen, I ask you,*
*What about your "salutory example?"*

*Make the scaffolds fearsome*
*Or do away with them entirely!*

Another notorious representation of the sadistically erotic guillotine was a graphic design by Adolphe Willette, a painter, illustrator, and cartoonist of anarchist leanings, associated with the Chat Noir. Authorities seized the December 4, 1887, issue of *Le Courrier français* in which Willette's illustration appeared showing a naked woman in a provocative pose, her right leg raised, one hand on her hip, the other behind her head, leaning back against the plank of a guillotine on a scaffold and waiting for the victim to "mount." The lunette forms a halo around the head of this decidedly unsaintly embodiment of the spirit of the guillotine. Particularly offensive to the government was the picture's comment on the French revolutionary heritage: the nude "Widow" wears a Phrygian cap, and the lantern hanging from the fatal machine bears the date 1793.

## THE GUILLOTINE AT THE GRAND GUIGNOL

When André de Lorde, the leading dramatist of the Grand Guignol, attempted to show an on-stage guillotining at the end of his horror play *At the Break of Day* (1921, written in collaboration with Jean Bernac), such a scandal broke out that the police intervened. Scrupulously researched to present authentically an execution "in its tragic horror," the drama was divided into three tableaux: murder, waiting for death in the cell, and execution. In the climactic scene, the audience heard the sounds of carpenters setting up the guillotine in total darkness, then were assaulted by ominous murmurings of the crowd, and finally witnessed the fatal machine as it went into operation at the break of day.

The prefecture of police reported in the press, "There is currently playing at the Grand Guignol a drama in which one scene shows the operation of the guillotine. The spectators are moved. The prefect of police has summoned the

*Scene from* A L'OMBRE DE LA GUILLOTINE *by Jean Bastia, 1930.*

director and the authors to his office this morning. It was agreed that a change would be made at the end of the third act and that the decapitation actually shown on stage would not occur." At the prefect's demand, *At the Break of Day* was rewritten so that it ended with the condemned man's arrival at the guillotine. During the initial performance, outraged critics screamed, "Shame!" Many in the audience—both opponents and defenders of capital punishment—hissed and hooted the guillotine, the play, and the authors. André de Lorde argued that he was objectively presenting the "dreadful instrument of human justice."

Vociferous protests led to a lengthy debate among French authors as to why it was so disgraceful to display the guillotine in action. The Catholic novelist François Mauriac pointed to the hypocrisy of an audience who not only tolerates but relishes the most ghastly horrors, such as the slashing of the young woman's throat at the beginning of the very same play, and yet is outraged by the sight of the instrument of legal punishment. Mauriac's explanation was that people "prefer to forget that after a hundred years of democracy [since the French Revolution], the guillotine continues to be in current use."

Two earlier Grand Guignol plays—*The Widow* (1906) by Eugène Héros and Léon Abric, and *The Shed on the rue Vicq-d'Azir* (1909) by Fernand Fauré and Edouard Helsey—had dealt with the guillotine without causing any scandal whatsoever, apparently because they were comic and no one was actually shown being decapitated.

*The Widow* takes place in the dark dungeon of a museum devoted to instruments of torture, which has recently acquired a new attraction: the guillotine. A group of British tourists passes through with a guide who tells them about the famous French guillotine which has been used by Deibler *père* to behead many notorious criminals. As they exit the chamber, a perverse young woman arrives with her lover. Obsessed with making love in weird places—the morgue, the catacombs, the crematorium oven—she is now determined to try the guillotine. She persuades her terrified lover to climb onto the plank. The lunette snaps shut and he is trapped. They cannot remember which lever releases the top panel of the neck collar and which releases the blade.

A locksmith, called to free the poor victim, is surprised to discover his wife in the dungeon. But recognizing her lover on the guillotine, he is delighted to have the opportunity to avenge his honor, and he raises his hand to release the knife. The returning group of British tourists are thrilled to see an execution in progress and shout, "Hurrah!" when the guide explains that the poor fellow is about to have his head cut off. The knife falls and the victim ludicrously cries out, "My head, my head!" in imagined agony as the curtain falls—the blade was only cardboard.

When a Grand Guignol revival was mounted in 1974 at the Théâtre de l'European, Gerard Croce's *Dr. Guillotin's Horrible End* was part of the evening of short plays. The haunted Dr. Guillotin dreams that the victims of his machine are pursuing him. When he wakes up from his nightmare, he is relieved to see that he is safe. However, he is somewhat uncomfortable, as the excitement of his dream has caused him to stretch his head out over the bedpost. Out of nowhere, a guillotine blade crashes down and chops his head off. Blood splatters and Dr. Guillotin's head rolls into the audience as the curtain falls. A real guillotine blade was used in the performance, and because of the dangers involved in the simulated guillotining, George Zicco, who played the lead, had his life insured with Lloyd's of London for one million francs.

## *LET 'EM EAT CAKE* AND THE AMERICAN MUSICAL GUILLOTINE

A guillotine, appropriately enough, provides the major comic business at the climax of *Let 'Em Eat Cake* by George S. Kaufman and Morris Ryskind, with lyrics by Ira Gershwin and score by George Gershwin, which premiered at the Imperial Theatre in New York in October 1933. A political satire of the depression years,

*Let 'Em Eat Cake* was a sequel to *Of Thee I Sing;* however, the new work did not enjoy the extraordinary success of the earlier musical, undoubtedly because its barbs hit too close to home in those hard economic times. The critics found *Let 'Em Eat Cake* angry and pessimistic, anarchistic, and full of undisguised hatred.

As the musical nears its conclusion, the play's protagonist, Wintergreen, proclaims a dictatorship of the proletariat, and the flag of Revolution is raised before the White House. The amiable but dim-witted Vice-President Throttlebottom (played by Victor Moore) has been tried before a military tribunal by the Revolutionary Army of Blue Shirts and condemned as a traitor, along with other convicts dressed in top hats and cutaways over striped prison trousers. The first man to be executed under the Revolution, Throttlebottom will be beheaded just as Marie-Antoinette and Louis XVI were. Since all the latest fashions are imported from Paris, the French Ambassador has provided a special guillotine for the occasion, for which the Americans were required to pay sixty thousand dollars.

The last scene of *Let 'Em Eat Cake* shows the veiled guillotine standing on a playing field surrounded by grandstands. An unruly, bloodthirsty mob fights for the best seats. The machine is unveiled, disclosing "a fantastic instrument in bright colors," with a block instead of a tilting bascule. The hooded executioner is General Snookfield, who has never executed anyone before and is afraid he'll prove inadequate to the task. The bespectacled Throttlebottom does all he can to assist in accomplishing his own execution, kneeling down in the right place and, when the blade repeatedly refuses to fall, obligingly getting up and making the necessary repairs.

THROTTLEBOTTOM *(Looking up from his point of vantage):* I see what's the matter. Look! You can see from here! *(He is addressing the General)*

GENERAL: Where? *(Puts his head in there with Throttlebottom)*

THROTTLEBOTTOM *(Graciously yielding the spot):* Now do you see it?

GENERAL: Oh, yeah! There's a little block of wood.

THROTTLEBOTTOM: That's it! Wait a minute! *(Standing on the block)*

*Scene from* LET 'EM EAT CAKE *by George S. Kaufman and Morris Ryskind, 1933.*

GENERAL: To your left a little! Now you got it! Now try it! *(The knife comes down with a bang, but sticks again about three inches from the General's neck. The General, with a hell of a yell, gets out)* Hey!

THROTTLEBOTTOM: It still doesn't work. It's all right up to here, but—*(Feeling around)*—there's something stuck here. *(He takes out a little piece of wood that had been causing the trouble—the knife falls all the way down)* Now we got it!

Throttlebottom is congratulated for his invaluable help and told, "If it wasn't for you we'd have had to call the whole thing off." The willing victim returns to his place on the block and bids a final farewell to everyone, but not before adjusting the basket and explaining, "I don't want to bump my head." At the last minute Throttlebottom is saved by the arrival of a "fashion show" that puts an end to the "passion show."

The image of Victor Moore as the overly compliant Throttlebottom getting up off the block and adjusting his glasses in order to fix the jammed blade was the comic high point of the musical. The guillotine became a brilliant gimmick in a Broadway vaudeville routine. *Let 'Em Eat Cake* inverted the comic beheading of the reluctant prisoner in Chavette's "Talked into Being Guillotined" and made the victim's foolish compliance in his own decapitation into a satiric commentary on American passivity in the face of the depression.

Fait divers *depiction of the capture of Ravachol, c. 1892.*

# ANARCHISTS
# CONFRONT THE GUILLOTINE

*They booed the executioner and they came within an ace of*
*setting fire to the jean-foutres' plaything, the guillotine.*
—Le Père Peinard

IN THE EARLY 1890s France was paralyzed by fear of anarchist terrorism. Enraged by the all too visible discrepancies between ostentatious wealth and widespread poverty, a small handful of activists from the ranks of the dispossessed began to practice "propaganda by deed" and attempted to bring about an overthrow of the state, as had for many years been advocated by the anarchist theorists. Through violence these terrorist misfits believed that they could usher in a golden age of equality and freedom. The lives of a few victims, innocent or not, seemed unimportant compared to their goal, which was nothing less than the future happiness of mankind.

From 1892 to 1894 a series of random bomb attacks reduced Paris to a state of abject fear and paranoia. Every bulging parcel was viewed with suspicion. Tourists fled, public places were deserted, buses empty, theatres barricaded. No one wanted to live near judges, politicians, or policemen, against whom anarchist reprisals for fallen comrades were sure to occur. Fantastic rumors circulated about plots to introduce deadly microbes into the water supply or blow up the sewers.

At the same time, artists and intellectuals seeking liberation from the constraints of bourgeois society saw these acts of violence as daring expressions of extreme individuality. Anarchism became intellectually fashionable. Symbolist and Decadent writers and painters on the left, drawn to dramatic gestures and the cult of romantic violence, sympathized with the anarchist assassins and glorified their revolt as a well-deserved attack on authority and a form of artistic innovation.

Four terrorists were condemned to death during this two-year period, and their trials and executions were the most widely publicized of all nineteenth-century French criminal proceedings. The anarchist press offered a radical new perspective on the guillotine. Written in the racy street slang of the Parisian working classes, Emile Pouget's *Le Père Peinard* advocated subversion and violence. With a circulation of fifteen thousand at its peak, and with contributing artists such as Pissaro, Steinlen, Willette, and Vallotton, Pouget's weekly had an impact well beyond anarchist circles. Scurrilous, witty, and ribald, it was as much an assault on middle-class language as on bourgeois morality and the government. *Le Père Peinard* glorified the heroic courage of the anarchist martyrs who were assassinated by the state and vilified the executioner Deibler and his "filthy contraption," the guillotine. The prison chaplain, or "sky pilot," was scorned as a servile tool of the oppressive bourgeois regime, and the newspapermen who reported these events were attacked as mercenary and bloodthirsty "pissers of ink."

The personal property of a despised functionary, the guillotine was made synonymous with the name of Deibler and scathingly ridiculed. It was "Deibler's blade" that cut the neck of anarchist heroes, not the "national razor" of revolutionary times. The perception of the condemned man underwent a similar revision in the pages of *Le Père Peinard*. Throughout the nineteenth century the convicted murderer on the scaffold, as depicted by the supposedly objective pen of bourgeois journalists, was only the passive victim of an inescapable fate. At best, a downtrodden working man sentenced to death might be judged picturesque and thus worthy of the compassion of a Chat Noir *chansonnier*. *Le Père Peinard* transformed this dominant image of submissive defeat into one of defiant triumph. The noble bearing of the terrorist on the scaffold and his ardent defense of anarchist principles challenged the entire system. Like a proud aristocrat during the Terror, the victim laughed at the guillotine, convinced that his cause would soon win.

The first and most charismatic of the anarchists to be executed in France was Ravachol (François-Claudius Koenigstein), glorified by the extreme left as a "saint" and a "kind of violent Christ" and condemned by the authorities as a counterfeiter, thief, graverobber, and murderer. Ravachol defended himself in court saying that he had committed acts of terror in order to call attention to the suffering of those who could not speak for themselves. "My object," he said, "was to terrorize so as to force society to look attentively at those who suffer."

He greeted his death sentence with the cry "Long live anarchy!" Head held high, he went to the guillotine singing what the authorities called "a profane and beastly" anticlerical song. His neck was severed as he was halfway through uttering a revolutionary exclamation. Ravachol quickly became a legend, the subject of poems and songs. A popular print shows the anarchist vanquishing the guillotine.

*French lithograph depicting Ravachol in triumph over the guillotine, late nineteenth century.*

An extraordinary account of Ravachol's execution appeared in *Le Père Peinard* under the title "Red Holiday." With bitter sarcasm, the editor pointed out that the "bastards" had taken the occasion of the national holiday celebrating the fall of the Bastille to guillotine Ravachol. "The 14th of July belongs to the bourgeois!" he wrote. "What is there strange in the fact that to celebrate the occasion they should treat themselves to a cascade of anarchist blood! For them no fireworks are worth the glug-glug of a rebel pissing his blood under the guillotine. No, the *jean-foutres* of the upper crust could not have given themselves a more thrilling spectacle than that of Ravachol's head dropping into the bucket full of sawdust."

From the viewpoint of anarchist counterculture, it is not the condemned man who shows fear; rather, it is the craven "guillotineers" who are terrified of the martyred hero. "Ravachol's nut has rolled at their feet: they fear it will explode, just like a bomb!" *Le Père Peinard* considered survival of consciousness after decapitation to be, in effect, the anarchist idea that would soon bring down bourgeois society. Transforming the imagery of a beheading into a subversive "guillotinade," the editor railed, "And for Christ's sake shut up about your whore of a society; it has no need of being defended—it's at its death rattle." For fear of the people's wrath the "bastards" advanced the date of the execution and conducted the "assassination" in secret, protected by a huge deployment of armed forces.

> You claim that his guillotination is an expiation. Well, why did you hide like bandits to do the trick? Why encircle the prison with thousands of troops, rifle in hand, fixed bayonets, complete with bandoliers. Why only one little spot left free: the one where Deibler was going to assassinate Ravachol? . . .
>
> And the guillotine-lickers are there surrounding him, never taking their eyes off him. If only he would have a moment of weakness. If only his eyes would have become misty for a moment or two and they could have bleated to their whores-papers: "Ravachol trembled."
>
> No, nothing doing. He is calm with just a faint hint of raillery in his eyes.
>
> Naturally the sky-pilot doesn't miss the bus. He appears on the scene and is spurned as he deserved: "Consolations at a moment like this, you can stick them up your . . . I don't care a f—— for your Christ: if you bring him anywhere near me I'll spit on him . . . Religion is alright for the idiots."

Approaching the guillotine, Ravachol began to sing the atheistic revolution-ary song "Père Duchene" in a strong voice without so much as a quaver.

> *If you want to be happy,*
> *By God!*
> *String up your landlord,*
> *Cut the priests in half,*
> *By God!*
> *Push the churches down*
> *God's blood!*
> *And the Good Lord in the shit*
> *By God!*
> *And the Good Lord in the shit.*

*Le Père Peinard* continued its eulogy to the indomitable singing hero. Ravachol does not stop singing, his eyes, wide open, resting on the guillotine. In spite of his struggles, they push him on to the moving plank; there is no way of resisting. He wants to continue speaking but his head is held in the lunette; one of the squad of executioners holds his head by the ears:

"You swine!" he shouts, still struggling. But the knife slips. Ravachol had heard its release. He defiantly shouts: "Long live the Re . . ."

The knife cuts the rest. The head rolls into the basket, the blood gushes in spurts. It's over.

What was Ravachol's last word?

All the entourage believed they heard, half issuing from under the knife, half from the basket, a formidable cry of: "Long live the Republic!"

Hum, hum! My view is that it was "Long live the Revolution!" that he wanted to shout.

In the next issue of *Le Père Peinard*, the outraged Pouget exposed the "abominable trick" that the authorities had played on Ravachol. The swine, the journalist declared, had "tied up his testicles and passed the cord through his legs and tied it tightly to his hands so that he couldn't move a step without a grimace of pain." But they had not counted on Ravachol's fortitude. The "bourgeois whorespaper men" who were also part of the hated state machinery, Pouget asserted, would have been only too glad to print derogatory lies about the prisoner.

On being sentenced, Ravachol had warned "I know I shall be avenged." His falling head turned out to be the explosive impetus for the next terrorist attack. In December 1893, Auguste Vaillant threw a bomb from the visitors' gallery of the Chamber of Deputies. Although no one was killed, the twenty-two-year-old anarchist was sentenced to be guillotined—it was the first time in nineteenth-century France that the death penalty had been invoked for any crime short of murder or treason. A massive display of armed might accompanied Vaillant's execution, including five hundred policemen, four companies of infantry, and a squad of cavalry. To show how an anarchist dies, Vaillant went to the guillotine with a firm step, head held high, humming an anarchist song, after refusing the customary offer of alcohol and the consolations of the chaplain. On the scaffold, Vaillant shouted the proud anarchist rallying cry "Death to the bourgeoisie! Long live anarchism! My death shall be avenged!"

The guillotined Vaillant became another martyr to the class war. Pilgrimages were made to his grave, where commemorative odes, fresh flowers, and even a crown of thorns were laid. The wicker basket into which his head had dropped was found in the bushes nearby, and lumps of blood-stained sawdust from inside the basket were knotted in handkerchiefs as holy relics.

Fait divers *illustration of the arrest of Emile Henry in the Café Terminus, c. 1894.*

Vengeance for Vaillant's death came five months later, in May 1894, when Emile Henry, the most militant and ruthless of the terrorists, threw a bomb into the crowded Café Terminus at the Gare Saint Lazare. Eighteen years old and the son of a Communard who had fled to Spain to escape the death sentence, Henry regretted only that his bomb had killed just one person. "If I have killed," he wrote his mother, "then it was for a great ideal." The more the state felt menaced, the greater its display of force. At Henry's execution there were five hundred Guardians of the Peace, four hundred Parisian guards, and one hundred sixty mounted guards. Behind the police barriers there was room for only several hundred ordinary spectators, mainly prostitutes and pimps. Among the hundred privileged spectators occupying the reserved area in front and consisting of newspaper men and official dignitaries were the novelist and politician Maurice Barrès, and the statesman Georges Clemenceau. And many eager onlookers stood at windows and on the roofs of the houses surrounding the square. According to Clemenceau, Henry, as cruelly trussed up as Ravachol had been, went to the guillotine "with the face of a tormented Christ" and shouting the obligatory "Long live anarchism!"

The finale to this rash of terrorist acts came in June 1894, when Santo Caserio, a twenty-year-old Italian baker's apprentice, stabbed and killed President Sadi Carnot in Lyons, where the president of the Republic had gone to visit the Exposition Universelle. For Caserio's execution there was unprecedented military pageantry, including three hundred police, one hundred security police, cuirassiers wearing steel casques, a battalion of the 98th regiment of infantry, and gendarmes both mounted and on foot.

Lyons was full of foreign tourists in town for the Exposition. National executioner Deibler had come from Paris, making a guest appearance with his "filthy contraption" and assistants. Elegantly dressed women sat on the roofs of houses facing the square where the machine had been set up during the night by the light of lanterns. The exorbitantly priced seats had quickly sold out.

Caserio did not die as a "good anarchist." Overcome with convulsive trembling, he staggered and had to be carried to the van. Once he had been pulled into position in the lunette, at the very last moment before the knife fell, the terrified victim was heard to mutter something that to some sounded like "Long live anarchy." But to others it sounded more like the words "I don't want to . . ." in his native Lombard dialect.

The terrorist wave of bombings and assassinations came to a close with the ignominious end of Caserio. In a fit of antiterrorist hysteria, the government passed repressive laws, closed many radical papers, including *Le Père Peinard*, and made mass arrests. The prestige of the national executioner had been seriously damaged; Deibler had been subjected to insult and his life constantly threatened; once he was almost kidnapped. For the first time ever the dignity of the executioner was challenged and his impartiality called into question. Deibler was evicted from his apartment; landlords refused to rent to such a notorious tenant. The anarchists and the anarchist press had succeeding in creating a scurrilous invective for denouncing public executions. But the guillotine and the guillotine lickers still remained firmly in power.

## FRANZ HELD'S *GOLDEN BOMB*

The German socialist writer Franz Held, father of Dadaist photomonteur John Heartfield, combined in his short story *The Golden Bomb* (1893) two turn-of-the-century motifs—anarchist bombings and medical experiments on severed heads—to create a fantastic guillotine tale of vengeance against the ruling class. Written in slashing proto-expressionist prose, *The Golden Bomb* is a politically seditious story in the spirit of *Le Père Peinard*.

At the fashionable Café Américain in Paris, rich whoremongers and fur-coated demimondaines try to ignore the masses of starving poor begging outside in the dark, snowy streets. Outraged at this injustice, the anarchist "Tête d'Or" brings his homemade bomb wrapped in blood red tissue paper like a bonbonnière, and blows the café to pieces. Body parts are scattered on the boulevard; "supple, shapely legs in tasteful, blood-speckled lace knickers" lie strewn about.

The trials that follow lead to a "few mistaken executions." Finally, in a big roundup the military court sentences twenty suspected bomb throwers, including "Tête d'Or," to be guillotined. After a mass execution at la Roquette, the twenty heads are rushed to the Ecole de Médecine and lined up atop a marble table in the anatomical amphitheatre, where a renowned physiologist wearing the Legion of Honor has invited a group of colleagues to witness his experiments, after first enjoying a sumptuous breakfast and Egyptian cigarettes.

The decapitated heads are subjected to a very strong "galvano-electric" current carried by "twenty copper wires [that] run out of a single mighty battery, one into each of the holes in the gaping brownish-red spinal columns." The face of "Tête d'Or" twists into its "old expression of fanatical disgust and frozen rage."

The eyes open and he gives the distinguished surgeon "a look of white, satanic hate." The other nineteen pairs of eyelids begin to twitch, and then the anarchist's "wrathful head, jaws stretched wide open, sticks out a scornful tongue at the doctors, and all the other heads follow suit." The terrified doctors lose self-control; they vomit, go mad, and drop dead. Before suffering a fatal stroke, the famed physiologist coats all of the heads in gold as part of his experiment.

Metamorphosed into golden balls, the heads hop around the marble slab screaming insults at their dead tormentors and spring out the window like rubber balls. Their brains having been transformed into dynamite by the electric charges, the severed heads crash and explode on the streets. "All the little heads roll together into one gigantic golden head," and melded together, they destroy all of Paris. Held's final apocalyptic vision is of "hundreds of thousands of cut-off heads" forming a huge colossus that exacts vengeance on all of the great cities of Europe.

## ZOLA'S *PARIS*

Emile Zola, the most hallucinatory of the naturalists, had first thought of describing an execution in *The Human Beast* (1890), a story of crime and passion in the Rougon-Macquart series offering a panorama of life in the Second Empire. But nothing came of the plan, and it was not until seven years later, influenced by anarchist trials and executions in the mid-1890s, that Zola depicted a guillotining, in his late political novel *Paris,* published in book form in 1898 shortly before he became involved in the Dreyfuss Affair.

Zola presents the execution of the fictional bomb-throwing anarchist Salvat, patterned after Auguste Vaillant, as "loathsome butchery" and "abject cutthroat work" relished by the worst scum "urged on by brutish fever, a hankering for death and blood." Zola's hatred of injustice is evident in his passionately contemptuous prose.

> But the instrument itself, how base and shameful it looked, squatting on the ground like some filthy beast, disgusted with the work it had to accomplish! What! those five beams lying on the ground, and those others barely nine feet high which avenged Society, the instrument which gave a warning to evil-doers! Where was the big scaffold painted a bright red and reached by a stairway of ten steps, the scaffold which raised high bloody arms over the eager multitude, so that everybody

might behold the punishment of the law in all its horror! The beast had now been felled to the ground, where it simply looked ignoble, crafty and cowardly.

Zola's bitter social criticism points out the appropriateness of the guillotine's being installed in a poor working-class district.

Each time that it was set up amidst those toilsome streets, was it not charged to overawe the disinherited ones, the starvelings, who, exasperated by everlasting injustice, were always ready for revolt? . . . And it was a tragical and terrible cooincidence that the bomb-thrower, driven mad by want, should be guillotined there, in the very center of want's dominion.

Thus the novelist creates sympathy for the naïve, self-destructive victim of poverty and ignorance who dies with dignity, crying, "Long live Anarchy!"

Then came a loathsome scramble, a scene of nameless brutality and ignominy. The headsman's helps rushed upon Salvat as he came up slowly with brow erect. Two of them seized him by the head, but finding little hair there, could only lower it by tugging at his neck. Next two others grasped him by the legs and flung him violently upon a plank which tilted over and rolled forward. Then, by dint of pushing and tugging, the head was got into the "lunette," the upper part of which fell in such wise that the neck was fixed as in a ship's porthole—and all this was accomplished amidst such confusion and with such savagery that one might have thought that head some cumbrous thing which it was necessary to get rid of with the greatest speed. But the knife fell with a dull, heavy, forcible thud, and two long jets of blood spurted from the severed arteries, while the dead man's feet moved convulsively. Nothing else could be seen. The executioner rubbed his hands in a mechanical way, and an assistant took the severed blood-streaming head from the little basket into which the body had already been turned.

The echo of the thud, Zola explains, "spoke of man's exasperation with injustice, of zeal for martyrdom, and of the dolorous hope that the blood then spilt might hasten the victory of the disinherited." But blood will have blood. In the crowd, another somber-faced anarchist, reminiscent of Emile Henry, witnesses the execution and plots his vengeance against society, which will bring him to the guillotine.

## ALFRED JARRY AND THE DISEMBRAINING MACHINE

Long interested in destructive machines capable of blowing up society, play-wright and poet Alfred Jarry was perfecting his *Ubu Roi* (first performed in 1896) during the years of the terrorist bombings, and he could not help but find black humor in the short, violent lives of Ravachol and Emile Henry. Indeed, a spirit of random, senseless terrorism animates Jarry's many works about Pere Ubu, who, as Jarry himself pointed out, is the near-perfect anarchist.

The guillotine is a frequent point of reference and subtext in Jarry's work, in which public executions and decapitations appear in bizarre and distorted forms. Chapter twenty-eight of Jarry's novel *Doctor Faustroll* is dedicated to "Monsieur Deibler, sympathetically." Since all the other dedicatees in the novel are poets and painters, such as Gauguin, Mallarmé, and Beardsley, it would seem that the executioner Deibler is to be considered as an artist too.

The notorious Disembraining Machine that appears repeatedly in Jarry's works is a modern Ubuesque version of the guillotine, medico-technological in its specifications and prophetically forecasting mass extermination in the death camps. The traditional guillotine is too old-fashioned in design, too much a product of the age of reason, too rectangular for the pear-shaped Ubu. Still, the two decapitating machines are closely related.

In "Visions of Present and Future," written in the spring of 1894, when Emile Henry's trial and execution were major news, Jarry compared the differ-ent methods of execution: hanging, impalement, and the guillotine ("the trian-gle of the blade that the two red arms carry up to sleep; plank, darkness.") The Disembraining Machine, Jarry maintained, was superior to the banal bomb, the gallows, and even to the guillotine, which effected separations that were tanta-mount to "paralogical vandalism."

The early guillotine, as portrayed by Lucas Cranach in a 1516 woodcut, was called the "French trap," Jarry explained, and thus it is that in *Ubu Roi* Ubu dis-patches his enemies—nobles, financiers, magistrates—"down the trap" where they will be disembrained. The lyrics of "The Song of the Disembraining" from *Ubu Cuckolded* describe the populace watching the democratic spectacle of the "machine revolving" and the "brain flying"—a show both morally edifying and blood splattering.

Jarry's surprising twist on the problem of talking heads is his suggestion that the sex organs of the decapitated victim may retain consciousness. Ever

*Alfred Jarry. Drawing for the cover of "The Song of the Disembraining,"*
*from* Ubu Roi, *1898.*

since Salome, there have been numerous heroines said to have knowingly kissed their lover's severed heads, an act emblematic of the survival of intelligence. Both Washington Irving and Dumas *père* wrote tales in which heroes make love, albeit unwittingly, to decapitated female corpses with imperfectly reattached heads. Only Villiers's Thermidor Moutonnet had preferred—at least in his imagination—a headless bed partner. Jarry took all this one step further in supposing that the genitalia survive the ordeal of the scaffold. With the Disembraining Machine, he created a highly idiosyncratic substitute for the guillotine and enlarged on its powers of human devastation to the point of absurdity.

## JACK LONDON'S "CHINAGO"

The French have no monopoly on black humor about the guillotine. Jack London's story "The Chinago" is as grimly ironic as any of Villiers's *Cruel Tales* and even more macabre than Chavette's "Talked into Being Guillotined." Inspired by London's visit to French Tahiti, the story effectively combines his socialist political views and his gift for exotic storytelling.

London first read "The Chinago" aloud to the crew of his schnooner *Snark* en route from Bora Bora to the Samoas in April 1908, and it was published in *Harper's* magazine in 1909. Fascinated with the withdrawal into self, the loneliness and terror of the individual confronted with imminent death, London had a planned a book-length exploration of the subject to be entitled *How We Die*. Although in public pronouncements he constantly warned of the dangers of the "Yellow Peril," in "The Chinago" his existentialist empathy with *homo mortalis* and his radical perspective on exploitation enabled London to portray the guillotining of the protagonist, Ah Cho, with penetrating insight.

A young Chinago, as Chinese coolies are called by native Tahitians, Ah Cho works in the cotton fields of an English-owned plantation run by a German overseer. He dreams of returning to China a rich man after working for five years and dutifully saving his wages of fifty cents a day. When a coolie is stabbed and killed in a fight, Ah Cho and four of his co-workers are arrested at the scene while the real murderer escapes. Passively and fatalistically the coolies accept the injustice meted out by the ever-incomprehensible white man.

Ah Cho is only condemned to twenty years of hard labor in New Caledonia, but Ah Chow, another of the falsely accused, is sentenced to die on the

*Dimitrios Galanis.* "WE MUST GO ON GUILLOTINING BECAUSE . . . , "
*in* L'ASSIETTE AU BEURRE *no. 310, March 9, 1907.*

guillotine, which Karl Schemmer, the German overseer, sets about building. "Schemmer had made the guillotine himself. He was a handy man, and though he had never seen a guillotine, the French officials had explained the principle to him." When the chief justice writes the order for the execution, he leaves out the last letter of Ah Chow's last name and so it is Ah Cho who is taken off in the wagon to be beheaded. Ah Cho protests, "I am not the Chinago that is to have his head cut off," but the gendarme only laughs, "Ah! So easy! Chck!—the knife cuts your neck like that. It is finished. The knife may even tickle. Who can say? Nobody who died that way ever came back to say."

The guillotine is erected at the scene of the crime as a salutary lesson for the coolies, and Schemmer himself volunteers to act as executioner. He demonstrates the machine on a banana tree about the size of a man's neck. On the first attempt, the blade neatly severs the tree, but on the second try it sticks two-thirds of the way through. While Schemmer attaches a twenty-five-pound piece of iron to the top of the blade, Ah Cho patiently explains, "I am not Ah Chow. I am Ah Cho. The honorable jailer has made a mistake. Ah Chow is a tall man, and you can see I am short."

On the third try, "the knife shot down with a thud, making a clean slice of the tree." The sergeant exclaims "Beautiful, my friend." Ah Cho submits to his fate. "Schemmer and the rest were doing this thing without malice. It was to them merely a piece of work." Contrary to the French practice, Ah Cho is lashed to Schemmer's guillotine lying face up. "He opened his eyes. Straight above him he saw the suspended knife blazing in the sunshine. . . . Then he heard the sergeant's voice in sharp command. Ah Cho closed his eyes hastily. He did not want to see the knife descend. But he felt it—for one great fleeting instant. . . . The knife did not tickle. That much he knew before he ceased to know."

## WE MUST GO ON GUILLOTINING

Adolphe Willette, Théophile Steinlen, and other left-wing artists were frequent contributors to the satirical magazine *L'Assiette au Beurre* (*The Butter Dish*, meaning graft in French slang). From 1901 to 1913 nearly six hundred weekly issues relentlessly exposed the sordid underside of the Belle Epoque and attacked abuses of wealth and power. One of its major themes was the corruption of bourgeois justice and the use of the guillotine to defend the interests of the ruling class against the poor and downtrodden.

"The Woman Who Had an Abortion" by Willette shows the culprit in court between two gendarmes, pointing one hand toward a jar containing the aborted foetus and the other toward a guillotine with a body lying prone on the plank. The caption reads, "Because of what you would have become at twenty."

*L'Assiette au Beurre* devoted the entire March 9, 1907 issue to the death penalty. Consisting of fourteen plates, it drew various connections between capital punishment and poverty, exploitation, profiteering, war, colonialism, imperialism, and the status quo. Each drawing has an ironic caption that begins either "WE MUST NOT DO AWAY WITH THE GUILLOTINE" or "WE MUST GO ON GUILLOTINING." One drawing shows a decadent upper-class couple renting a room from a tavern keeper so that they can observe a guillotining in the square below.

The outspoken artist and social critic Aristide Delannoy depicted two prosecuting attorneys near the bloodied blade of a guillotine, their robes reddened, and a freshly severed head in the basket below. "WE MUST GO ON GUILLOTINING BECAUSE the prosecutors' robes have to be dyed anew every so often," reads the caption. The Greek artist Dimitrios Galanis portrayed a defenseless half-wit standing before the decapitating machine; to the right is the top-hatted executioner and in the background a crowd of witnesses and observers. "WE MUST GO ON GUILLOTINING BECAUSE society must be avenged—by the death of a dumb brute, a madman, or an idiot."

# FANTOMAS
## AND THE TRIUMPH OF EVIL

*It is decreed that executions be public, and then each time that justice is*
*put into effect, they drive back as far as possible those who come to watch.*
*Once and for all it should be decided to hide the guillotine in the prison*
*courtyard as something hideous, or to admit that, on the contrary,*
*watching it has a moral effect, and then let the crowd feast their eyes on it.*
*—Marcel Allain and Pierre Souvestre,* Fantômas in Custody, *1912*

A S THE BELLE EPOQUE drew to a close, the guillotine began to appear frequently as a horrific accessory in popular French fiction, especially sensational crime and detective novels. The most celebrated of these chilling mystery stories is the thirty-two-volume *Fantômas*, produced in exactly thirty-two months by two Parisian journalists, Marcel Allain and Pierre Souvestre.

The first volume of *Fantômas* was written by conventional means and published in 1911; by 1913 thirty-one sequels had been published, all of which were produced by dictation without the authors ever putting a single word down on paper. This high-speed method of composition, not unlike surrealist automatic writing, tapped directly into the unconscious of the two authors and let their imaginations play freely, unleashing secret desires. For nearly three years, a new novel of 382 pages appeared monthly in an edition of six hundred thousand copies.

As a silent film serial, made in 1913 by Louis Feuillade, *Fantômas* reached an even wider audience, increasing the already immense popularity the "Emperor of Crime" had enjoyed in book form. The success of the novel was so great that it was even held responsible for the terrifying exploits of the "Bonnot gang," a motorized band of American-style criminals with anarchist leanings whose bank heists and gunning down of people in the streets dominated the news of 1912. Soon there were impassioned calls for government suppression of the *Fantômas*

*Gino Starace. Cover illustration for* Fantomas in Custody
*by Marcel Allain and Pierrre Souvestre.*

series, which glorifies its unpunished and unrepentant hero, the killer of over fifty victims, and revels in anti-social violence.

*Fantômas* quickly became a favorite among artists and intellectuals, including Guillaume Apollinaire, Jean Cocteau, and Pablo Picasso. Novelist and poet Raymond Queneau called the series a modern *Aeneid*, and its masked criminal hero was exalted as a desacralized divinity of evil. The American theatre artist Richard Foreman has frequently paid homage to *Fantômas;* his *Hotel for Criminals* (1974) includes the "Master of Fear" as one of the dramatis personae.

Dreamlike images of nihilistic violence materialize in the hallucinatory poetics of *Fantômas*, but contrived horror is matched by outrageous black humor. Although the guillotine recurs throughout this criminal epic, only once in the entire thirty-two volumes, at the climax to the first volume, does a court-ordered execution actually take place. It is not, however, the malefactor who goes to the scaffold, but a look-alike actor, the involuntary stand-in for the evil genius of crime.

"On the Scaffold," the concluding chapter of volume one of *Fantômas*, gives a vivid moment-by-moment account of a guillotining. The precise, realistic rendering of the high melodrama on the scaffold begins with Fantômas sentenced to death for the murder of Lord Beltham and operating under the alias Gurn. He succeeds in bribing a guard to let him out of prison for a short visit in a neighboring building with his mistress, who is none other than Lady Beltham, widow of his victim. Simultaneously, Lady Beltham has sent a note proposing an assignation to Valgrand, a leading actor then very much in vogue. For his role in a sensational new play Valgrand has made himself up to look just like the murderer Gurn, knowing that his appearance as the famous criminal will create a sensation among the theatre-going public.

Valgrand receives Lady Beltham's summons to meet her at 2 A.M. in a room facing la Santé prison, where the condemned Gurn languishes in his cell. The actor is thrilled by the perverse theatricality of the proposition. "The choice of the spot and the desire to see me in my costume as Gurn are evidence of positive refinement in erotic delight! See! The lady and I—the double of Gurn— and right opposite the real Gurn in his cell!" Valgrand is drugged by Lady Beltham, and two prison guards, believing that he is the criminal scheduled to be executed at dawn, drag him off semiconscious to Gurn's nearby cell.

Cheers, applause, and joyous shouts break out as the "light-hearted, singing crowd" welcomes the arrival of the guillotine. "Drawn by an old white horse, a heavy black van arrived at a fast trot, escorted by four mounted police with drawn swords. . . . A shabby brougham came into view, from which three men in black proceeded to get out." Excitement mounts with the arrival of Anatole Deibler and his men, who have only half an hour to set up the guillotine.

> The assistants took out of the van some long cases, wrapped in gray canvas and apparently very heavy. They laid these on the ground with the utmost care; they were the timbers and frame of the guillotine and could not be warped or strained, for the guillotine is a precisely accurate machine!
>
> They swept the ground thoroughly, careful to remove any gravel that might have affected the equilibrium of the framework, and then set up the red uprights of the scaffold. The floor timbers fit one into another and were joined by stout metal clamps fastened together by a bolt; next the men set the grooved slides, down which the knife must fall, into holes cut for the purpose in the middle of the floor. The guillotine now raised its awful arms to the sky.

Deibler now sprang into action.

> With a level he ascertained that the floor was absolutely horizontal; next he arranged the two pieces of wood, from each of which a segment is cut so as to form the lunette into which the victim's neck is thrust; then he tested the lever, to make sure that it worked freely, and gave a curt order.
>
> "The knife!" . . .
>
> Deibler leaned calmly against the guillotine; fit the shank into the grooves in the two uprights; and, setting the mechanisms to work, hoisted up the knife, which glittered strangely. He looked the whole thing over and turned again to his assistants.
>
> "The hay!"
>
> A truss was arranged in the lunette, and Deibler faced the instrument and pressed a spring. Like a flash the knife dropped down the uprights and severed the truss in two.
>
> The rehearsal was finished. Now for the real drama!

The assistants arrange the baskets filled with hay, one for the severed head, the other for the body. Deibler puts on his coat and informs the officials that it will soon be sunrise and is therefore time to awaken the prisoner. The public prosecutor must inform the prisoner that his appeal has been rejected, but the condemned man seems stupefied and can only mutter, "I'm not—" His eyes are

mad and haggard; he moves like an automaton; his face twitches. The chaplain
and the prison doctor are horrified, but the sun has risen and the ceremony must
proceed. The prison governor nervously signs a warrant authorizing delivery of
the prisoner to the public executioner.

> Deibler took the scissors and cut a segment out of the prisoner's shirt and cut off
> a wisp of hair that grew down his neck. Meanwhile an assistant bound the wrists of
> the man who was about to die. The executioner looked at his watch and made a
> little bow to the public prosecutor.
>
> "Come! Come! It is the time fixed by law!"
>
> Two assistants took the wretch by the shoulders and raised him up. There was
> a horrible, deep, unintelligible rattle in his throat.
>
> "I—I—"
>
> But no one heard him, and he was dragged away. It was practically a corpse
> that the servants of the guillotine took. . . .

At last the supreme moment has come. The first rays of dawn gleam on the
great triangular knife. A carriage leaves the prison and pulls up to the guillotine.

> All eyes were fixed, and a deep silence fell upon the crowded boulevard. . . .
> M. Deibler jumped down from the box and, opening the door at the back of
> the vehicle, let down the steps. Pale and nervous, the chaplain got out backward,
> hiding the scaffold from the eyes of the condemned man, who the assistants
> managed somehow to help out of the carriage. . . . The chaplain, still walking
> backward, hid the dreaded vision for still a few seconds more, then stepped aside
> abruptly. The assistants seized the condemned man and pushed him on to the
> bascule. . . . The executioner's assistants had bound the man upon the plank; it
> tilted upward. Deibler grasped the head by the two ears and pulled it into the
> lunette, despite one last convulsive struggle of the victim.
>
> There was a click of a spring, the flash of the falling knife, a spurt of blood, a
> dull groan from ten thousand mouths, and the head rolled into the basket!

Inspector Juve, who has devoted his career to an endless pursuit of Fantômas, suddenly realizes that the wrong man has been executed. Springing forward, he plunges his hand into the basket and seizes the severed head by the
hair. Staring into the actor's face, the detective sees the makeup and exclaims

*left: Henri-Désiré Landru.*

*right: Charles Chaplin in* MONSIEUR VERDOUX, *1947.*

in horror that an innocent man has been unjustly killed, and what's worse, Fantômas has escaped.

The hapless leading man has undergone the ultimate guillotine nightmare. A vain performer who chose the wrong role, Valgrand was tricked into acting out Fantômas's death for him. Like all the Evil Genius's victims, he is an easily duped puppet, and despite his inarticulate suffering, little sympathy goes out to him.

Last-minute substitutions on the scaffold have had currency in the popular imagination at least since *A Tale of Two Cities*. When the serial wife-killer, Henri-Désiré Landru (the model for Charlie Chaplin's *Monsieur Verdoux* [1947]) was guillotined in 1922, there arose a persistent legend that another man had been executed in his place. The first volume of *Fantômas* anticipated such conspiratorial mythologies.

Deibler and his sinister machine reappear in volume eleven, *Fantômas in Custody*. The episode is a variation on the classic narrative device of turning the tables in which a bloodthirsty guillotiner perishes by the very blade he was preparing for others. In need of an additional assistant for a coming execution, the practical bourgeois Deibler hires the brutal criminal Jean-Marie, a horse flayer by trade, on the assumption that a man who loves the sight of gore will make a good servant of the guillotine. "I have only one passion," the vicious thug declares, "blood, the smell of blood, the warmth of blood."

To introduce his new apprentice to the secrets of the profession, the executioner brings Jean-Marie to the "Red Hangar" on the rue de la Folie-Regnault (near the Père Lachaise cemetery) where his two machines are stored. The whole neighborhood seems marked by the sinister shed and the ghastly objects that it jealously guards; children cross the street and dogs howl whenever they pass by. On the nights before executions the shopkeepers in the area make extra money by informing the newspaper reporters of the telltale activity that is the only announcement of the coming event.

Jean-Marie is excited to see the Red Hangar "where the guillotines slept, the killing machines, the 'widows' who, always, call their lovers, hold them tight against their breast once and then cast them off into the oblivion of the cemeteries."

Deibler and his men set about their work of preparing the guillotine— "dressing up the Widow"—as if it were the most normal, mundane task in the world. Showing how to install the blade, Deibler remarks, "It's child's play." As he completes the demonstration, Deibler rationalizes, "I'm just the executioner. . . . I'm not the brain, I'm the hand. . . . Whether I'm for or against capital punishment doesn't matter."

Intoxicated by the blood-soaked uprights, Jean-Marie returns alone to the Red Hangar later that night, long after Deibler and his men have left. He caresses the hideous machine, passionately addressing his new mechanical mistress.

Jean-Marie coos, "So there you are, death machine, killing machine, who loves blood as much as I do, more than I do. Your blade, in a flash of steel, cuts necks, gnaws flesh, crushes bones, and spreads rivers of that red blood that you and I love to smell. There you are, red machine, in whose presence everyone is unnerved, in whose presence everyone is terrified, in whose presence everyone sweats with fear, and yet I contemplate you with calm indifference, with joyful curiosity, with voluptuous desire."

In a state of frenzied exultation, Jean-Marie throws his arms around the guillotine, hugs the plank, and proclaims himself servant to the blade. "In three days, do you hear, guillotine? In three days. You will function, you will fulfill your calling as killer, you will kill, and it will be me, your lackey, who will have the honor of wiping your bloody lips, of sponging your splattered blade."

Suddenly a figure in a black mask, black tights, and black gloves steps out of the shadows. It is the legendary Master of Fear. He pushes the treacherous Jean-Marie onto the guillotine and tells him he must die.

"You loved your guillotine," Fantômas sneers as Jean-Marie pleads for mercy, "By god, you're going to die by your love."

Before he propels his helpless victim forward, the King of Fear makes the wretched *apache* suffer the worst agonies, "Open your eyes wide, I'm lifting my finger, my hand is searching for the lever, I'm pressing it. In a second the blade is going to glide the length of the uprights and you'll be dead, and you'll have your neck cut, and your body will be nothing but two misshapen stumps from which the blood—which you love—will spurt in thick and heavy jets."

At last Jean-Marie is decapitated. His body, "convulsed by frightful twitchings, twisted for a few seconds on the plank, then, rigid, remained motionless." When Deibler and his men return, they hear a slight splashing sound. It is Jean-Marie's blood "dripping drop by drop from the uprights of the Red Machine, the Red Machine which that evening was still redder from all the blood that it had drunk."

In another celebrated episode, Fantômas acts out a recurrent fantasy of the European dramatic imagination: the actual killing of someone on stage disguised as an exceedingly artful simulation. The seventeenth-century Dutch scholar Gerhard Vossius had suggested that real criminals be executed in tragedies to heighten the dramatic effect, as was in fact done in Roman mimes during the decline of the empire. In volume eighteen of the epic, *Lady Beltham's Assassin*, Fantômas adopts the alias of a venerable actor, calling himself Talma Junior, and plays the role of the Great Sanson opposite his chosen victim, Rose Coutureau, who is appearing as Marie-Antoinette in a somber historical drama, *The Loves of the Executioner, or the Child of the Guillotine*.

The final tableau is the queen's execution. Fantômas's sudden appearance on the scaffold—swathed in an ample red cloak, face hidden behind a red mask, hands covered with red gloves—causes a sensation. As he releases the real steel blade, which he has secretly substituted for the cardboard stage prop, the King of Terror declares, "My vengeance is beginning." Actors and actresses scream and faint or run in panic from the stage. The audience's enthusiasm for the brilliant simulation soon becomes horror. "Black blood gushed on the stage, spurting everywhere, splashing the spectators as well as the performers. It was real blood, human blood. . . . The guillotine had functioned in earnest." Theatre, the favorite place of entertainment in *Fantômas*, makes for a spectacular scene of violent crime when the Master of Fear cleverly exploits dramatic illusion to destroy his enemies.

## *FANTOMAS* ON THE RADIO

The multiple personalities of Fantômas and the havoc and disorder that he spread throughout the world endeared the evil genius of crime to the surrealists, who made a cult of this icon of popular culture and often included him in their art and literature.

On November 3, 1933, at 8:15 P.M., the Paris station of French National Radio broadcast *La grande complainte de Fantômas, a Ballad for Radio* by the surrealist poet Robert Desnos. It was later played by regional stations and reached audiences all over France. Employing the *complainte*, a lyric form going back to the Renaissance and used in the nineteenth century for popular ballads about the lives of criminals, Desnos recounted the exploits of Fantômas in twenty-five quatrains. In other poems, Desnos refers to Deibler as "the sinister archangel of vengeance in a top hat" and pays his respects to decapitation, executioners, guillotines under the Terror, Robespierre, and the Marquis de Sade.

The radio dramatization of *La grande complainte*, which lasted only fifteen minutes, was a monumental production with a cast of over one hundred, including cabaret and music hall artists, buskers, accordionists, whistlers, and clowns, as well as opera singers and recitalists. Organized by *Le Petit Journal* to publicize the paper's new serial, *If It Was Fantômas!* by Marcel Allain, this celebration of the Emperor of Crime created an unlikely meeting of artistic talents. Antonin Artaud directed, Kurt Weill composed the music, and the Cuban musicologist and author Alejo Carpentier, who twenty years later would write the extraordinary guillotine novel *Explosion in a Cathedral*, conducted the ensemble. Unfortunately, the music has been lost, although in 1951 the *Complainte de Fantômas*, as adapted by Guillaume Hanoteau, was performed at La Rose Rouge Cabaret in Paris.

# THE GUILLOTINE
# IN THE SILENT FILM

*If we possessed a series of cinematographs of all the executions during
the Reign of Terror, they might be exhibited a thousand times
without enlightening the audiences in the least
about the meaning of the revolution.*
—George Bernard Shaw, *Preface to* Three Plays by Brieux, *1909*

FIN-DE-SIECLE PARIS was intrigued with decapitated heads. They appear in many branches of the popular arts, including magic shows, which featured routines with severed heads that continued to live and carry on conversations. In his earlier career as a magician, the pioneer filmmaker Georges Méliès featured crowd-pleasing decapitation illusions that even attracted the attention of the national executioner Deibler. When Méliès switched from theatre to cinema, he improved on the hallucinatory image of the severed yet living head, which he now was able to make photographically convincing. In short trick films, the magician-turned-filmmaker showed roving severed heads mysteriously appearing and disappearing, engaged in aggressive horse-play and violence, and often replicated as mirror images of his own head.

*Harry Kellar poster,*
*1897.*

Although the guillotine itself played no part in Méliès's macabre, zany, and blackly humorous

*Le Meutre.*

*L'Arrestation.*

*La Confrontation.*

fantasies, it was not long before it began to appear in the new art of cinema, where it immediately became a popular favorite. The context of the guillotine's film debut was not that of fantasy, however, but of the pseudodocumentary story of crime and punishment, based on a sensational news item and developed as a naturalistic melodrama.

The most popular of these early thrillers was *The Story of a Crime*, made in 1901 for Pathé by Ferdinand Zecca. It was inspired by a narrative exhibit that had opened in 1889 at Paris's famous wax museum, the Musée Grévin. Wax figures told the story of the crime in a series of seven tableaux: murder, arrest, confrontation, prison, the *toilette du condamné*, last day of the condemned man, and execution. Basing his film on the scenario from the wax exhibit, Zecca ingeniously made each of the episodes part of a dream experienced by the condemned man in his death cell. On the back wall, above the prisoner sleeping on his bed of straw, was a large opening in which the dream scenes appeared as on the stage of a theatre. The past reckless misdeeds of the prisoner are juxtaposed against his present plight. The final scene within the prisoner's dream shows him about to be executed. At precisely the same moment that the blade of the guillotine falls, the condemned man suddenly wakes up. The vision dissolves as the executioner and prison officials enter the cell door.

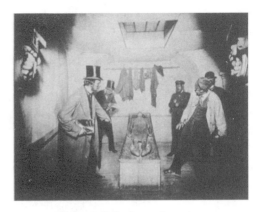

*La Cellule du condamné.*

Although in 1902 the Parisian prefect of police personally intervened to suppress Zecca's final scene of execution, the subject remained popular, especially in itinerant fairground cinemas. As early as 1900 someone in Paris had succeeded in filming an actual execution, and in 1904 Ferdinand Zecca planned to make a film called *Capital Executions,* designed to show the principal means of punishment around the world. Unable to find willing cameramen on location (Villiers's Baron Saturn would certainly have accepted the challenge), Zecca reconstructed in a Parisian studio four modes of execution: hanging in England, decapitation by axe in Germany, garroting in Spain, and electrocution in the United States. The acting, settings, and

*La Toilette du condamné.*

*L'Execution.*
*Musée Grévin, Paris, c. 1889.*

*La Guillotine, Musée Grévin, Paris, c. 1889.*

*Scene from* A DESPARATE CRIME, *1906.*

trick photography were so persuasive that thrilled audiences believed they were seeing actual killings, not simulations.

Méliès made a brief and uncharacteristic venture into the genre of realism with *A Desperate Crime* (1906), also known as *Incendiaries, or The Story of a Crime,* titles indicating the work's close kinship to Zecca's film. Having committed acts of arson, a criminal is apprehended, tried, and guillotined for the brutal murder of a farmer and his family. The final episode presents his execution in full detail, including the decapitation and the tossing of the head and trunk into the basket. Because of its too-faithful reproduction of the guillotine ritual, the film was apparently suppressed at the time of its release.

When a band of criminals who had terrorized the northern districts of Picardy and Artois were apprehended in 1908, the quadruple execution which took place in January 1909 was eagerly followed by the press and public. Cameramen from the *Pathé-Journal,* an immensely successful French newsreel, succeeded in filming the event, despite inept government attempts to prevent them. A sweeping interdiction against any filming of the guillotine resulted, and film censorship was instituted by the Ministry of the Interior.

The directive, which applied to simulations as well as to actual executions, stated: "It is imperative to forbid categorically all cinematographic showings of this genre which are capable of causing manifestations disturbing the public order and tranquillity." Even so, at a triple execution at Valence that same year, an enterprising still photographer took a number of pictures, including one with the blade in midcourse. A set of twelve postcards of the execution was issued and proved commercially successful.

Thus it was that the supreme instrument of justice that owed its continued use to its reputed effect as an example to potential criminals could not be directly shown in the French cinema. This prohibition kept filmmakers from doing treatments of books about the French Revolution (such as Anatole France's *The Gods Will Have Blood* [1912]) which virtually demanded as the key image a stark silhouette of the fatal machine. In her autobiography, *Links in the Chain of Life,* the Baroness Orczy complains that the British film version of her *Scarlet Pimpernel* (1934) was cut in France because the censor "would not permit any scene to be shown in which the guillotine could be seen, except quite small and nebulous in the distance."

*Lillian Gish in* ORPHANS OF THE STORM, *1921.*

## FANTOMAS IN THE CINEMA

"Around the Scaffold," the final episode in Feuillade's silent film version of *Fantômas* (1913) tells the story of the actor Valgrand and Lady Beltham, but compared to the novel, the film ends in a morally and aesthetically conventional manner. In the film version, Fantômas exults on hearing the hammer blows signaling the erection of the guillotine and beats time with his hand while the conscience-stricken Lady Beltham stops her ears. She looks on in horror as the Master of Fear mimes the coming execution. As dawn approaches, he opens the window and looks out at the guillotine (which is painted on a backdrop) while Lady Beltham draws away in horror.

Valgrand, still made up as Gurn, waits with his knees bound and hands tied behind his back in the cell of the condemned. Surrounded by officials in top hats, the hapless victim is about to have his hair cut and collar cut off in preparation for the execution. The scissors are already against his neck when Inspector Juve recognizes the switch that has been made and rips off Valgrand's wig and false mustache, rescuing the actor from the guillotine and the film from the censor. By 1980 it was finally possible for Claude Chabrol to present the entire Valgrand episode when he made his television film version of *Fantômas*, titled *The Magic Scaffold*, which included the detailed mounting of the guillotine and Valgrand's execution.

Nineteenth-century fascination with antisocial killers like Lacenaire and Troppmann, and with anarchist terrorists like Ravachol and Vaillant, found its ultimate fulfillment, freed from any punitive consequences, in the fantastic adventures of the Master of Fear. During World War I, when civic and patriotic virtue was obligatory—and hundreds of thousands were being slaughtered on battlefields in the name of the state—the *Fantômas* film serial was banned in certain municipalities for encouraging immorality and violence.

## THE GUILLOTINE IN SILENT FILMS
## ABOUT THE FRENCH REVOLUTION

Historical melodrama and spectacular epic were two popular cinema genres of the 1920s, and the guillotine and its sensational impact on the screen attracted many early filmmakers to the subject of the French Revolution. More often than not the climax of such films occurred on the scaffold at the place de la Révolution, as is the case in D. W. Griffith's *Orphans of the Storm* (1921) starring the Gish sisters. Griffith adapted Adolphe Dennery's *Two Orphans*, a nineteenth-century melodrama set in the prerevolutionary period, advancing his film version to 1789 at the outset and adding motifs from Dickens's *Tale of Two Cities* to create a tumultuous picture of the Terror.

Accompanying each descent of the guillotine blade is Griffith's baroque, alliterative title card reading "Death's down-dropping gesture." The image of Robespierre making a menacing gesture with his finger, starting as a throat cutting and ending as an adjustment to his lace neckpiece, sets the tone of alternating horror and comedy typical of American melodrama.

At the denouement, Henriette, the orphan, played by Lillian Gish, is sent to the scaffold by Robespierre. Strapped to the plank and tipped into the lunette before she is saved by Danton in an exciting last-minute rescue, Henriette kicks and struggles and makes faces indicating her unwillingness to submit. The effect is a rare instance of comedic response by a victim actually locked in the collar beneath the suspended blade. Fighting back against impossible odds was intrinsic to the American melodramatic heroine's vitality and resourcefulness, and the high spirits and optimistic humor of the diminutive Henriette/Lillian Gish are not overpowered by the towering guillotine. The New World instinct for survival was altogether different from European fatalistic heroics on the scaffold when confronted with "Death's down-dropping gesture."

Censorship in French cinema during the first half of the twentieth century prohibited showing the guillotine in detail as Griffith had done. The guillotine appears repeatedly in Abel Gance's epic *Napoleon* (1927), and while its image is so fleeting as to be scarcely noticeable, it nonetheless creates a strong subliminal impression. The very filming of Gance's *Napoleon* employed a "guillotine camera," so named by the crew because of its construction and its descending apparatus. Attached to a moving bar between two uprights on a platform which itself could be slid back and forth, this special camera allowed the cinematographer to catch the actors in motion. Metaphorically the decapitating machine could likewise be said to be taking pictures when it took off its patients' heads—as witness the member of the guillotine team known as the "photographer."

In *Napoleon* the guillotine makes its first subtle appearance as a small tattoo beneath the words *Mort aux Tyrans* (Death to the tyrants) on the torso of a bare-chested guard standing by the door of the revolutionary Cordeliers Club. During an extended scene of factional wrangling at the Convention, as the deadly struggle for power intensifies, an image of the guillotine with its blade dropping on an

*Poster for* NAPOLEON, *1927.*

empty lunette is rapidly superimposed three times on the heaving sea of faces. Later in the film, as a tumbril bearing prisoners approaches the scaffold, the guillotine comes into view, its plank standing vertical and the lunette open, waiting for its prey. In another scene Robespierre sits at a table, a book titled *Cromwell* before him (portending his own ruthless rise to the position of dictator). An object not visible in the frame casts the shadow of a guillotine on the book, literally foreshadowing the tyrant's doom. The fifth and final view of the guillotine occurs in a brief scene showing Danton standing on the scaffold.

The guillotine in Gance's *Napoleon* is little more than a shadow, a negative reflection of the revolutionary leaders' divisiveness. Through these subliminal images Gance reinforced the film's thesis that only Napoleon could bring unity to France and preserve the ideals of the Revolution.

*Abel Faivre. Satirical drawing in* LE RIRE, *1898.*

# APHORISTS, POETS, AND PLAYWRIGHTS

*The guillotine is the masterpiece of plastic art*

*its click*

*creates perpetual motion*

*—Blaise Cendrars, "The Head," 1914*

HENRI BERGSON's theory that laughter is the sudden perception of the mechanical imposed upon the living (*Le Rire*, 1900) finds a sinister and unexpected application in the case of the guillotine, which instantly reduces human beings to marionettes and in one swift chop divides the puppets in two. Humorists of a sardonic bent have long recognized a grim comedy in this artfully designed machine put in the service of removing people's heads, and aphorists, satirists, and cartoonists have admired its efficiency, speed, and finality. The guillotine's art is like their own.

Finding in the guillotine a metaphor for style, Alfred de Vigny declared in *Stello* (1832), his novel of the Terror, "I feel that my narrative must be as strong and swift as the blade that is lifted still smoking from a severed head." In *Opium* (1930) Jean Cocteau explained, "I do not talk of my works. Each one guillotines the other. My only aim is to spare myself Napoleon." He called Saint-Just "the delightful throat-cutter with the cut throat." The Austrian satirist and aphorist Karl Kraus found the machine most useful to express his boundless misanthropy: "I'd like to apply for a permit to run a hand-operated guillotine. But oh, that income tax!"

Ambrose Bierce, an American author of horror stories and sardonic epigrams, defined the guillotine in his *Devil's Dictionary* (1906) as "A machine which makes a Frenchman shrug his shoulders with good reason." Bierce considered this characteristic gesture to be "directly referable to the Terror inspired by the guillotine during the period of that instrument's activity."

A Polish aphorist with a taste for the fantastic and the macabre, Jerzy Lec was confined in a German concentration camp from 1941 to 1943, lived from 1950 to 1952 an émigré in Israel, and returned to Poland, where he remained during the Stalinist era. Lec was unable to publish until after the thaw in 1956. Like many modern Polish writers who underwent similar repression and displacement, he was fascinated by the dialectics of terror and by the complicity of victim and victimizer.

Executioners and guillotines amplify the menacing irony in several of his brief vignettes. "People can be divided in various ways. We know that. Into human and inhuman, for example. Said the astonished executioner: 'I just divide them into heads and trunks!' "

Decapitation gives rise to mordant reflection in Lec's dislocated universe. "People don't always recognize the value of something 'in context.' They'll say of a person: 'He had a head on his shoulders!' when they see it separately in the basket under the guillotine."

Reminiscent of the revolutionary cartoons and engravings of 1793 and 1794, Lec's black humor often found expression in his aphorisms, as in the quatrain "When Called Upon."

> *The guillotine grows rusty*
> *If it stops cutting heads off.*
> *The model citizen-executioner*
> *When called upon—sticks out his own.*

## POETS OF THE APOCALYPSE:
## GEORG HEYM AND MAXIMILIAN VOLOSHIN

In the opening years of the twentieth century, two poets, one German, the other Russian, were drawn to the apocalyptic landscape of the guillotine. In his poems and dramatic sketches about the French Revolution written in 1910 and 1911, the early expressionist Georg Heym anticipated the disasters of war and the violent social changes soon to come.

Heym expressed his horrified fascination with the mechanical brutality of the guillotine in his sonnet "Louis Capet," about the execution of the King. A frenzied beating of drums sounds all around the scaffold draped in black like a coffin when suddenly turmoil and shouting signal the imminent entrance of the principal actor in this grim drama.

> *In his carriage there arrives Capet, all bedraggled,*
> *Pelted with muck, his hair disheveled.*

> *Quickly he is pulled forth and stretched out.*
> *His head lies on the block. The blade whizzes down.*
> *Blood spurts from his neck stuck firmly in the collar.*

Historical accuracy is secondary to emotional intensity, and in Heym's account the violence done to the king by the brutish mob exceeds anything that occurred in actuality. The poet's impulse is to seek in the chaos and destruction of revolution a vital acceleration of life and renewal of human existence. Heinrich Eduard Jacob, a contemporary of Heym's, recalled the mood of this tumultuous prewar period in his memoirs, *Berlin* (1961).

> We were filled with the future, and never did just "being there" seem more attrac-
> tive that at the *Aktion's* "Revolution Ball." The ambiguous title of the theme was
> just a colorful theatrical gag. One after the other the couples fell on their knees
> before a laughing guillotine as if it were a bed of love—this was the extraordinary
> thing—to be beheaded.

Heym confessed, "In my daydreams I always see myself as Danton or a man on the barricades; I cannot really imagine myself at all without my Jacobin bonnet. I hope now at least for a war!" For Heym the lightning-fast descent of the guillotine blade forecasted the impending cataclysm that was to engulf Europe. But the poet did not live to see the violence he longed for; he drowned in a skating accident in 1912, two years before the outbreak of the Great War.

The Russian symbolist poet and painter Maximilian Voloshin repeatedly drew an analogy between the Bolshevik and the French revolutions. A series of his poems, written in 1917 and published in the collection *Demons Deaf and Dumb* (1919), portrays the bloody ritual of the guillotine during the Terror as a blasphemous inversion of Christian worship. The final lines of the poem "Thermidor" describe the Revolution as a human sacrifice to a monstrous deity.

Robespierre's death is the last mass to be celebrated. Amidst a graveyard of ghosts represented by all the other heads that have rolled, the high priest ascends the altar bearing his head as though it were an offering.

> *Now the furies dance the Carmagnole,*
> *Raising a howl before the guillotine.*
> *For the last time like a throne*
> *She reigns over the violent mob.*

The last tumbril of "Thermidor" bears the remnants of power and of shame—the bodies of the executed terrorists.

> *And amongst them, to the burial ground of phantoms*
> *Robespierre makes his final journey.*
> *The bells ring for the last mass in the temple.*

> *And the people pray to the guillotine . . .*
> *Piously, as though a casket with offerings,*
> *He bears his head to the scaffold.*

Having experienced both the failed uprising of 1905 and the Bolshevik victory in 1917, Voloshin knew that for the true believers in revolution, violence was the holy sacrament needed to purify the nation.

## ROUSSEL'S *LOCUS SOLUS*

Raymond Roussel's proto-surrealist novel *Locus Solus* (1914) presents the ultimate experiment with a decapitated head. The erudite scientist Martial Canterel suspends Danton's partially decomposed head (which the professor's great-great-grandfather had secretly obtained from the executioner Sanson) in a diamond-shaped tank full of specially oxygenated water. The depilated white Siamese tomcat Khóng-dek-lèn sends electrical charges into Danton's brain. The eyes turn, the lips move, and disjointed fragments of speech can be deciphered.

> Certain muscles appeared to make the absent eyes turn in all directions, while others periodically went into action as if to raise, lower, screw up or relax the area

of the eyebrows and forehead; but those of the lips in particular moved with wild agility, undoubtedly due to the amazing gift of oratory that Danton once possessed. . . . The intense twitching of the other facial muscles . . . showed how expressive Danton's hideous snout must have been on the platform. . . . Under the influence of the powerful animal magnetism . . . the facial muscles trembled and the fleshless lips began to move distinctly, vigorously pronouncing strings of noiseless words. By lip-reading, Canterel managed to make out various syllables just from the way they were articulated; then he discovered chaotic snatches of speech following one another disconnectedly or, sometimes, repeated *ad nauseam* with strange insistence.

## ANOUILH, IONESCO, HOCHWÄLDER, AND WEISS

For postwar playwrights, the guillotine seemed a permanent fixture of civilization and a perfect symbol of its mechanized killing at the most basic level, illustrative of the way modern states liquidate their own "undesirables." In the light of mid-twentieth-century European history—fascism, Stalinism, death camps, the Final Solution—the guillotine inevitably became metaphoric: political, metaphysical, and existential in its resonances.

Jean Anouilh's play *Poor Bitos* (1956), features contemporary Frenchmen masquerading as leaders of the Revolution at a costume dinner party, at which one of the guests explains, "In France we dine off severed heads. It's the national dish." The other half of decapitated victims appears in Eugène Ionesco's *A Stroll in the Air* (1963), when the principal character Beranger has an apocalyptic vision: "I saw columns of guillotined men marching along without their heads, columns of guillotined men . . . crossing enormous plains."

In several central European plays ostensibly dealing with the French Revolution, the guillotine's role as an emblem of totalitarian violence is clear. *The Public Prosecutor* (1948) by the Austrian playwright Fritz Hochwälder is a "devil's comedy" set in Paris during the last days of the Reign of Terror after the fall of Robespierre. The dreaded public prosecutor Antoine Fouquier-Tinville, responsible for sending thousands to the guillotine, believes he will be able to save his own head by fabricating charges against an anonymous enemy. But once the execution orders are signed and sealed, he discovers that he has condemned himself to the scaffold.

As depicted by Hochwälder (whose parents perished in the Holocaust), terror by guillotine bears striking resemblance to the terror of the Nazi system. The efficient bureaucrat Fouquier-Tinville, like the executioner Sanson, is ready to serve all masters and always has the defense that he was only carrying out orders. The process of selecting victims is utterly arbitrary; everyone is suspect and subject to immediate detention. The public prosecutor arrests anyone whose name bears the slightest relation to the names of those who have been denounced.

All distinctions among people come to a quick end in the prison cells. "Down there personality, rank or influence no longer exist." The assault on human dignity is completely egalitarian. "I've had millionaires among my clients," Fouquier-Tinville explains, "believe me, the man who picked their heads out of the sack gave them no special consideration."

Condemnations come about so quickly that there is soon a large backlog of prisoners waiting to be beheaded. Unfortunately, the executions take too long. It is not the fault of the "maestro," as the public prosecutor calls Sanson, but of the old-fashioned equipment. A new model of the decapitating machine is desparately needed.

After the execution, Fouquier-Tinville is determined that all evidence of the victims be obliterated. The hair is made into wigs, the skin tanned for ornaments. "The guillotine and then the lime-pits. Quick, efficient, leave no trace. Future historians will not be able to resurrect their bones, bury them in pious monuments. . . . What is done is done."

In Peter Weiss's *Marat/Sade* (1964), the inmates of the Charenton asylum under the direction of the Marquis de Sade perform the persecution and assassination of Marat, as well as other episodes of the French Revolution. As conceived by the Marquis, Paris during the Terror is a slaughterhouse and the mob in the streets are participants in a grotesque dance of death. Two patients covered with a cloth represent a horse, and they pull a tumbril filled with the condemned receiving last rites from a priest. Two other patients represent the guillotine, where preparations for an execution are rehearsed in gruesome detail.

As a procession of nobles lines up to be decapitated, Charlotte Corday comments that high upon the scaffold you can see further than the eyes of your executioner. Sade points out to Marat that the aristocrats have turned defeat into victory. Now that their pleasures have been taken away from them, the guillotine saves the idle nobles from endless boredom and allows them to offer their heads as if for a coronation. Taking pride in one's own decapitation, Sade observes, is the height of perversion. Death by guillotine is painless when com-

*Scene from* THE MARAT/SADE *directed by Peter Brook.*

pared to the hideous tortures that were inflicted for many hours on end on the would-be assassin of Louis XV, Robert François Damiens, in prerevolutionary days. Yet the revolutionary beheadings presided over by the Marquis in his play within a play, enacted by the mad inmates of the asylum, are themselves cruel rituals of vengeance.

Peter Brook's famous production of *The Marat/Sade* turned the march to the scaffold into a mimed sequence lasting two minutes. The unusual guillotine simulation was one of the high points of the performance and a great moment in modern theatre. To the rasping sound of a broomhandle pulled across a grate, suggestive of the whoosh of the blade's descent, the inmates playing aristocrats stepped forward toward the center trap, where each in turn jerked his or her head down, as though it had just been cut, off and dropped into the pit. The gaping hole appears to fill with severed heads, their mouths twisted, tongues protruding, and eyes bulging.

To suggest the ceaseless flow of blood, one of the four singers poured paint from one bucket to another. "The execution of the king" was effected by the decapitation of a dummy made of broomhandles and scraps of clothing with a cabbage head and carrot nose, which is then thrown into the pit as another bucket of blood is poured out—but this time the blood is blue paint. Brook's realization of Weiss's play embodied the sinister emblem of revolutionary violence not by the customary wooden structure and steel blade, but by two connected images: pouring blood and a pit full of heads. Metaphorically Brook transcended the French Revolution to reach into our own era of holocaust and genocide.

## GEORG LICHTENBERG REDISCOVERED

In 1988 a passage from a letter by the eighteenth-century German philosopher Georg Christoph Lichtenberg about the guillotine blade was reworked into dialogue for a scene in Robert Wilson's theatrical spectacle *The Forest*, written by the East German playwright Heiner Müller.

When the new French mechanism for removing heads had first appeared in the late 1700s, it had immediately caught the eye of Lichtenberg, an aphorist and physicist equally adept at science and literature. A small, sickly hunchback, Lichtenberg addressed the nature of infirmity in his vignettes and maxims. He is best known for his probing aphorisms, admired by Goethe, Nietzsche, Freud, and Wittgenstein.

" 'How's it going?' the blindman asked the cripple. 'As you can see,' was his answer."

"The healthiest and handsomest, the best-built people are in accord with the whole world. As soon as one has any kind of physical defect, he also has his own opinion."

The French Revolution and its new method of execution provided Lichtenberg with subjects for reflection, and in the cool and critical judg-

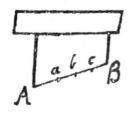

*Lichtenberg's diagram.*

ment of this satirist, revolutionary France seemed to have gone mad. "No one in the Convention has yet proposed to eat the bodies of the guillotined; but that, too, will come," he speculated. Yet in July 1793, the philosopher-scientist sent a letter to his friend Jeremias David Reuss, accompanied by a diagram in which he expounded enthusiastically on the operation of the guillotine blade, dispassionately treating the matter as a problem in geometry. It is this letter that provided dialogue in Müller's play.

Up until now I have seen only one really good illustration of the guillotine, and that was in an English engraving. The neck does not rest on a block, but simply in a circular opening cut in a rather thick board. This board is not struck by the falling blade, but only lightly grazed as it passes by, so that the head is, as it were, planed off. To facilitate this, the cutting edge is not placed along the horizontal, but is inclined at an angle to the horizontal, wherein lies the elegance of this splendid concept for cutting, and whereby the blow is transformed into a cut. For if $A\,B$ represents the blade and the neck lies in the opening $C\,D$, then all points of the blade $a$, $b$, $c$ hit the neck, but $a$ earlier and at different spots than $b$, and $b$ earlier and at different spots than $c$. After the operation, the blade rests at $a\,b$ and the head really has been cut off, and this occurs with the greater ease the more the blade is inclined at an angle to the horizontal. . . . If the administration of justice is definitely resolved on decapitating and must do so, I truly know of nothing more ingenious than the guillotine. But there is probably very little chance of its being adopted here in Germany, on account of the abominable and murderous use to which it was put at the time of its inauguration.

Wilson choreographed and directed a musical spectacle for the July 13, 1989, inauguration of the new opera house on the place de la Bastille as part of the ceremony marking the bicentennial of the French Revolution. At one end of the stage in the opening scene there stood a giant chair. Sitting in the audience, Wilson observed to his amusement, "Some people think it's the guillotine."

Having introduced Lichtenberg's inclined blade in his earlier production of *The Forest*, Robert Wilson now paid indirect homage to the absent decapitating machine, officially ignored in all the other festivities celebrating the principles of Liberty, Equality, and Fraternity.

*Artist unknown. Illustration of Karl Valentin's Panoptikon, c. 1934.*

# THE NAZI GUILLOTINE

*Kürten asked me particularly about the execution in detail—whether, his
head chopped off, he would still hear the gushing of blood. That would
be for him, he said, the pleasure of all pleasures.*
—*Dr. Karl Berg,* The Sadist, *1932*

"THE PUBLIC IS INVITED TO
Valentin's Panopticon! The Most
Original Museum in the World! Daily at the Hotel Wagner, Sonnenstrasse 23.
Admission: 60 Pfenning. Children and Soldiers Half Price. Weekdays from 4–12
P.M. Sundays from 4–12 P.M."

In 1934 Karl Valentin, a Bavarian cabaret artist who directly influenced his
great admirer Bertolt Brecht, opened in his native town of Munich a Museum
of Curiosities featuring a Chamber of Horrors and Collection of the Weird.
One of the main exhibits was a guillotine scene "the last moments of the
murderer and robber, Peter Kürten (executed by means of a guillotine)."
Kürten was a German psychopathic serial killer after whom Peter Lorre's role
in Fritz Lang's film *M* (1931) was modeled. A wax figure of the murderer lay
beneath the guillotine and a hooded figure stood beside the bascule. Next to
the guillotine was a sign: "The executioner guarantees quick relief for
headaches of all kinds." Also exhibited in the Panopticon's Chamber of
Horrors was a display showing the results of such a cure: an impeccably
dressed figure without a head.

Karl Valentin himself often explained the functioning of the machine to visitors, but since he could not always be present, he hired Donderer, the assistant
to the state executioner Johann Reichart, to demonstrate the operation of the
guillotine based on professional experience. The Bavarian state ministry was

outraged and forbade Donderer to engage in such unbecoming activity. When he persisted, he was promptly dismissed. "The former Assistant Executioner Donderer shall not engage in the carrying out of death sentences in the future," the ministry of justice declared in a notice of December 4, 1934.

The Panopticon guillotine was particularly provocative because of its striking similarity to the machine still in use at that time in the Stadelheim prison. Police officials in Munich wanted to prohibit the public showing of the guillotine, but afraid of creating an uproar, they abandoned the idea of intervening directly. Instead, they confiscated Valentin's construction plans. Valentin's Panopticon was closed in December 1934, less than a year after its opening. It reopened briefly the next year, but never proved a success.

The Bavarian comedian eventually erected the wooden scaffold of the guillotine in his own garden in Planegg so that, as he ironically explained, "my grandchild would have something to play with."

## THE NAZI GUILLOTINE

Germany in 1935 was hardly the place for Valentine's disabusing performance. Under Hitler the guillotine was given free reign such as had not been seen since the height of the Terror in France. But the many thousands sent to the guillotine by the Nazi regime have passed virtually unnoticed in the overwhelming slaughter of World War II, when greater atrocities and mass exterminations were carried out by more efficient modern means.

The figures are staggering. As recorded by the Nazis themselves, between 1933 and 1945, there were 16,500 executions by guillotine in Germany. Shortly after coming to power, Hitler, wishing to see his "revolution" inaugurated by the guillotine, ordered twenty additional machines to be built and began recruiting executioners. In a ten-month period during 1944 to 1945, over 10,000 heads fell. At Plotzensee, seventy executions were carried out in eleven hours during a single night, necessitating the use of several guillotines. During the year of 1944, one Nazi executioner decapitated 1,399 victims, an average of nearly four a day.

*The Diary of a Man in Despair*, written by the anti-Nazi Prussian aristocrat Friedrich Percyval Reck-Malleczewen, who was shot in Dachau in 1945, draws a direct parallel between the use of the guillotine in Paris under the Terror and during Hitler's reign.

We live now as people must have lived before Thermidor and the overthrow of Robespierre. . . . The Summary Courts, presided over by sadistic and bloodthirsty Nazi Jacobins, make quick work of sentencing people to death, and five-minute trials suffice. . . . The victim is shoved out a back door, where the executioner already awaits him. In fifteen minutes it is all over, trial, sentencing, everything. Next comes the towering guillotine, and in university dissecting rooms the cadavers of the decapitated are piling up so high that university officials have refused further shipments of these silent guests. . . . And we now have, as I am informed by the Traunstein public prosecutor, eleven guillotines in Germany. Recently, when the one in Munich went out of order, the Stuttgart guillotine was borrowed to help out.

It is the executioner's duty loyally to cut off heads, no matter who is in power. This principle was dramatically illustrated by Jules-Henri Desfourneaux (incumbent from 1939 to 1951), who four days before the Germans took Paris in June 1940, guillotined Fritz Erler, a Nazi spy. Erler's mistress and accomplice, Carmen Mory, was pardoned and went on to earn infamy as the notorious "Black Angel" of Ravensbruck.

The conquering Nazis found Erler's execution highly objectionable, since political prisoners normally were shot, and they lodged a complaint against the French, not so much for executing their spy as for executing him in the wrong way. Even so, the occupying forces accepted Desfourneaux, and the grateful executioner served the collaborationist regime well. During the occupation, in addition to his regular roster of murderers, Desfourneaux guillotined various communists and resistance fighters (who sometimes spat in his face) in reprisals for the slaying of Nazis.

The last execution of a woman in France prior to the German occupation had taken place in 1893; from 1893 to 1941 all condemned murderesses had been pardoned. Under Marshal Pétain's collaborationist regime, with its emphasis on restoring "family" values to defeated France, all this changed. Between 1941 and 1943 five women were guillotined. They did not go to their execution submissively but struggling, screaming, and cursing. The last of these five victims, Marie-Louise Giraud, a *faiseuse d'anges* (literally, "maker of angels" as abortionists are called in French), was the most celebrated—sentenced to death under a harsh new law against abortion passed by the Pétainists in the name of moral rebirth and decency.

Claude Chabrol's film *The Story of Women* (1988) dramatized in fictional form the life and death of Marie-Louise Giraud, exposing the moral hypocrisy of a corrupt society that watched indifferently as Jewish children were sent to their death in concentration camps. Based on Francis Szpiner's study of the case, *Une Affaire de femmes* (1986), and with a screenplay by Colo Tavernier, the film depicts the occupation under the Vichy government as an era of utter degradation and heartlessness. Chabrol's abortionist-heroine (played by Isabelle Huppert) is amoral and acquisitive but more generous in spontaneous human emotion than the world around her. In her martyrdom at the hands of a male-ruled society in which church and state were allied, the abortionist becomes a moving victim.

The climactic guillotining in the prison courtyard is preceded by an elliptical march to the scaffold, represented largely by shots of the heroine's feet in chains clanking on the stone floor, and a *toilette du condamné* that is suggested by locks of hair falling on the rough floor. Flanked by officials and the priest, the heroine approaches the guillotine where the executioner Desfourneaux stands waiting. The blade descends, and suddenly the *mouton*, the heavy weight above the blade, lies at rest at the bottom of its course between the uprights. The mother of two young children has been executed in the name of the family.

After the liberation, in spite of having beheaded many innocent victims, Desfourneaux and his assistant executioners were cleared of any charges of collaboration and resumed their duties in 1946. In the remaining five years of his life Desfourneaux reportedly had terrifying visions and when he died at the age of seventy-four in 1951, he was said to be nearly insane.

Similar powers of survival were displayed by the German master guillotiner Johann Baptist Reichart, scion of a dynasty of executioners going back eight generations. Reichart faithfully served the Nazis before and during the war and continued to perform his function under the new democratic regime. According to his own careful record keeping, from 1939 to 1945 Reichart guillotined 2,876 victims (almost all of them political), setting the world record for the number of heads severed, far surpassing any of the Sansons and Deiblers of the past.

In 1943 Hans and Sophie Scholl, the young anti-Nazi brother and sister of the White Rose underground, were executed for treason by Reichart in Munich's Stadelheim prison. "These despicable criminals deserve a speedy and dishonorable death," the verdict read, reflecting the stigma the Germans attached to a shameful and degrading death on the guillotine as opposed to the dignity of dying by firing squad. The execution of the Scholls was depicted in the 1983 German film *The White Rose*, directed by Michael Verhoeven, which ends with the beheading of the heroic Sophie (played by Irena Stalze). The final shot shows the blade falling above her bare neck.

Following what appears to be an unwritten law that guillotiners always receive protection, the Allies used the services of Reichart after the defeat of Germany and had him prepare the gallows for the Nuremberg war criminals and give instructions to Sergeant John Woods, the hangman for the American forces.

*Antonio Recalcati. Detail,* 31 Janvier 1801, *1975.*

# THE GUILLOTINE SAILS FOR
# THE NEW WORLD

*At Pointe-à-Pitre the horrible instrument had at first been set up*
*in the Market Square, but the blood, which lacked any outlet,*
*gathered in pools and infected the air. Hugues had the guillotine*
*moved to Victory Square where it was erected facing the sea,*
*a ditch having been dug to let the blood flow out.*
—*Sainte-Croix de la Roncière*, Victor Hugues, *1937*

"I SAW THEM ERECT the guillotine again tonight. It stood in the bows, like a doorway opening on to the immense sky." So begins the most lyrical and inventive of all guillotine novels, *Explosion in a Cathedral* (1962), written by the Cuban musicologist and author Alejo Carpentier. The passage continues: "The Door stood alone, facing into the night above the tutelary figurehead, its diagonal blade gleaming, its wooden uprights framing a whole panorama of stars." Emblem of freedom and of death, the "guillotine-door" is both a threshold and an exit.

From 1928 to 1939 an exile in Paris, where he associated with the surrealists, Carpentier had directed the orchestra for the Artaud-Weill radio production of *La grande complainte de Fantômas* in 1933. He employed surrealist techniques in *Explosion in a Cathedral*, blurring the frontiers between dream and reality. The mixture of the everyday and the fabulous is central to his "Lo real-maravilloso" —"the marvelous-real." The concept, often called magic realism, which Carpentier first introduced in 1949 in his prologue to *The Kingdom of this World*, integrates the myth, magic, and religion that are an essential part of daily life in the fantastic history of Latin America. To Carpentier, art does not simply imitate but adds to an already magical reality.

*Explosion in a Cathedral* (*El Siglio de las Luces* in Spanish, or *The Age of Enlightenment*) is a novel about the neglected historical figure Victor Hugues, who brought the French Revolution to the Caribbean. In addition to the heroic

ideals of Liberty, Equality, and Fraternity, this strange adventurer—son of a
baker from Marseilles— also brought the means to liquidate the past and impose
the Revolution. The gift of freedom to the slaves could always be given and
then taken back, but the colonial guillotine would stay on and undergo metamorphoses. The European killing machine managed to take on local coloration,
go native, and become exotic.

Based on Carpentier's study of documents in Guadeloupe and historical
records in Barbados libraries, the novel traces Hugues's career from the sincere
revolutionary zeal of his days as a commissioner of the Republic in the Antilles
to the cynical opportunism of his service to the Directory and Napoleon.
Throughout the rise and fall of Hugues's fortune, the guillotine is on center
stage, sometimes playing a sinister, commanding role, at other times assuming a
shabby, grotesque bit part.

Hugues's mission to the Antilles is a dangerous one: the commissioner
must wrest back from recent British conquest the French royal colonies and
establish the new revolutionary order. He keeps a portrait of Robespierre the
Incorruptible in his cabin, but as his voyage nears its end, an even more powerful talisman is needed. As an envoy from the Convention, Hugues puts on
his glittering republican uniform one moonlit night and goes out onto the fore-
deck where workmen are setting up the guillotine.

> The carpenters . . . were carrying planks up into the bows, followed by sailors
> laden with large, oblong crates. When one of these was opened, a steely, triangular
> shape glinted in the moonlight. . . . These men, silhouetted against the sea,
> seemed to be performing some bloody and mysterious rite, as they laid the bascule
> and the uprights out flat on the deck, following a sequence determined by the
> sheet of instructions, which they consulted in silence by the light of a lantern.
> What was being set out there was a geometrical projection from the vertical, a false
> perspective, a configuration in two dimensions of what would soon take on height,
> breadth and a terrible depth. With something of the air of Aztec immolators, the
> dark figures toiled at their nocturnal joinery, taking parts, runners and hinges from
> the coffin-like crates.

Victor Hugues proclaims the guillotine and the printing press the two essential items on board. The great gift of the French to the men of the new world is
absolute equality of rights without regard to race, and as the ship enters the har-

bor in Guadeloupe, Hugues orders the printing of hundred of posters bearing the decree abolishing slavery. At the same time he unveils the guillotine, which until now has remained shrouded in a tarpaulin to keep the blade from being corroded by the salt air.

> Then he strode decisively across the deck, and going up to the guillotine, he tore off the tarpaulin sheath which covered it, revealing it to the sunlight for the first time, its finely tempered blade gleaming.
>
> With all the insignia of his authority sparkling, Victor Hugues stood motionless, turned to stone, his right hand resting on the upright of the Machine, suddenly transformed into a symbolic figure. Together with Liberty, the first guillotine was arriving in the New World.

Once Hugues has become the undisputed master of Guadeloupe, the guillotine begins to function publicly—an opening long awaited by the impatient and curious inhabitants of the island.

> The day it made its debut—on the persons of two monarchist chaplains—the entire town herded into the marketplace, where a sturdy platform had been erected with steps at the side, supported, as in Paris, by four cedar-wood stanchions. And since Republican fashions had already found their way into the colony, the mestizos appeared dressed in short blue jackets and white trousers with a red stripe, while the mulattas displayed new headdresses in the colours of the day. It would be hard to imagine a more joyful or ebullient crowd, with the splashes of indigo and strawberry which seemed to ripple in time to the flags in the limpid morning sunlight. The servants from the Commissariat were leaning out the windows, shouting and laughing—and laughing still louder when the trembling hand of an officer slid up over their hams. Many children had clambered up on to the roofs of the buildings to get a better view. . . . When Monsieur Anse [the sensitive, artistic mulatto executioner imported from France] showed himself on top of the scaffold in his best ceremonial clothes—the excellent shave the barber had given him showed how seriously he took his work—he received a prolonged ovation. Pointe-à-Pitre [the capital of Guadeloupe] was not Cap Français, where, for some time past, there had existed an excellent theatre, supplied with new shows given by companies on their way to New Orleans. Here they had nothing of that sort; they had never seen a theatre open to all, and, for this reason, the people were now

discovering the essence of Tragedy. Fate was present among them, its blade waiting, with inexorable punctuality, for those who had been ill-advised enough to turn
their arms against the town. And the spirit of the Chorus was active in every spectator, as strophes and antistrophes, occurrences and apostrophes were bandied
across the stage.

Suddenly a Messenger appeared, the Guards fell back, and the tumbril made
its entry on to the bedecked expanse of the public square, bearing the two condemned men, their hands joined by the same rosary tied round their wrists. Solemn
rolls on the drum were heard, the bascule took the weight of a fairly corpulent man,
and the knife fell in a clamour of expectation.

Minutes later the first two executions had been performed. But the crowd did
not disperse, perhaps temporarily disappointed that the spectacle had been so
brief—the liquid blood was still draining away through the cracks in the stage. The
merrymaking must continue longer, on this new holiday and day of rest. They
must show off their new clothes. And as figure-dances were best for displaying cos-
tumes, and for swirling many-coloured carmagnole skirts, they all began to form in
quadrilles, advancing and retiring in line, changing partners, holding each other
round the waist, bowing and ignoring the self-appointed leaders of the dance.

The joyous and exuberant dancing lasts until nightfall.

That day marked the inauguration of the Great Terror on the island. The guillotine
functioned ceaselessly now in the place de la Victoire; the tempo of its blade
increased. And since the desire to witness executions was kept alive in a place
where everyone knew everyone else, at least by sight, if not from business dealings—one man harboured a grudge against another, who, in his turn, had not forgotten some humiliation he had suffered—the guillotine became the centre of the
life of the town. The crowd from the Market migrated to the pretty harbour square
. . . and since it was now a very good place for doing business, the square became a
running exchange for bric-à-brac and things abandoned by their owners. . . . The
scaffold had become the hub of an exchange, of a forum, a perpetual auction sale.
The executions no longer even interrupted the haggling, importuning and arguing.
The guillotine had begun to form part of normal everyday life. Among the parsley
and the marjoram, miniature guillotines were sold as ornaments, and many people
took them home. Children exerted their ingenuity to construct little machines for
decapitating cats. A beautiful mulatta . . . offered her guests liqueurs in wooden

flasks made in the shape of people; when placed on a bascule they ejected their corks—which naturally had prettily painted faces—as a toy knife came down on them, operated by a tiny automatic executioner.

Elevated to the rank of French citizens, the former black slaves are quickly condemned to death if they prove troublesome or protest against doing forced labor. Under the commissioner's firm hand, Guadeloupe prospers beyond all expectation. Even though Robespierre has fallen and the Terror has come to a close in France, the guillotine continues to travel from village to village on the little island. "Swift and relentless, endowed with military genius, fearless as few men are," Victor Hugues enjoys a success that far exceeds most other men's achievements in the Revolution. Now Governor of Guadeloupe, Hugues authorizes piracy against the British and their allies, profits greatly from his armed Caribbean privateers, and marries a rich heiress.

Learning of the island's newly acquired wealth, an international opera company touring the Americas decides to conclude its tour in the capital of Guadeloupe. But since Pointe-à-Pitre has no theatre—save that of the guillotine—the opera is obliged to share the platform used for executions. The guillotine is moved to a nearby yard where hens roost on the uprights. Monsieur Anse the executioner, who happens to be a good violinist, helps coach the orchestra. A gala performance of Jean-Jacques Rousseau's popular *Village Soothsayer*, given on the very scaffold where the guillotine had recently severed heads is an outstanding success.

But a new regime has come to power in Paris and in 1798 Victor Hugues is relieved of his post, arrested, and recalled to France by the Directory. The guillotine is promptly dismantled by Monsieur Anse's assistants. "The Machine had concluded its fearful task in the island. The gleaming steel triangle was returned to its box. The Narrow Gate was taken down, through which so many had passed out of the daylight into that darkness whence there is no return. The Instrument, the only one to have reached America as the secular arm of Liberty, would now gather rust amongst the scrap metal in some warehouse."

Gifted with the ability to come out on top whatever the circumstances, the former revolutionary commissioner succeeds in returning to America as an agent of the Directory in Cayenne, French Guiana, appointed by Bonaparte. The Age of the Scaffold is over but so is the Age of the Tree of Liberty. Several years after his arrival in Guiana, Victor Hugues reads out a new proclamation canceling the previous decree that had granted freedom to all and announcing the reinstitution of slavery in the French colonies in America.

What follows is a wholesale manhunt. "The Negroes who had not surrendered, or who were insubordinate, were whipped to death, dismembered, beheaded, or subjected to appalling tortures. Many of them hung by the ribs from the hooks in the public slaughter-houses."

Victor Hugues, who eight years before had shown "a persistent, an almost superhuman energy in abolishing slavery," now displays the same energy in restoring it. "I'm a politician," Hugues explains, "and if the restoration of slavery is a political necessity, then I must bow to that necessity." Yesterday's political exiles become slave owners. "We're progressing gentlemen, we're progressing," the former republican commissioner declares.

### A WOMAN NAMED SOLITUDE

An epilogue to the story of Victor Hugues is found in the lyrical novel *A Woman Named Solitude* (1985) by the French author André Schwartz-Bart, which covers the events following the reinstitution of slavery in the West Indies, as told from the point of view of a woman slave. The fate of Solitude is determined by the revolt of the blacks and the bloody manhunt that the uprising sets in motion. Solitude becomes a fugitive slave, and although executed, presumably by hanging, after she is captured, she preserves her dignity to the very end.

Schwartz-Bart describes the guillotine's impact on the lives of slaves. "It was said that when the blacks of Saint-Domingue saw the first head fall, they had rushed at the machine and torn it to pieces. But those of Guadeloupe had soon got used to the new entertainment: They came and went at all hours, ate, drank, and laughed, savored the sweet air of freedom [the abolition of slavery] and blinked sagely at the sun as they watched white men cutting white men's heads off. It was just like France, they were told; and in taverns French soldiers would show them books bound in aristocrat-hide."

The blacks are soon to get a taste of another aspect of liberty. The former slaves, free under the Republic, now must work on plantations under the surveillance of brutal National Guards who beat them with whips decorated with tricolored ribbons. As many resolve to "take refuge from liberty, equality and fraternity in the deep dark-woods," the guillotine leaves Pointe-à-Pitre to haunt the countryside. "It climbed the steep, desolate hills in pursuit of citizens who did not understand their new duties. . . . Special detachments hunted them day and night." The heads of those caught soon begin to roll under the guillotine.

In 1802 slavery was officially reestablished and the revolt brutally put down by the republican army. The guillotine proved far too slow for the demands it then confronted. The rebellious former slaves, turned into citizens and then turned back again into slaves, are hanged by the hundreds, just as had been done in the days before the Revolution.

*Scene from the filming of* LIFE, LOVE, DEATH, *1968.*

# THE CAMPAIGN AGAINST
# THE DEATH PENALTY—
# EXISTENTIALISTS AND FILMMAKERS

*"They question my right to the title of philanthropist," Marat exclaims . . .*
*"Ah, what injustice! Who cannot see that I want to cut off a few heads to*
*save a great number" . . . But Marat, making his final calculations,*
*claimed two hundred and seventy-three thousand heads.*
—Albert Camus, The Rebel, *1951*

AFTER WORLD WAR II French philosophers and filmmakers called attention to capital punishment and demanded that society acknowledge its responsibility for state-sponsored killings. During the time when literature and the arts were redefined by existentialism, the guillotine was no longer a subject for joking.

## SARTRE'S SONG FROM HELL

In his one-act play *No Exit* (1944), Jean-Paul Sartre included a guillotine song, "La rue des Blancs Manteaux." The author gave his lyrics and music in 1964 to the cabaret artist Juliette Greco, who made it one of her best-known hits, although to a different musical setting by Joseph Kosma.

Sartre's philosophic drama presents an existentialist hell in which three characters, already dead, must relive the past and endlessly torment themselves and one another. One of the trio, the cruel lesbian Ines, sings a song that tells of a crowd that has come to the rue des Blancs Manteaux (street of the White Cloaks), where the scaffold has been erected, the knife suspended high above, and the bucket of bran placed down below. The executioner arises early; he has many heads to chop off—those of generals, admirals, priests, nobles, and elegantly dressed ladies, all the highest and mightiest in the land.

The eternal penal colony of *No Exit* needs no executioner. In this existential environment, the guillotine becomes superfluous. There is no punishment that can exceed the characters' mutual mental torture.

## TWO FILMS FROM THE 1950s

Released in France in 1952, *We Are All Murderers* and *Golden Marie* (*Casque d'Or*) are both stories of crime and punishment based on actual characters. The first is a polemical argument against capital punishment, while the second is a lyrical recreation of fin-de siècle Paris and its underworld.

*We Are All Murderers* was written and directed by the lawyer and novelist André Cayatte. Essentially it describes a situation much like that of Victor Hugo's *Last Day of a Condemned Man.* The point of focus in Cayatte's film, however, is not the isolated individual viewed almost abstractly as he faces death alone, but rather a cross section of representative figures, the social causes of their plight, and the collective responsibility for the futile legal system that can only respond to violence with more violence. As the title suggests, we are all murderers; we are all capable of committing terrible atrocities and yet we habitually acquiesce in society's judicial killings.

An uneducated young drifter, René le Guen learned to kill during the Nazi occupation while serving in the Resistance. But after the liberation he continues to kill, failing to understand that such behavior is no longer condoned. Convicted of the murder of a policeman, René is sent to la Santé prison, where he becomes the cellmate of a Corsican who killed to defend his family honor, a doctor accused of poisoning his wife, and a worker who beat his crying baby to death. A tense drama unfolds in the cell as these four men may at any moment be guillotined, while in the corridors and chambers of the prison their legal murder is being contrived with a relentless logic.

The condemned live in a state of agonizing suspense, uncertain as to whose turn is next. Particularly terrifying are the scenes in which the warders at la Santé take off their shoes, stealthily tiptoe to the cell to surprise the sleeping prisoners, and suddenly burst in and grab the victim, who is dragged out screaming to his death. The guillotine itself is never shown.

Although some of his cellmates are executed, René's fate remains unknown. His lawyer appeals to the president of the Republic for a pardon, but the film ends with the matter unresolved.

A passionate argument against capital punishment, *We Are All Murderers* shocked some critics and irritated others with its polemical tone. It stirred controversy both in France and England, where the death penalty was then under debate. Cayatte was striving to portray a kind of documentary realism and truth, although the characters and situations are necessarily fictionalized. French censorship laws and governmental restrictions prohibited the filming of actual condemned prisoners awaiting execution in their cells. Cayatte was allowed to shoot only exteriors and certain passageways at la Santé. To create an authentic atmosphere that would compel his actors to behave like animals confined in a small cage, the filmmaker had cell walls constructed of cement against which he had the performers beat their fists and he had the actors wear chains around their ankles during the entire shooting of the film.

Cayatte maintained that he knew the real-life prototypes of all the characters in *We Are All Murderers* and that their stories were absolutely true. The power of the film was so great that the actual prisoner who had served as the model for René obtained a pardon from President Vincent Auriol. However, the executioner André Obrecht maintained in his memoirs that the film was "false from beginning to end" and that none of the four cases illustrated in the film would have led to the death penalty.

Jacques Becker's *Golden Marie*, based on a sensational *fait divers* from 1900, is a loving evocation of the turn-of-the-century Parisian underworld and one of its famous queens who was known as "Casque d'Or" because of her beautiful blond hair. Becker called up pictures from his childhood in his re-creation of the pre-1914 atmosphere of Feuillade's serials and old news items from the *Petit Journal Illustré*. Simone Signoret gave an outstanding performances as "Casque d'Or."

When Manda, the hero of the film, is released after a short jail term, he tries to earn his living honestly as a carpenter but ends up drawn into a world of pimps, prostitutes, and petty thieves because of his passion for Marie, the mistress of a criminal. As a result of his involvement with her, Manda kills his rival in a fight and then commits a second murder as an act of vengeance against a treacherous enemy. The honest but impulsive carpenter, loyal in love and in friendship, is condemned to die on the guillotine.

An outstanding example of cinematic montage, the guillotine scenes are the high point of *Golden Marie*. Manda appears through prison doors, dressed only in pants and a shirt from which the collar has been cut off, his hands tied behind

*Casque d'Or, c. 1900.*

his back. The priest clutches the condemned man in one hand and a crucifix in the other. They are followed by a group of prison guards and gentlemen in frock coats and top hats—the executioners. The crowd murmurs indistinctly.

Marie stands watching at the window of a room that she has rented on the square. The priest speaks inaudible words to Manda and the condemned prisoner weeps silently, tears streaming down his cheeks. The murmuring crowd is shown again before the scene switches back to Marie, alone at the window, compelled to watch the action below that fills her with horror.

Manda moves forward and two men spring forward from opposite sides, each grabbing one of his arms. Suddenly they push the condemned prisoner against the plank, to which they fasten him. Marie's eyes widen and she screams to her lover. The echo of her voice reaches Manda and makes him shudder. At just the same moment the plank tilts down and Manda's head passes out of the frame. From below, the uprights of the guillotine and the knife are shown. The blade begins its descent and slides the length of the uprights.

Marie hears the dull thud. Her head shakes convulsively as if she had just been struck by the blade. Losing consciousness, she collapses, hitting her forehead against the windowsill as she falls. Only her golden hair is visible, glowing in the light of the day, which grows brighter and brighter.

The final shot is of Marie and Manda when they were first falling in love, gazing deeply into each other's eyes as they waltz at a country tavern. This poignant image slowly recedes and the sordidness and obscene haste of the execution are powerfully contrasted with the rhythms of life that must ultimately triumph over the senseless death dealing of an obsolete legal code.

The actual events took a somewhat different course. The real Casque d'Or was an obscure prostitute who became an overnight celebrity due to the murder her lover Manda committed. Her hairstyle was imitated, artists vied to paint her portrait, plays were written about her, and a revue was staged, called *Casque d'Or, or The Apaches of Love,* in which she was scheduled to appear until stopped by the prefect of police. She posed for postcards—in some, semi-nude, in other, writing her memoirs—and for a series of ten narrative cards retelling the murder that led her lover in actuality not to the guillotine, but to life imprisonment. Manda was condemned to the dry guillotine in Guiana, where he died in 1936 at the age of fifty-nine. In a newspaper interview in 1902, she declared, "They all want me for their theatres, for their newspapers, for their books and for the chance to take my photograph. . . . What a terrible bore!!!"

## CAMUS'S COMMITMENT TO FIGHT CAPITAL PUNISHMENT

Albert Camus contributed a long essay, "Reflections on the Guillotine," to the collection *Reflections on Capital Punishment* (1957), which also contains a study by Arthur Koestler of the death penalty in England. Camus cited the stereotyped, ritual language used to mask the shameful act of capital punishment as a major obstacle to the repeal of the death penalty. A condemned victim was called "the patient" who "pays his debt to society." Such conventional phrases, Camus believed, dulled the imagination and kept society from seeing the horror of the guillotine.

"But if people are shown the machine, made to touch the wood and steel and to hear the sound of a head falling, then public imagination, suddenly awakened, will repudiate both the vocabulary and the penalty." Camus included in his argument medical evidence that suggested the survival of consciousness and the reality of suffering after the fall of the blade. Drawing upon images of premature burials and decapitated heads answering to the call of their names—as documented in scientific experiments conducted as late as the 1950s—Camus created Gothic pictures of horror in support of his abolitionist stand against the death penalty.

The concept of capital punishment as a deterrent is what Camus most urgently refuted. He asked, "How can a furtive assassination committed at night in a prison courtyard be exemplary?" Moreover, the supreme penalty, based on fear of death, would have no effect on the homicidal mind and its "dark regions of consciousness," because the desire to kill so often coincides with the desire to destroy oneself. The criminal kills in order to die. Camus persuasively demonstrated that the revolting ceremonies of decapitation served only to provoke displays of perverse vainglory in hardened criminals.

Capital punishment, in Camus's view, was the most premeditated of murders, an unacceptable form of societal revenge. Most of the condemned went to their deaths passively, in a state of utter despondency mistaken for courage by journalists. All that such supposed bravery signified was that the victims had willingly facilitated their own annihilation rather than struggled against it. "The compliments and certificates of courage belong to the general mystification surrounding the death penalty."

Since society and its institutions had lost all contact with the sacred, execution could no longer serve as a redemptive act. In a totally secular world, Camus argued that it was the individual who must be defended against the ambition for absolute power displayed by the state in each fall of the guillotine blade.

Camus reminded readers that it was the humanitarian dreams of the eighteenth century that had led to the bloodstained scaffold of his day; executioners were always humanists. He opposed capital punishment not on the basis of humanist ideals, but because of his pessimistic view of human nature and the need he saw to place limits on the state's excessive power.

The guillotine was revolting butchery, a sordid and obscene exhibition from a brutal past age. "That truncation, that living and yet uprooted head, those spurts of blood date from a barbarous period that aimed to impress the masses with degrading sights." Ultimately, Camus declared, even the most "humane" form of capital punishment—by anesthesia or injection—is intolerable; the death penalty itself must be outlawed.

## "THE CALVARY OF A CONDEMNED MAN"

Claude Lelouch's 1968 film, *Life, Love, Death,* continued the attack on capital punishment that André Cayatte had begun with *We Are All Murderers.* Inspired by a book against the death penalty written by the celebrated defense attorney Albert Naud, Lelouch originally wanted to make a television drama of the last half hour of a condemned man's life, to be shown worldwide. However, when this project failed to materialize, he resolved to make a film with Naud as his technical advisor—an absolutely authentic re-creation of an execution according to the lawyer's eyewitness account.

During the relatively liberal period of the late sixties, the courts and prisons were generally open to the filmmaker. The scenes of incarceration and the execution scene in *Life, Love, Death* were shot in an actual prison, and the director of la Santé permitted the set designers to replicate exactly in both dimension and materials the famous guillotine. Even the blade was real. Lelouch explained his obsession: "A wooden blade covered with silver paper won't fall, won't kill anybody. A slide that's not made of real copper will look phony. Death calls for a visually lethal piece of solid workmanship. With respect to materials, the cinema won't permit any cheating."

In keeping with these principles of verisimilitude, the filmmaker hoped to engage the actual Grand High Executioner of the Fifth Republic. A letter was written to André Obrecht asking him to play the role of the executioner, but

*Albert Naud in* LIFE, LOVE, DEATH, *1968.*

nothing came of this interesting proposal. Naud objected that, as a lawyer who had tried to save victims from the guillotiner, he was not prepared to collaborate with the enemy.

*Life, Love, Death* presents the fictional story of François Toledo, a worker in an auto factory in Nîmes whose marginal existence provides only meager satisfactions. Seeking a sense of freedom denied by his drab marriage, Toledo turns to women of the street, but suffering from impotence, he murders three prostitutes in psychopathic fits of rage and is eventually caught and condemned to be guillotined.

The film carefully builds sympathy for Toledo before revealing that he is a killer. His impoverished life, related in painful detail, acts as extenuating circumstances. The defense attorney, actually played by Albert Naud in an unusual self-performance, argues that Toledo is mentally ill and needs to have his head treated, not cut off.

Once the death sentence is handed down, the film suddenly changes from color to black and white. Just as all color has been drained from the protagonist's bleak life, so it is removed from the film. The condemned man waits, awake in his cell night after night and dawn after dawn. Early one morning while it is still dark, a group of gentlemen, some in dark suits and some in black uniforms, comes to claim the prisoner. Although the top hats are gone, the grim ritual remains. The prison chaplain celebrates a mass and the condemned man is forced to kneel to receive absolution. Futilely trying to resist, he is pushed and pulled down the prison corridors. The collar of his shirt is cut off. He refuses the proffered cigarette and glass of rum.

To achieve the greatest possible realism, Amidou, the actor playing Toledo, was locked in a cell for twelve hours and made to feel like a condemned prisoner. He was not allowed to set eyes on the guillotine until the last moment so that his terror and physical recoil at the final moment would be painfully genuine.

Overcome by animal fear, Toledo fights with all his strength when he does at last see the guillotine, recently sharpened and gleaming in the gray courtyard of the prison. The two assistant executioners must drag him to the foot of the machine and throw him brutally onto the plank. A dull thud, a jump of the basket when the head lands, and it is all over. The film ends with the fading frozen image of the witnesses petrified in horror, and from the darkness Albert Naud's voice is heard, reading an indictment of capital punishment.

In an interview given while he was preparing to shoot *Life, Love, Death*, Lelouch explained his purpose.

> This will be an entirely subjective film. For an hour and thirty minutes the spectators will become prisoners condemned to death. I am going to try to show the Calvary of a condemned man, whether he has been condemned by a judicial decision or as the result of a sickness. When a man knows that he is going to lose his life, that unleashes a whole series of traumas within him and we quickly perceive that that man dies well before the hour of his death. . . . Thus I am going to film the life of a living corpse. I shall, in fact, be making a film about life. . . . I hope that the spectators at the end of the showing will take a position. For those that see it, the film should be an experience that forces them to take a stand against the death penalty.

Cayatte, Becker, and Lelouch demystify the guillotine and its servants. The execution of a condemned prisoner is no longer viewed as a solemn ritual; it is a squalid and disgraceful affair done with as quickly as possible in secret behind high walls and locked doors. The victim no longer cooperates or attempts a heroic stand. The mechanism of the law serves not to protect the prisoner but to assure that the decapitating machine gets its victim. The executioner is a nameless functionary, the priest a paid vulture. The camera neither theatricalizes nor mythologizes the horror. That which is ugly and frightful looks ugly and frightful.

## DEFENSE ATTORNEY VERSUS THE GUILLOTINE

Of all the participants in the modern drama of the guillotine, the lawyer for the condemned fighting to save his client's life stands out as the most dynamic and eloquent. In the final quarter of a century leading up to the abolition of the death penalty in France, the defense attorney took part in a relentless duel with the fatal machine that ultimately ended in the dreaded instrument's defeat.

Priests, servants of the state, dutifully reconciled the prisoner to his destiny. Doctors had always played an unsavory role, first devising the machine and then conducting experiments on the mutilated bodies of the condemned. Journalists were forever looking for a sensational story. Only the defense attorney can be said to have been wholeheartedly committed to saving his client.

A constant visitor to the death cell and intimate witness of the prisoner's suffering, the defense attorney was able to describe authoritatively the horrors of the ordeal and express the anguish of the condemned. Attacking the senseless barbarity of society's vengefulness, asking compassion and forgiveness for despised murderers, the lawyer assumed a heroic role in the battle against hostile public opinion, against the entrenched judicial system, and against a killing machine that embodied the bloodthirsty *lex talionis*.

Eventually it was attorneys such as Albert Naud and Robert Badinter, through their writings, lectures, and social and political activities, who became the vanquishers of the guillotine. Their books vividly recorded the powerful hold their foe had on the French and the ways in which it shaped their own imaginations. For the defense attorney, losing his case and his client was a bitter and heartbreaking experience, which he had to endure down to the gruesome end as a witness at the execution. Lawyer and client were bound together by what Albert Naud called a "desperate tenderness."

In his book, *To Defend Them All* (1973), Naud described the singularly horrifying execution of twenty-three-year-old Michel Watrin, guillotined in Metz in 1950 for killing a taxi driver in an armed robbery. This was the young lawyer's first execution and it turned him into a formidable opponent of capital punishment.

Because Michel Watrin had agreed to leave his eyes to the French Eye Bank, the condemned prisoner had to make a stop on his march to the guillotine and sign the release papers brought by two medical technicians from Paris who would shortly perform the extraction. Suddenly terrified at the thought of having his eyes plucked out after having his head cut off, Watrin turns to Naud and, trying to smile, asks if he thought it possible that one's suffering could continue after death. "One last request," he implores. "Can I ask you to be present when they pull out my eyes? Maybe I'll still see you, who knows? That way I'll have more courage."

The mass and communion in the prison chapel seem interminable, and afterwards the condemned prisoner is taken into a tiny room containing only a stool. From here the lower part of the guillotine in the adjoining courtyard is visible. His arm touching the prisoner, the lawyer feels the body of his client stiffen and recoil at the sight.

The executioner and his two assistants enter. Desfourneaux, the Grand High Executioner of the Fourth Republic, who has faithfully served one regime after the other, looks absolutely indifferent. He is dressed carelessly, in a garish blue shirt and red tie and a seedy, chestnut colored hat clapped on his head at an angle.

The prisoner's collar is cut off and he is rapidly trussed up. Michel briefly draws away from the executioners and throws himself into the lawyer's arms, telling him he has loved him like a father, before he is thrust onto the machine. The blade falls and Naud watches in horror as blood spurts everywhere, splattering even the wall of the courtyard. Looking down, he notices a red pool that has formed and is spreading out in all directions in the cracks of the pavement, suggestive of the geographical outlines of islands, peninsulas, isthmuses, and straits.

The lawyer watches Desfourneaux carrying Michel's head by the hair like an inconsequential package to the surgeons' table. Naud wants to vomit, scream, weep. As though "serving a cannibal dinner," the Grand High Executioner sets the head on a little table covered with a white cloth. One of the men from the eye bank turns the head over so that the eyes are looking up.

To Naud, the freshly severed head and soon to be extracted eyes are still Michel, the human being he knew and tried to save. Without realizing it, he murmurs words of pity and encouragement to the head as the doctors remove the eyes. All the while, the executioners continue their work. They throw the prisoner's trunk in a wicker basket and one of the assistants methodically washes the blade and all the bloodstained parts of the guillotine, squeezing out the sponge in a bucket and drenched by the reddened water that drips down his arms.

Naud recoils. "In the back of this courtyard with its impenetrable walls, a clandestine slaughter has taken place; a human being has been cut in pieces, human blood has been waded in, the smell of human blood has risen to the nostrils." Overcome by anger and nausea, he wonders how other people can take the hands of these three executioners into their own without being sickened; whether these hands caress loving women; if an animal about to be petted by these hands would not instinctively sense the truth and pull away; if these hands do not give their owners nightmares.

When the surgeons have finished their work, Desfourneaux again grasps Michel's head by the hair, which to Naud suddenly appears to be the head of a decrepit old man with pink eye sockets, and tosses it into the basket.

At the provincial graveyard the assistant executioners, their fingernails caked with clotted blood, pull Michel's body out of the basket. Without even removing the ropes binding his arms, they heave the trunk stomach-down into a coffin so flimsy that it looks like an egg crate. The Grand High Executioner grabs the mutilated head and sets it on the left shoulder of the torso, so that the eyeless sockets stare up at the dawn as it grows brighter and brighter. No effort is made to arrange the remains to resemble a human body. One of the assistants shovels blood-soaked sawdust onto the face while the other tilts and shakes the wicker basket to empty out its contents. This final outrage fuels Naud's rage and he reflects bitterly that of course the executioners had to get rid of the hardened clods of sawdust somewhere. What better place than the condemned man's coffin?

In disgust, Naud asks the president of the criminal court, who has done his "duty" by seeing the prisoner's punishment carried out to the final moment of burial, if he is prepared to shake hands with the executioners. But denied an answer, he must leave the cemetery and face the bright new July 14, a time for celebrating fraternity and the Revolution. To combat this barbarity, Naud asserts, the guillotine must be revealed for what it is and the executioners exposed as callous butchers.

## DENOUEMENT FOR THE GUILLOTINE

The double execution on November 28, 1972, of Claude Buffet and Roger Bontemps, convicted of the murder of two hostages taken in a failed attempt to win their freedom from the prison in Clairvaux, proved to be the last use of the guillotine in Paris, though there were four subsequent outings for the machine in France—three to Marseilles and one to Douai. Even though it was apparently Buffet, a convicted murderer serving a life term, who actually killed both victims, Bontemps was also sent to the guillotine as an accomplice. So great was the public outcry and demand for vengeance that President Pompidou, who in five previous instances had issued pardons for death sentences, felt compelled to let the executions take place.

Driven to reexamine what it was that led to such a disastrous outcome for his client, Bontemps's defense attorney Robert Badinter wrote a book about the case, *The Execution* (1973). It was Badinter's first execution, and his teacher had told him that going to the guillotine with a client was the true baptism for a lawyer, an idea that he at first rejected, finding it ghoulish and sinister. The experience proved instrumental in bringing him to the forefront of the opposition to capital punishment.

The future minister of justice responsible for abolishing the death penalty, Badinter analyzes the deadly drama in terms of role playing. While the public demands theatricalization, only rarely does the criminal play the role expected of him, that of a monster. Lacenaire, for example, became such an actor in his own tragedy, giving the public the performance that they secretly desired, and so did Buffet, assuming the character of a cold-blooded killer. He seemed possessed by death lurking silently within him and was drawn towards the guillotine as though it had cast its fatal spell upon him. "The man that I am wants to die by the guillotine," Buffet wrote. "Let it be known that Claude Buffet commits suicide by the guillotine."

The day the double death sentence is pronounced, the crowd in the courtroom and out in the street cheers wildly. Such hatred always gives the worst criminal an unexpected dignity, Badinter observes. Little seems to have changed since the time of the Revolution. "The crowd undoubtedly would have applauded, screamed with delight, if the executioner, in the manner of Sanson, had held up the two heads in front of them." Such hate-filled court sessions struck Badinter as a marionette theatre in which wooden puppets knocked each other about until death appeared and sent them all down the trap.

Next came the drama of quietly waiting for notification in the middle of the night. Only at the end of the week can the lawyer feel temporarily secure, knowing that executioners do not work on weekends, and thus executions are never scheduled for Sunday or Monday morning.

The dreaded call inevitably arrives. Awakened at three in the morning and summoned to come to the prison, Badinter describes dressing and preparing for his first execution. Pursued by photographers, he makes his way to the prison, where he enters the courtyard and is suddenly confronted by the guillotine. Somehow he hadn't expected it to be standing there, right in front of him. He is overwhelmed by the sinister poetry of the guillotine.

> There it was, just the way I—like all the rest of us—had seen it in so many old photographs and prints. But still I was surprised by the uprights, so very tall and slender. . . . In contrast, the body of the machine struck me as small, like a compact chest. But just as it is, with its two thin arms raised high, it expresses death so perfectly that it seems to be death itself, become a thing, materialized, in this bare space. The impression was reinforced still further by the huge black canopy, stretched like an awning or cover over the whole courtyard. Thus it concealed the guillotine from intrusive stares from above which could have spied down upon it. This canopy hid the entire sky and transformed the courtyard into a sort of

immense chamber where the guillotine stood all alone like an idol or a malevolent altar. The assistants busied themselves around it. The symbol was also a machine. And this mechanical aspect, this utilitarian side, linked to death, which it so powerfully expressed, made the guillotine something terrible and vile.

A large group of officials and bureaucrats sets off down the corridor, moving faster and faster until finally they are almost running. "It was grotesque and sinister at the same time," Badinter remarks.

The condemned prisoner is moved from point to point—here writing a letter to his mother, there confessing to the chaplain—as though from station to station of the cross, an image suggestive of Christ's agony. Everyone, including Badinter, wears a fixed grin on his face, rendered ghoulish by the electric light. "They all had, at this moment, the mugs of killers. Only the priest and Bontemps, who was receiving absolution, still had human faces. Crime had physically changed sides." The condemned prisoner drinks the glass of cognac offered; it is his last act of human volition. The ruddy-faced executioner, hat on his head, approaches and together with his assistants takes complete possession of Bontemps. The prisoner is rapidly tied and trussed. The defense attorney fleetingly embraces his client before he is carried through the door that opens onto the courtyard. The dry sound of the blade striking the buffer is heard. Buffet's turn is next. In no time an assistant executioner was washing the floor around the guillotine, while the canopy above seems to bear down with all its black weight. So ended Badinter's initiation.

Claude Buffet, who like Lacenaire became an author in prison, had proposed an original way of letting those being guillotined die happily. A few months before his own execution, the murderer wrote, "Once the condemned prisoner has got his head in the guillotine, there should be a moment of silence before the knife falls. The director of the prison hands a letter to the executioner, who tells the condemned man, 'It's your pardon!' Then he lets the knife drop. Thus the prisoner dies in a state of joy."

The guillotine had reigned in the place de la Révolution, the place de Grève, the place de la Roquette, and many other squares and courtyards in Paris for almost two centuries. Although no one knew it at the time, this double execution in 1972 was to be the final inglorious performance of the guillotine in the capital. But it was not until September 1981 that a successful motion for abolition of the death penalty was proposed by Robert Badinter in the name of the new Socialist government: "I have the honor, in the name of the government of the Republic, to request the National Assembly to abolish the death penalty in France. The death penalty is contrary to what, for the past two thousand years, constitutes humanity's finest thoughts and noblest dreams. It is contrary to the spirit of the Revolution." The motion was overwhelmingly accepted by both the National Assembly and the Senate. The blade of the guillotine would fall no more.

# GUILLOTINES
# IN UNEXPECTED PLACES

*You tell the truth*
*You go to the guillotine*
*You lose your head*
*But your conscience is clean.*
*—J. G. Thirlwell, "Ramrod"*

*La Guillotine Belgian beer.*

SIMILARITIES BETWEEN the executioner and magician have often been noted. "Death on the guillotine," wrote Dumas *fils*, "is only a bit of sleight-of-hand that makes life vanish: a trick with a goblet in which there's a head displayed."

In "Notes of an Executioner," which appear in Roger Grenier's novel *The Monsters* (1951) as authentic revelations related to a journalist, the assistant executioner explains that, as in the circus, it's all done with a smile. He describes the finale on the guillotine as a consummate bit of hocus-pocus. "The body slides into the basket; the head, rapidly reclaimed from the bucket, joins it immediately, the lid is closed. Two buckets of water, prepared in advance, are thrown on the groove and the blade to wash away whatever blood had time to spurt. When the spectators approach, there is no longer anything to see—no body, no head, no blood. It's prestidigitation."

*Illustrations from Louis Tannen, Inc.'s magicians' supply catalog.*

Given these affinities, it is hardly surprising that the guillotine has often been featured on the vaudeville stage and in the variety show and circus. The French illusionist François Steens (1881–1939), known as the "man who plays with death," specialized in a guillotine act, and it has become part of the American magician's repertory. Catalogs from both Abbott's and Tannen's, two leading magic companies, carry a wide list of "choppers," ranging from the small finger chopper to the larger leg, wrist, and head models, as well as a thirty-five-page booklet, *Chopper Capers,* describing "new and different routines, bits of business, jokes and gags," to accompany the guillotine acts. Under the Giant Guillotine (which appears in George Marshall's film *Houdini* [1953]), it is claimed that

Audiences will gasp at the magician's daring in presenting this grim spectacle. The Giant Guillotine, seven feet in height, breaks down for packing and can be set up in three minutes. It is awe inspiring in appearance. First, a cabbage or other type of vegetable is placed in the head opening. The release lever is pulled and the blade travels at lightning speed downward, dividing the vegetable into two parts. Sensationalism at its peak! The blade is raised and the lever is reset. The head stocks are unlocked, the victim kneels and brings his head into the opening and the stocks are relocked in position around his neck. A carrot is placed in each cutout alongside the victim's head. Just imagine the suspense as the magician takes his place, ready to pull the lever. A dramatic pause, then a pull on the lever and down comes the blade . . . right through the stocks cutting the carrots but with no injury to the victim.

The New French Guillotine stands almost six feet high. "The large heavy blade ZOOMS down through the neck stock and OUT THE BOTTOM CLEAR TO THE FLOOR!" The magician is advised to employ it in "a comedy presentation [for] a dramatic, sensational climax." Despite its name, this and all the other magic guillotines are always two-dimensional and lack the tilting plank of the authentic French machine; in this respect they resemble the earliest European pre-guillotines.

Still more imposing is the Monster Guillotine.

This feature Death Thriller stands 9 feet in height, with a huge solid steel knife which falls with sufficient force to sever a 1 by 3 [board] at one blow. A girl is

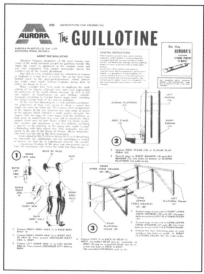

*Aurora Plastic Co.'s toy guillotine model and assembly instructions.*

secured—with head and hands exposed to view at all times. The blade falls.
Girl's head may be removed in a box and placed elsewhere. . . . The girl may be
reproduced alive and unharmed. This illusion is capable of being a great money
maker, as nothing of a greater thrilling nature has ever been conceived. Our
improved safety feature is 100% positive.

The fanciful advertisement provides different views of the machine. A
dream vision depicts the Monster Guillotine in operation during revolutionary
times. A crowd stands beneath the scaffold as a soldier with a musket pushes
forward one victim, whose hands are tied behind his back, while the executioner
stands ready to release the blade suspended above a second kneeling victim
whose head and hands are locked in place. A basket stands waiting below.

Implying that audiences at the magic show can—at least vicariously—
experience the thrills and terrors of the dark and dangerous period when the
guillotine held sway, the manufacturers stress that such reenactment is, of
course, "100% safe." Popular culture has transformed the deadly drama that
formerly was presented on the place de la Révolution and the place de Grève
into a lucrative Monster Guillotine show. One may well wonder what Saint-
Just would have thought.

## ALICE COOPER'S GRAND GUIGNOL

The American rock star Alice Cooper began using a monster magic guillotine
in 1973 for his spectacular stage show "Billion-Dollar Babies." While the performance focuses on violence, sex, and death, its morality is pure Old
Testament. After committing horrible crimes, Cooper, the son of a minister,
is always punished.

For his act he uses a hatchet to bludgeon and hack to pieces baby dolls,
which ooze blood. Dressed entirely in black, he rapes a large, armless and leg-
less female mannequin. Singing "Dead Babies" and the necrophiliac "I Love
the Dead," Cooper is taken away to the giant guillotine, which has replaced
the gallows and electric chair used in his previous shows. After his head falls
into the basket, the band members kick it around the stage. Finally, he reappears, now dressed in a white suit, still singing, "I Love the Dead." Cooper
described the effect:

*Alice Cooper in "Billion-Dollar Babies," 1973. Photo © Mark Weiss.*

For "Billion-Dollar Babies" I gave up the noose and had a guillotine designed by the Amazing Randi, a magician who went on the road with us and played the part of the dentist and executioner. The guillotine had a real forty-pound blade in it. After "I Love the Dead," Randi led me to the guillotine. As always the audience got quiet, waiting breathlessly for the sound of the falling blade. From my hiding place behind the set I could always tell when the dummy's head got lopped off and fell into the barrel from the cheering in the audience. The rest of the band retrieved the bloody head from the basket and kicked it around the stage as a football.

Cooper had long been interested in magic, and when he found James Randi, who was working at the time as the "Amazing Randi" and whose specialty was the trick guillotine, he bought the prop and hired the magician. Randi later embarked on a career debunking alleged psychic phenomena and became a founding editor of *The Skeptical Inquirer*.

A more detailed description of Alice Cooper's beheading, provided by an eye-witness, reveals both retribution for sin and grim humor to be central to the act.

For the guillotine scene Randi wears an executioner's hood of fur around his head and shoulders and Alice is dragged to La Guillotine wailing "I Love the Dead" while he postures like Richard the Third.

The stage twilight deepens except for a circle of light on his head, which is fastened between two planks of wood.

Randi pulls on the piece of rope—even at the rehearsal everyone was breathlessly quiet—and the broad cleaver head, made of thick, heavy metal, falls swiftly.

All in an instant the light appears to shut off and then on again, and instead of Alice's tangled head of hair there's only a round, black hole.

Then, as "I Love the Dead" creaks once more with passable eeriness, the executioner dips into his basket set before the guillotine and pulls forth a rubber facsimile which even at close quarters bears a very good likeness to the original. There are trickles and smears of blood from the lips. He carries this out to center stage and then tosses it to the rest of the band, who pat it around among themselves like gleeful, malicious urchins.

It resembles nothing so much as the final scene in *Suddenly Last Summer:* an act of lip-smacking cannibalism.

Alice Cooper's "popular-culture" reveling in horrible fantasies of evil and perversity followed by his own hideous decapitation provided the same fin-de-siècle thrill for millions of teenagers as was once offered a more elite audience by Maurice Rollinat at the Chat Noir and André de Lorde at the Grand Guignol. His themes and grotesqueries are equally morbid and histrionic, and despite all the cultural differences of time and place, the hysterical reactions of the audience are quite similar.

To stage his own decapitation, Alice Cooper availed himself of the advanced theatrical technology of the sort that the Grand Guignol was already pioneering in the early 1900s. The tradition of black guillotine romanticism in its most horrific forms survives in such American rock music spectacles. A leftover from the property room of Western civilization, the guillotine appears fleetingly as an iconographic element in rock lyrics and videos, as a proof of one's daring or the seal of one's eternal damnation for unspeakable crimes.

## CHARADES ON EAST FOURTH STREET

A surprise encounter with the guillotine occurs in the black American dramatist Lonne Elder III's *Charades on East Fourth Street,* a play about police brutality first performed at Expo 67 in Montreal. While upstairs in an old movie house in New York's Lower East Side a dance and a meeting are being held to protest police treatment of members of the community, downstairs more direct action is in progress as five teen-age youths in white face masks hold a police officer chained and handcuffed to a chair.

The "charades" that the youths enact are not merely a subterranean reflection of the more rational discourse going on above them. They are also a parody of the interrogations of suspects routinely conducted in police stations. Snapping pictures with a camera, waving guns, brandishing knives, threatening beatings, the youths intend to force the officer to confess to brutalizing Cliff's brother and raping Manuel's sister.

What they stage is not a trial but a kind of sporting event or game. The issue of police brutality has been transposed into theatrical exercises in violence. There is "fun" to be had with murderous threats, and the use of lethal weapons is likened to playing with toys. "No game is a game without a surprise," observes Adam, master of the bizarre ceremonies.

When the biggest death-dealing toy of all becomes the centerpiece of

*Charades on East Fourth Street*, its entrance on stage is far from awe-inspiring. "They roll out a rusty old guillotine. . . . It creaks and rattles." The performance that the dilapidated decapitating machine gives is even less impressive. For a rehearsal, they place a dirty old mannequin on a table and position the head in the guillotine, but when the cord is pulled, rather than cutting the head off, the blade stops at the neck. The mechanism is too old.

A discard, a relic, an abandoned piece of machinery, this guillotine has undergone cultural displacement. "It's my machine," Cliff declares. "I found it." Cut off from its roots, Cliff's comically grotesque guillotine has no memory of the French Revolution, France, or even capital punishment. It can function only as a funny "scary" contraption.

On the guillotine's second "dry run" the blade sticks in the grooves halfway down. The boys reposition the dummy's head in the slot and prepare for a third try. "The blade falls on the dummy's head, severing it from the body part. It falls to the floor, rolling about, making awkward, clunking sounds."

Having succeeded in their rehearsal, they now adjust the police officer on the table so that his head sticks through the slot of the guillotine. After arguing about who will get to pull the cord, Adam delays the action further, pointing out that they can't just let the policeman's head roll all over the floor, bloodying up everything. "I'm not going to let you cut his head off, without a basket." Faced with the dilemma of where to get a basket at that time of night, two of the boys rush off to steal "mama's clothes basket from the bathroom." At last Adam takes the cord in his hand, saying, "If you don't tell me the truth I'm going to pull this cord myself." The policeman confesses to the crimes he has been accused of and is freed, only to be beaten and perhaps killed later.

A sequence of macabre gags, visual and auditory, repeatedly mounts to a perpetually postponed climax, much in the spirit of slapstick film comedy. But the slapstick has a decidedly sinister underside. While comically conceived, such guillotine games are ultimately ambivalent and disturbing.

## KENNETH BERNARD'S *NIGHT CLUB*

A guillotine also makes a surprising appearance in the apocalyptic conclusion to *Night Club* by the American playwright Kenneth Bernard. First performed by the Play-House of the Ridiculous at La MaMa Experimental Theatre Club in 1970 and directed by John Vaccaro, *Night Club* takes place in Bubi's Hide-Away, where the cruel and androgynous Master of Ceremonies stages a series of bizarre and degrading "routines" for the onstage audience of adoring patrons, culminating in mass copulation, while ominous sounds of bulldozers and jackhammers can be heard outside.

A Young Man on his honeymoon who refuses to participate is dragged to "a makeshift guillotine" and beheaded as he screams, "No! . . . No! . . . The Menu says there is no cover charge!" Bubi picks up the severed head and places it on a table. "Slowly the eyes in the Young Man's head open, the head moves and turns almost upright. With great difficulty, the mouth moves, then speaks." The severed head hoarsely croaks Bubi's name until drowned out by the noise of approaching bulldozers and jackhammers signaling total demolition. The magic guillotine of a night club act and its talking head become part of civilization's descent into the abyss.

## TADEUSZ KANTOR'S THEATRE OF DEATH

For the 1990 Avignon Festival, avant-garde Polish theatre artist Tadeusz Kantor staged a brilliantly ironic narrative play, *Oh, Gentle Night*. Using a cast of twenty apprentice actors, Kantor delves into the realms of birth and death, crucifixion and resurrection. In the fifth part of the play, "The Time of Cut-Off Heads," a mob suddenly bursts into the poor room of the imagination singing the revolutionary anthem "Ça Ira" and pushing a guillotine. The machine is operated by the prostitute-commissar-executioner while the priest gives a benediction. Soon, the plaster head of a would-be Marie-Antionette falls. The blade rises up and down repeatedly signifying both the end of this world and the creation of a new one.

## *THE MISANTHROPE* REVISITED

Another startling transposition of the guillotine into a contemporary milieu occurred in a production of Molière's *Misanthrope* (1989) at the San Diego Playhouse. Director Robert Falls moved the play's heroine, Célimène, to a high-tech Hollywood apartment befitting a fashionable pop star. In the center of the room he wanted to place a large exercise machine, so the set designer George Tsypin, who had never seen such a device, visited a nearby gym, where he was particularly impressed by an ominous-looking mechanism with chrome upright bars and

*George Tsypin's set design for Robert Fall's production of*
THE MISANTHROPE *by Molière, 1989.*

a weight attached to cords to be pulled up and down while lying on an attached bench. Based on this design, Tsypin created an imaginary guillotine–exercise machine that looked like a piece of sculpture and stood decoratively at center stage, creating a "sense of impending doom."

Not until well into the middle of the play does Célimène climb onto the bench, where she lies face up and pulls the rings attached to weights, making the blade rise and fall—almost to her neck. In confrontation with the envious prude Arsinoe, Célimène is sitting upright on the bench when the blade, released by her jealous rival, suddenly crashes down beside her. After being exposed as a deceptive flirt and deserted by all her suitors, Célimène again lies down on the bench of her guillotine–exercise machine and pulls the blade up and down. Alone with her futile vanity, she metaphorically commits suicide on the bench of her stylish self-decapitator.

## THOMAS BRASCH'S *STEEL ANGEL* AND
## THE BERLIN EXECUTIONER

In his first film, *Steel Angel* (1981), the German playwright, poet, and novelist Thomas Brasch delves into a bizarre episode from the early postwar history of Berlin to explore the forces that shaped his life and those of his compatriots. Brasch was born in England in 1945 of Jewish émigré parents who settled in East Berlin after the war, where his father became an official in the Ministry of Culture. The writer moved to West Berlin in 1976.

The published script of Brasch's *Steel Angel* is accompanied by extensive documentary material providing the historical background to the film. In its quest for the truth about this forgotten and unsettled period in the new life of post-Hitler Germany, *Steel Angel* metaphorically linked the violence and anarchy of 1948 and 1949, to the horrific Nazi past that was being systematically repressed and buried in the prosperous, complacent present.

During the blockade and airlift in 1948 and 1949, Gustav Völpel, the former executioner in Berlin, became involved in armed robberies perpetrated by a vicious band of gangsters led by the seventeen-year-old Werner Gladow. The steel angel of the title is not only the German nickname for American planes breaking the Berlin blockade in 1948, but also for Völpel's guillotine, recently retired from active service and kept locked away in a cell in the basement of the prison. The compact and efficient modern decapitating machine in its clean white "execution room" resembles a surgical instrument or slaughterhouse device.

Capital punishment was not suspended in West Berlin until May 24, 1949, when the new Bonn constitution went into effect. Two weeks earlier the twenty-four-year-old Berthold Wehmeyer had been guillotined in a prison cell on Lehrter Strasse for murdering an old woman in the Soviet zone and stealing her potatoes. From the end of the war until its formal abolition in 1951, the death sentence was handed down twenty-five times in West Berlin courts, and nine executions were actually carried out. Brasch was particularly fascinated by the role of the executioner in a world in which justice and the law were so ambiguously interpreted and illogically implemented.

Imprisoned during the war as a conscientious objector (or perhaps as a deserter), Gustav Völpel was a photocopier by training. Finding himself unemployed in 1945, he was happy to be accepted for the job of executioner. According to Völpel's own account, between 1946 and 1948 he carried out forty-eight executions in both halves of Berlin, receiving a thousand marks per head (unlike the salaried French executioners who did not receive any bounty). He executed his "patients" with a guillotine in West Berlin and with an axe in East Berlin. Völpel carried the thirteen-pound axe inside a small green suitcase and always took it home with him to his apartment in the Eastern sector, where he kept it in a kitchen cabinet, under the biblical injunction "Love thy neighbor as thyself."

Implicated in the activities of the Gladow gang, which had terrorized Berlin with shootings, killings, and robberies from May 1948 to summer

*Gustav Völpel in mask, c. 1948.*

1949, Völpel stood trial in spring 1948 with three others for highway robbery and assault. During the trial he was granted a leave of absence from the court by the authorities in the Eastern sector so that he could execute three condemned prisoners in Dresden. Returning to the courtroom late, the executioner opened his green suitcase to give the judge proof of his official business: an axe, a pair of black gloves, and a yellow fabric mask with a black cross above the eyes and a hanging black cloth to cover the lower face and entire neck. Völpel wore this mask at executions so as to appear to be what he called an "anonymous instrument of justice."

Arrested again in 1949, Gustav Völpel was sentenced in the Western sector to seven years imprisonment. Werner Gladow, known as the "Little Doctor," and his two accomplices were executed by axe in East Germany in 1950. Völpel died in 1959, two years after his release, a broken man. His tools still remain in existence, the well-oiled guillotine in a prison basement in West Berlin, the axe in a museum in East Berlin.

Brasch's *Steel Angel* explores both the metaphysical anguish and the social chaos that made Völpel an executioner and Gladow a ruthless killer and gang leader who patterned himself after Al Capone. A crucial confrontation

*Scenes from* STEEL ANGEL, *1981.*

between the two takes place in the antiseptic, white-tiled cell where the guillotine stands. Of his old job the former executioner says, "It's nothing special, just another job." Pointing to the machine, Völpel remarks, "Some die standing up, others like this."

Fascinated by the death machine, the teenage killer Gladow climbs on the guillotine, lies on his back, and closes the collar around his neck. The criminal tells the former executioner, "Come on, strap me down properly." Bound to the plank, Gladow looks up at the blade. Following the nineteenth-century tradition of scaffold bravado, the social outlaw measures himself against the mechanical nemesis that may one day overtake him. Later in Völpel's apartment, Gladow, fascinated by the emblems of state violence, looks pruriently at the axe in the green suitcase and compels the executioner's wife to put on the mask, which she discloses is her own handiwork.

Völpel claims that that he is no more a killer than the next person. If it were legal, he proclaims, everyone would have his own guillotine in the kitchen to get rid of his wife, his servant, his boss. In the jumble of civilizations and wreckage of legal codes in occupied Berlin during the blockade, the axe and mask of the executioner in Brasch's film represent a primordial layer of existence. Policemen, soldiers, and gangsters roam the surface of a city still partly in ruins. A sparkling guillotine waits in the basement, beneath a cruel "civilization" above.

## A JAPANESE GUILLOTINE:
## HIDESHI HINO'S *PANORAMA OF HELL*

The Tokyo illustrator-author Hideshi Hino in 1982 created *Panorama of Hell*, a new volume in his "Shocking Theatre," a thirteen-volume series of graphic novels ("manga" in Japanese). Presented in the form of "vile confessions," the narrative tells the story of a painter who has descended into hell because of his "obsession with the exquisite beauty and the intoxicating smell of blood."

A child of the atomic bomb, the hell painter was conceived on August 6, 1945, the day Hiroshima was incinerated. A radioactive beam from the bomb struck his mother, and thus he claims the "Emperor of Hell," the bomb itself, as his true father. Even in the womb, the embryo was already privy to visions of the inferno.

In the apocalyptic landscape inhabited by the hell painter, a guillotine towers over his house and is one of the principal subjects that he represents in his work. Against a burning sunset sky filled with soaring crows, "the guillotine blade rises, freshly cleansed in holy water."

> Fireworks light up the night sky, marking each execution. All the severed heads are collected in a large hopper, from which they are dumped into a gondola car. This hideous work goes on all night.
>
> The screech of skyrockets, shrieks of the condemned, and the crash of the guillotine blade echo ceaselessly through the night.

After the severed heads drop down through a chute into the platform cars waiting below, they are taken off by train. All along the tracks stained red with blood sprout the crimson flowers of hell, whose fruit when eaten is said to cause madness. The headless corpses of the guillotined prisoners are burned in the crematorium next door to the hell painter's house.

Two children, who turn out to be only puppets created by the hell painter, watch the heads fall under the blade and sing guillotine songs:

*Hideshi Hino. From* PANORAMA OF HELL, *1982.*

*Guillotine, Guillotine,*
*Drops one head.*
*Guillotine, Guillotine,*
*Drops another head.*
*Guillotine, Guillotine,*
*Now you have a whole mountain of heads!*

By igniting all of the world's bombs, the artist believes he can finally produce the ultimate hell he has been yearning for. He exclaims that the end of the world will be a "moment of awesome beauty." Linking the guillotine with the atomic bomb, the crematoria of the holocaust, and impending nuclear apocalypse, Hideshi Hino removes the decapitating machine from its historical eighteenth-century context and places it squarely in the hell of our own age.

*Pierrette Dupoyet in* MADAME GUILLOTIN, *1988.*

# RECENT PLAYS AND FILMS
## ABOUT THE FRENCH REVOLUTION AND
## THE HISTORICAL GUILLOTINE

*For the fifth year, pastry chefs competed in a Bastille Day contest,*
*"Let Them Eat Cake." . . . Prizes of Laurent Perrier were awarded*
*for . . . "The Spirit of Bastille Day," a chocolate guillotine*
*by Prunelle in New York.*
—The New York Times, *July 18, 1990*

EVER SINCE Peter Weiss's landmark *Marat/Sade*, the guillotine has played a different role in many contemporary plays about the French Revolution. Weiss's influence is highly evident in these newer works, with their emphasis on play, reenactment, and games with heads. The moral fervor once connected with the Revolution has finally died away. The Terror and its fatal machine are seen ironically, even sarcastically.

The Hungarian dramatist Géza Páskándi's *Hiding Place*, written in 1972 and first produced in 1979, is one of only a few plays in which Dr. Guillotin appears as a major character. Although not actually shown, the guillotine is an indispensable accessory in a revolution grown increasingly brutal and senseless.

Set in 1794, the play uses the Reign of Terror as a potent mirror image of Stalinism and its paralyzing grip. A group of bored and terrified bourgeois and aristocratic suspects hiding in a Jacobin boot maker's workshop play cards to while away the time as they "wait out" the failure of the Revolution. Frequent screams are heard from the other room as the drunken sansculotte (as extreme republicans of the lower classes were called) shoemaker Simon "educates" his young charge, the former Dauphin, who, had he lived, would have become Louis XVII. Danton drops in to make love with the Curious Princess (curious primarily about the erotics of power). Even Robespierre pays an occasional visit.

Everyone in *The Hiding Place* seeks a way out, a little breathing space, a respite from the ghastly killings out in the streets, for which no one will take responsibility. "This isn't our Revolution. This isn't our France," Dr. Guillotin offers as a disclaimer—not unlike the French Ministry of Culture's wish to disown the guillotine during the 1989 bicentennial. But the good doctor is reminded that his decapitator will certainly outlive this Revolution. "Because it's all the same to the guillotine. The guillotine has no mind. It doesn't engage in politics, it obeys its operator, whoever that happens to be." The present operator happens to be the mob. Power has been given to the rabble, the slackers, the drunken illiterates, Danton complains. His most eloquent portrayal of the situation is sexual. "If I were a woman," he tells Robespierre, "I'd be afraid to go to bed with you, because every time you caressed my neck, all I could think of would be the guillotine." For the sensual Danton, having one's head chopped off by the guillotine is like coitus interruptus.

### MADAME GUILLOTIN

A one-woman show, *Madame Guillotin* was written and performed by the French actress Pierrette Dupoyet for the Festival of Avignon in 1988. During the bicentennial year it was presented as part of the officially sponsored celebrations in Tunisia, Congo, Switzerland, Poland, Spain, Iceland, Madagascar, Equatorial Guinea, and Cameroon, among other places.

Using only a table, several toy guillotines, and a basket of vegetables, Dupoyet brought to life the principal events of the Revolution as seen from a feminist perspective. One night in Paris during the Terror, Dr. Guillotin, offstage behind a screen, groans and snores as he sleeps uneasily. His wife, wearing a lace nightcap, skirt, and house jacket, dozes at a table on which are a number of small models of guillotines. Candles provide the sole illumination throughout the play. Suddenly awakened by the noise of passing tumbrils bearing the latest victims to the scaffold, Madame Guillotin tells the story of the horrible machine that has ruined both her life and her husband's. Ever since the device to which her husband's name has become forever attached was first used, the doctor has withdrawn into himself, seeking a hiding place in oblivion.

Madame Guillotin can find no such escape. Lonely and friendless, she is insulted and ridiculed in the streets during the day and tormented by ghastly visions during sleepless nights. Reflecting on the tragic losses of such brilliant personalities as Desmoulins, Madame Roland, and Danton, she recounts their executions, playing with the models in front of her, peering through the openings between the uprights and arranging the blades on the table.

Her evocations of the horrors of the machine are complex and inventive, alternatively lyrical, macabre, and humorous. At times she is an ordinary practical housewife, peeling and chopping vegetables for the meals that have to be prepared, since life must go on even in the midst of the Terror.

As she speaks, she grabs hold of one of the miniguillotines on the table and tries to cut her vegetables by releasing the blade, but in vain.

" 'Joseph! You might think about repairing my vegetable cutter! It's really beyond belief to have so many guillotines in the house and not be able to slice the carrots!' "

The tolling of the funeral bells remind Madame Guillotin of the omnipresence of death, which permeates her entire body.

My nights are haunted by relentless nightmares. Once dusk falls I am possessed by hallucinations. While you sleep soundly, Joseph, I have the sensation that prowling guillotines have surrounded the house. I can hear their trousers brush against the wall. . . . Someone bangs on the door. It is forced open and as I watch, a terrifying army bursts into our bedroom and lurches toward me. Their fetid breath blows down my neck.

(*She seizes a large kitchen knife, spears a cabbage on it, and marches up and down the room brandishing this improvised pike.*)

Each carries his head on the point of a pike, they dangle like disjointed marionettes . . . sinister puppets.

And suddenly I feel Madame Tussaud's nails caressing my neck. That carcass waxer does a good business in guillotined heads; she's on excellent terms with the executioner. She runs after the tumbril, her cloak billowing behind her, she retrieves the freshly cut heads and begins her grisly work. She wipes the blood and bran from the face, then smears it with a mixture of linseed oil and litharge . . . and makes an impression of the features . . . (*She takes the speared cabbage off the end of the knife, sits down, and in a state of delirium, begins painstakingly to remove the cabbage leaves one after the other, as though fixing the hair of a severed head.*)

La Tussaud is waiting for our turn to come. Every night I feel her crouching there, in the shadows of our bedroom, with her basket, her tongs, her needles, her linens and her hot wax.

*Scene from* THE SECOND YEAR OF LIBERTY *by Alexander Buravsky, 1988.*

Even more appalling is Madame Guillotin's version of childbirth.

> Last night I had a dream that was much more terrifying than usual: I dreamed that I
> gave birth to a headless baby . . . and much later out came a head with a sad little
> look of utter desolation . . . and suddenly I found myself surrounded by children
> who were kicking their own heads along in front of them. . . .
>
> At night, the dead are tireless in their attempts to touch hands with the living. . . .
>
> My dreams are full of the sound of clicks, of locks, of the blade that bites. My
> nights are metallic to the point of sheer horror.
>
> I hear guillotine blades sharpening themselves against one another, counting
> their dead. (*She sharpens two knives violently one against the other.*)

At the end of the play, Madame Guillotin pushes over the model decapitating machines on the table and voices the hope that what ultimately will be remembered about the French Revolution is not the guillotine but the Declaration of the Rights of Man. As she blows out the candles, the words of the Declaration can be heard amid hoofbeats on the pavement outside.

### THE SECOND YEAR OF LIBERTY

Alexander Buravsky's play *The Second Year of Liberty*, subtitled "A Guillotine for Robespierre," is the first Soviet play about the French Revolution to appear since 1931. Until 1988, when Buravsky's drama was staged in Moscow, the entire subject—and especially the Terror—was something Soviet writers felt it was safer to avoid in such a public forum as the theatre. It was too easy to draw dangerous parallels between past and present, France and Russia.

But Buravsky rejected this cautionary stance to give a penetrating analysis of the failure and betrayal of the Revolution of 1789 widely applicable to the present. In *The Second Year of Liberty* the mummification of the Revolution, the hollow slogans and empty glorification by state-sanctioned artists fail to mask the government's inability to meet the material needs of its citizens or lessen the ever-present reality of fear, suspicion, and informing.

A corrupt, self-serving politician, Danton would prefer that the Revolution were forgotten once and for all so that he could get on with his drinking and womanizing. The disillusioned, dedicated Robespierre still hopes to save the Revolution, but to do so he realizes that he must become a scapegoat, taking the blame for all the horrors upon himself. Robespierre's introspective anguish is contrasted with the opportunism flourishing everywhere. Life goes on in the midst of death and disaster. Hawkers sell food and drink to a rowdy mob gathered around the guillotine, which is festively decked with flowers.

Combining the guillotine rehearsals of imprisoned aristocrats during the Terror with the victims' balls after the Terror, Buravsky creates a provocative scene of perverse guillotine erotics based on the historical figure Jean-Marie Collot d'Herbois. An actor and playwright who deserted the stage for violent political theatre, Collot was a vicious terrorist responsible for the death of thousands. He helped plot the downfall of Robespierre and was sent to the "dry guillotine" in Guiana.

In the play, Catherine, secretary to the ruthless Collot, seductively reveals her passion for the blade.

COLLOT to CATHERINE: You know what our fashion plates have come up with, Here, right here . . . (*he passes a finger across his neck*) just under the neck, they draw a fine scarlet stripe, all jagged—razor thin. Quite arousing, don't you think?

CATHERINE (*tearing off her collar*): Like this? (*She shows him her stripe.*)

COLLOT: What a neck! (*He caresses it.*) And that stripe!

CATHERINE: Blow out the candles! (*She starts undressing.*) But leave one burning. Then you'll see I'm covered with red stripes. Breasts, belly, even there! Yes, Collot, even there! As if the blade had dropped a thousand times all over me, all over me!

### THE PASSION ACCORDING TO CHARLES-HENRI SANSON

A virtuoso piece for a single actor, *The Passion According to Charles-Henri Sanson* by Christian Drapron was staged in 1989 at the Theatre of the Eclipse, in Juvisy sur Orge, near Paris, directed by the author and starring Christian Jehanin. Based on the recently published memoirs *The French Revolution as Seen by Its Executioner, Charles-Henri Sanson*, the play presents a poetic self-portrait of the executioner of Louis XVI and Marie-Antoinette as a sensitive public servant driven half-mad by the brutal demands made of him during the Terror. A gifted amateur violinist, Sanson plays duets with the German harpsichord maker Schmidt, who describes the new decapitating machine he is creating.

The mass executions are a nightmare. To help him control the unruly crowds, Sanson hires Jacot, a mountebank from the fairground who does turns and lazzi on the scaffold mocking the condemned.

As Sanson describes the vicious caricatures that show him guillotining himself, he constructs a strange amorphous machine on stage and climbs on it, ready to sacrifice his own head. A very old man perched on his instrument and surrounded by bundles of the clothes of the dead, the executioner intones the names of the victims of the guillotine, both famous and obscure. Before being swallowed by the darkness, Sanson speaks his last words:

> *They have left me alone*
> *On this raft of the dead*
> *Each free to find music*
> *In the gesture by which I brush the flies*
> *Off their faces*

## PLAYING WITH HEADS

Presenting a panorama of the French Revolution in the form of a British Christmas pantomime, *Sweet Liberty*, like *The Second Year of Liberty*, is an irreverent treatment of the Terror and the guillotine. Written and composed by Jeff Clarke for the Chipping Norton Theatre, this burlesque musical pageant was first performed in the summer of 1989 as part of the bicentennial celebration of the French Revolution.

*Sweet Liberty* is full of macabre horseplay. Two grimy sansculottes wearing red caps and blood-stained butcher's aprons and both called Jean play games with dismembered body parts and squirt blood in one another's faces. For the "Musical Guillotine" number, the executioner's assistant calls out the names of all those to be executed. The shadow of the victims are seen mounting the steps to the scaffold, and the blade rises and falls without the decapitations actually being visible. A game with heads follows; each one is tossed from the wings to Colline onstage, who tosses it to Nelly, who brings it downstage and lobs it into a basket. The fall of the blade and the deft throws are in perfect

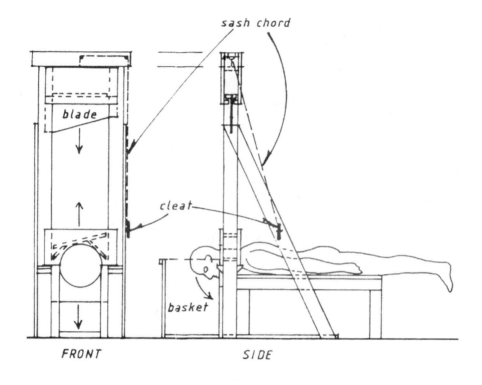

*Drawing for* Sweet Liberty *by Jeff Clark, 1989.*

synchronization with the music. Nelly and Colline comment on the original owners of the heads as they go about their work.

British criticism of French decapitations goes back almost two centuries. In the tenth book of his autobiographical poem *The Prelude,* William Wordsworth likens the bloodthirsty revolutionaries across the channel to a child with a toy, playing with "head after head, and never heads enough." However, the poet's disillusion with the excesses of the guillotine during the Terror did not prevent him from an enthusiastic endorsement of capital punishment English style, and in his old age he wrote a series of fourteen sonnets in defense of hanging.

In Beverley Cross's 1985 updating of the Baroness Orczy's stage version of *The Scarlet Pimpernel,* starring Donald Sinden, the resourceful British aristocrat and his fellow fighters against revolutionary terror suddenly throw off their disguises as nuns, free the prisoners about to be guillotined, and beat the French scoundrels carrying out the slaughter. The Pimpernel and his men begin a rugby game with the freshly decapitated heads, using the resulting confusion as a means of getting away safely with the noble victims whom they have saved.

The Pimpernel vanquishes French tyranny and, in the spirit of fair play, transforms the horrors of the guillotine into good clean English sport. A tradition of British self-mockery of the Scarlet Pimpernel already existed. In the 1966 film *Don't Lose Your Head,* producer Peter Rogers and the "Carry On" team parodied the heroics of Sir Percy Blakeney and his antirevolutionary conspirators.

The East German playwright Heiner Müller included a grotesque playing with heads in *The Task* (1979), a drama about the export of revolution to Jamaica based on Anna Seghers's story "The Light on the Gallows." In a game they call "Theatre of the Revolution," rebellious slaves wear a Danton head and a Robespierre head, which they knock off, chuck back and forth, put under their arms and between their legs, and use for playing soccer.

## FILMS OF THE 1980s ABOUT THE FRENCH REVOLUTION

Anticipation of the 1989 bicentennial of the French Revolution stimulated the production of historical films on the subject throughout the eighties. The guillotine inevitably figures in many of these, and with the abolition of capital punishment and the removal of censorship, it was at last possible for French cinema to show the decapitating machine in action.

*Gerard Depardieu in* DANTON, *1983.*

The guillotine is the fate toward which the hero is inexorably drawn by the mechanism of the Revolution in Andrzej Wajda's *Danton* (1983) starring Gerard Depardieu, a joint Polish-French production based on the play *The Danton Case* (1929) by Stanislawa Przybyszewska. The towering machine standing on the place de la Révolution is briefly shown three times before Danton's final appearance on the scaffold.

Early in the film Paris is shown as a grim, fearful city full of informers and secret police agents. Suddenly, through the driving rain, the huge machine comes into view, draped in a dark tarpaulin, which parts like curtains to disclose the raised blade beneath the arched canopy. Later, after Danton has been excluded from his own trial and before he is sentenced, an old woman, lying almost prone, scrubs the scaffold, the blade still raised high under the canopy covering the machine. When Danton is finally imprisoned, he looks out the window just as the cover is being removed from the guillotine and workmen are shoveling hay underneath the scaffold that awaits him.

A brutal *toilette du condamné* follows. The hair of Danton, Desmoulins, and their confederates is cut and their collars ripped off. The executioner-barber cautions one of his clients not to move: "Look out, I'll cut you." The prisoners ironically cite Dr. Guillotin's "soothing" comment that decapitation by his machine produces "only a pleasant sensation of cold on the neck."

In no film has tension surrounding the guillotine been more ominously built, and the final scene of Danton's execution is unsurpassed in horror. Danton stands on the scaffold, his hands tied behind his back, as the executioners thrust him against the plank. His head appears in the lunette, and the blade falls, blood dripping down on the hay, and quickly rises again, blood-drenched. Danton's head is shown to the crowd, but filmed from the vantage point of the execu-tioner so that his face is never visible.

Later, the tarpaulin is raised over the machine again to protect it from the elements. Watching is the distraught Lucile Desmoulins, who pulls and ties a thin red cord to fasten her hood tightly around her face. Twisting this cord, she makes a delicate red line appear around her neck. Wajda's subtle allusion evokes the violent death that Lucile Desmoulins's husband has just met and which soon awaits her. To the Polish director, the guillotine is the very emblem of the inexorable mechanisms of revolution.

Alexandre Mnouchkine's two-part, six-hour, $50 million production, *The French Revolution* (1989), used a multinational cast and was shot simultaneously in French and English. The star horror actor Christopher Lee, known for his portrayal of Dracula in the Hammer films, plays Charles-Henri Sanson. An early scene portrays the apocryphal meeting between Louis XVI and Dr. Guillotin (recounted by Dumas *père* and others), at which the king studies the good doc-tor's model machine and suggests the crucial improvement of making the blade slope instead of having it be horizontal. The six-foot-four Lee creates a portrait of the celebrated executioner as a gaunt, silent figure doing his job with quiet dignity, whether it be decapitating his king or later beheading the king-killers Danton and Robespierre.

## GUILLOTINE SIMULATIONS

The French company Le Théâtre de l'Unité created a traveling street show called *The Guillotine: An Execution Ritual*, which they have been presenting in public squares in France since 1987. For this complete simulation, an authentic scaffold and guillotine are set up, much as they might have been on the place de Grève in the early nineteenth century. The Theatre provides a description for anyone who might wish to book *The Guillotine* at $2,500 a performance. "The show freely reconstructs what public executions may have been in the era when

LA GUILLOTINE *by Théâtre de l'Unité, 1989.*

they were considered as the most popular form of mass entertainment. The machine is eight meters high, equipped with an impressive blade and a superb and macabre beauty." Le Théâtre de l'Unité can't restrain from including a few humorous observations on the refinement and the humanity of this machine. "The public participates, boos the executioners, and demands grace for the victim. Needed is a public area with a flat space 24 feet square for the installation of the scaffold, one local policeman's uniform, and one live piglet (to be returned alive)."

The machine itself is the work of Claude Acquart's stage workshop, constructed "according to the authentic drafts of Dr. Guillotin," and the performance, we are assured, is "full of irony, provocation, cruelty." Ironic indeed is the fact that no designs by Dr. Guillotin ever existed. And if the audience were truly to assume the role of spectators at revolutionary public executions, they certainly would not be demanding grace for the victim.

Even with its concessions to modern sensibilities, when the Théâtre de l'Unité performed *The Guillotine* in Texas, the American audience grew so concerned for the fate of the piglet that they almost refused to let the show go on.

## A NOTE ON ANIMAL EXECUTIONS

During the Middle Ages, animals were actually tried, imprisoned, and executed for crimes. There are cases recorded of sows being condemned to death for infanticide—the killing of human children, not their own. Of course, such superstitious rituals no longer existed in the enlightened times that produced the guillotine. According to one story, however, a dog taught to howl upon hearing the word "republican" is said to have been executed by the decapitating machine along with his master during the height of the Terror.

Animals have in fact been guillotined. The first live victim of the new mechanism at its initial demonstration in 1792, a sheep preceded the human corpses in having its neck placed in the lunette. And sheep were sometimes decapitated at special private shows arranged for British tourists.

At present, an Italian medical supply firm manufactures a "rat guillotine" for use by laboratories engaged in experiments on animals. The machines cost between $400 and $600, depending on size. The "Small Animal Decapitator" (8 × 6 × 8 in., 4 lb.), as described in the catalog, "is constructed of a pair of hardened and ground surgical stainless steel blades, a cast aluminum base and stainless steel

*Small-animal decapitator,* HARVARD APPARATUS BIOSCIENCE CATALOG, *c. 1989.*

hardware. The decapitator cuts cleanly through bone and tissue, and is still sharp enough to cut hair. . . . For use with rats, mice, and other small animals." The "Large Animal Decapitator" (14 x 9 x 17 in., 9 lb.) is of comparable design, but intended for "use with rabbits, small monkeys, and similar sized animals."

Today's guiltless experimental animals are condemned without even a trial or the possibility of a pardon, unlike those in the Middle Ages. Only in sixteenth-century Scotland were animals given the opportunity to play the executioner themselves, when cows were used to release the blade of the Maiden on the necks of cattle thieves.

# THE GUILLOTINE
# BETWEEN WORD AND IMAGE

*It is not as an instrument but as a symbol*
*that the guillotine terrorizes today.*
—Ian Hamilton Finlay

S A CULTURAL ARTIFACT, the post-
modern guillotine floats freely in
the popular consciousness, liberated from any single historical context or meaning. The American painter Robert Motherwell has created an almost abstract canvas in oils called *Guillotine* (1966) scarcely recognizable as the instrument of
death. Rather than representing any actual or ideal decapitating machine, the
painting gives form to an idea of violence. A piece of furniture, a wooden vehicle,
an art object might call forth similar shapes, but not the violent mood. The stark
colors of Motherwell's machine are red, black, and violet. The choice of the guillotine as the occasion for the composition reflects the artist's long involvement
with France and its culture. Motherwell infuses the ambiguous shape on canvas
with a surprisingly powerful haunting aura.

## GUILLOTINE AND PAINTING: HOMAGE TO TOPINO-LEBRUN

An exhibition entitled Guillotine and Painting opened in June 1977 at the
Beaubourg Center in Paris. Organized by Alain Jouffroy, the exhibit was dedicated to making known the life and work of the long-forgotten Jacobin painter
François Topino-Lebrun, who was guillotined on January 31, 1801, accused of
having collaborated in a plot against Napoleon Bonaparte. A pupil and friend
of Jacques Louis David, the leading artist of the Revolution, Topino emulated

*Wicar.* FRANÇOIS TOPINO-LEBRUN, *c. 1791.*

the master in his choice of neoclassical subject matter and style.

On view at the exhibition was Topino's long-suppressed and ignored masterpiece *The Death of Caius Gracchus* (1797), newly restored and surrounded by works on the theme of art and history, specially created to honor the memory of Topino by seven contemporary artists. Jouffroy and the "friends of Topino-Lebrun" saw a relation between the failed student-worker rebellion of 1968 and the tragic playing out of the French Revolution.

Among those paying homage to the artist executed for his radical politics was Antonio Recalcati, who created a series of canvases in which his own easel has become a guillotine standing in his studio. Historical risk taking begins with the work of solitary creation, and the suspended blade in Racalcati's work expresses his vision of the relation of art and politics. Daniel Arasse in his book *The Guillotine and the Terror* (1989) points out that a whole life can be revealed in a severed head's expression, as was the case with the mortuary masks made by Madame Tussaud at the graveside. Like a camera, Racalcati's easel-guillotine takes such pictures, which are in fact essences.

Vladimir Velickovic presented the contrast of the guillotine directly as a "still life" (*nature morte*) in a series of paintings showing the headless corpse being thrown from a balcony and lying on a low wooden platform, blood dripping from the neck. This homage to Topino replays the brutal moment of decapitation that ended his life.

## VISUAL POETRY OF THE GUILLOTINE

As an image and as an object, the guillotine is rich in cultural and historical associations. In Max Ernst's collage novel without words, *One Week of Kindness; or The Seven Capital Elements* (1934), the lion-headed protagonist is brought to the scaffold to be guillotined for committing sadistic sex crimes and dismembering a woman's body. As base pictures, Ernst used illustrations from popular French fiction of the late nineteenth century, altering them with pasted-on additions.

To unleash "the mind's hallucinatory faculties" by a free association of images, Ernst introduced bestial figures into the confines of civilization, changing the perspective from anthropocentric to zoocentric. The intrusion of the beast into the familiar world of old engravings creates a disorienting parody of the stereotypes of popular culture.

In the 1970s and 1980s two artists whose special province is visual poetry, Cozette de Charmoy and Ian Hamilton Finlay, have been drawn to the decapitating machine, its blade, and its traditions. Their creativity encompasses realms of the imagination that traverse all boundaries of genre. That which lies on the borderline between word and image and defies expression in either sphere alone is at the heart of their concerns. The guillotine is such an object-concept.

## COZETTE DE CHARMOY

A writer, painter, poet, and sculptor, Cozette de Charmoy creates works in visual and concrete poetry and in pictorial narratives, stressing the interconnection of word, image, and graphic notation. Incorporating heterogeneous materials and assaying different media, she breaks barriers and transcends norms. Her boxes, postage stamps, assemblages in wood, masks, and sculptures to be photographed and then destroyed, as well as her paintings of hunters and bears, shamans, birdmen, and armed warriors, create an imaginary world that can be now ironic and playful, now mythic and primordial.

For de Charmoy, "found objects" in *The Illustrated London News* and other nineteenth-century journals and catalogs become iconographic discoveries—she has absorbed the lessons of Dada and surrealism. Old drawings, photographs, announcements, ads, technical diagrams, and medical instructions provide images to be archeologically recovered from the past and recreated in new contexts.

Her collage-novels *The True Life of Sweeney Todd* and *The Voyages of Sweeney Todd* are a journey through the underside of Victorian society. Her Sweeney Todd is a hero of the industrial revolution, a believer in progress and science whose talent as an inventor enables him to create a barber chair with a devilish trap door and machine for making meat pies that usher in a masterful economy: man eats man.

*The Colossal Lie* (1973), a compendium of technological monstrosities, is de Charmoy's commentary on the the world of fraudulence and phantoms upon which we are nurtured. A world overflowing with delusions and running red

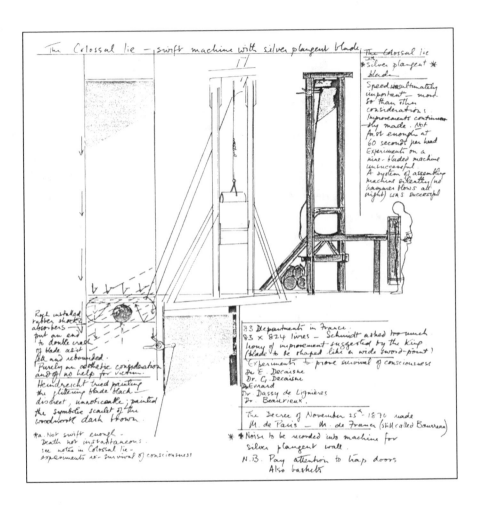

*Cozette De Charmoy.*

THE COLOSSAL LIE—SWIFT MACHINE WITH SILVER PLANGENT BLADE, *1973*.

from spilled blood, her "museum of the imagination" is a figurative version of Karl Valentin's Chamber of Horrors. Featured prominently in *The Colossal Lie* is the guillotine, with diagrams and illustrations accompanying texts from Alistair Kershaw's history of the machine. Its triangular blade, trap doors, baskets, technical refinements, and the experiments done to test the survival of consciousness (Dr. Lignières pumping the blood of a dog into Louis Menesclou's decapitated head) are among the most preposterous and fantastic inventions of modern civilization that de Charmoy elaborates through her associative alliance of words and images.

## IAN HAMILTON FINLAY

The multitalented Scottish artist Ian Hamilton Finlay approaches the guillotine through eighteenth-century gardens and temples, pastoral ideals, and the mythical and philosophical concepts underlying revolutionary change. A concrete poet, short-story writer, playwright, publisher, toy maker, gardener, and constructor of environments and installations, Finlay explores the heroic and the sublime, the violent and the catastrophic through a system of complex transcultural and transhistorical references. Cubism, Dada, modernism, and the avant-garde are just parts of his comprehensive perspective, which extends back to the classical and finds in the French Revolution and its aesthetic a crucial moment in the tissue of artistic and cultural continuities.

At his home in Stonypath, Scotland, which he calls Little Sparta (in tribute to the antique ideal), Finlay has created a garden to serve as the context for his work. Transformed into a temple, his gallery is adorned with heroic emblems celebrating the classical and pastoral values of the French Revolution and giving rise to meditations on Virtue and Terror.

Finlay's neoclassical rearmament consists of reworking models and values, reinventing forms and discovering unsuspected cultural connections. Visual puns and plays on images suggest new configurations, associations, and interrogations about art and politics. Working in collaboration with other artists who realize his concepts in diverse media, Finlay is able to create expertly crafted works of unusual variety that are by nature public and in essence somewhere between nature and culture: tree columns, plaques, monuments, and sundials. The scale varies from the epic to the minimal, and the context invites viewer participation in interactions between the meanings of words,

*Ian Hamilton Finlay, with Gary Hincks, Keith Brookwell, Nicholas Sloane,*
*Sue Finlay, Andreas Gram, Markus Gnüchtel.*
A VIEW TO THE TEMPLE. *Installation for the 1987 Documenta, Kassel, Germany.*

their formal organization, and the media in which they are inscribed. In all his creations, Finlay is attentive to composition, scale, material, and placement and to the relationship between the constituent elements. Because the works have many collaborators, stylistic appearance is depersonalized in the interest of a public classicism.

Challenging our notions of power and freedom in Western civilization, Finlay has made Louis Saint-Just the deity of his Temple. The Apollo of new age, Saint-Just was the youngest, the most beautiful, and the most extreme terrorist of all the major figures of the French Revolution, dedicated to the swift justice of the guillotine (by which he himself was to perish). In the neoclassical idiom, the artist has created emblems, medallions, plaques, and constructions that bear maxims by Saint-Just and other revolutionary leaders. A single citation may appear in different media and contexts. For example, the aphorism "The Present Order Is the Disorder of the Future, Saint-Just" is inscribed word by word on eleven monumental stones weighing several tons and set in the countryside near the garden. The same words are reproduced on a card with the instructions "Cut around outlines. Arrange words in order." The stones are immense; to rearrange them would be virtually impossible. Yet their text is broken. The fragile and the enduring, the fragmentary and the solid are ingeniously juxtaposed. Finlay's version in paper offers a rather different commentary on Saint-Just's utopian vision.

Revolutionary maxims adorn Finlay's scythes, and his Saint-Just axe carries the phrase "He spoke like an axe." Finlay has designed a Virtue medal embossed with an arch and a Terror medal embossed with a guillotine. For the 1987 Documenta exhibition in Kassel, Germany, in the setting of an eighteenth-century park, Finlay installed four life-size (or might it be more accurate to say death-sized?) guillotines, on the blades of which appeared short texts by Saint-Just, such as "Terror is the Piety of the Revolution."

Like classical arches, the four guillotines surrounded a small neoclassical temple on an island at the back of the park. The perspectives offered literally through the uprights of the towering machines and figuratively through the inscriptions induce the viewer to meditate on the nature of the classical and the sublime. The eye, the judgment, and the imagination are all brought into play in this concrete poem in action. The four inscribed guillotine blades were later exhibited separately in different media: on slate, on cards, on folding paper.

As a reflection on the bonds between the pastoral and Revolution, Finlay created a print of a bright yellow guillotine-trellis entwined in honeysuckle, bearing the inscription: "Both the garden style called 'sentimental,' and the French Revolution, grew from Rousseau. The garden trellis, and the guillotine, are alike entwined with the honeysuckle of the new 'sensibility.'"

In *Aphrodite of the Terror*, Finlay modified the familiar Greek statue with one small addition. His goddess of love wears a red ribbon around her neck in mourning for her brother and sister gods, killed by the secularization effected by the Terror and the Age of Enlightenment (the new goddess of reason). The artist explains: "In the Terror, a red silk thread worn around the neck intimated that friends or relatives had been lost to the guillotine. Aphrodite (or Venus) being a goddess, the same adornment signifies the loss of Olympian relatives and refers not to the Revolution's 'Sublime' Terror, but to the subsequent, secular Terror directed against the Ideal." Commentary and documentation are an integral part of Finlay's aesthetic.

Reworking Pierre Puvis de Chavannes's classic pastoral canvas "Oh, Nature, how sublime and delightful is your power!" Finlay added a guillotine in the far right corner of the picture. Visual rhymes showing the correspondence between two forms belonging to different domains are part of Finlay's strategy of confronting cultural values in unexpected ways. A waterfall and a guillotine are juxtaposed in an engraving as two examples of the sublime. And in a completely different scale, Finlay has designed and inscribed inkwells, flower pots, jam jars, and other everyday objects. A ceramic teapot in republican red, white, and blue has a blue handle and spout, a red lid with a small red guillotine set on top, and a white body upon which is lettered: *Il y a Deux Aspects de la Révolution Française: L'Épique et le Domestique—la Guillotine et la Theière.* ("There Are Two Aspects of the French Revolution: The Epic and the Domestic, The Guillotine and the Teapot.")

The brevity of the aphorism suits Finlay's aesthetics well. His terse mottoes combined with striking images inscribed on stone or printed on colored paper acquire a visual identity. "In the Picturesque landscape of the Revolution the wildest of banditti were all ex-lawyers." "Revolutions conceived in the fields are very different from Revolutions conceived in the cellar." "For the best of the Jacobins the Revolution was intended as a pastoral whose Virgil was Rousseau."

Finlay's Little Sparta revives ancient heroic virtues as understood by the French Revolution and its neoclassicism. Joining these concepts with the spirit of Dada and the "happenings" of the 1960s, Finlay created the Saint-Just Vigilantes, a group of the artist's supporters who conducted guerilla activities in defense of the Temple during the artist's clashes with the Scottish Arts

Council. The mythical Saint-Just Vigilantes had made their first appearance in Finlay's fictional *Third Reich Revisited*. Now in a battle with the sheriff, who intended to seize works from the garden Temple, the Saint-Just Vigilantes bombarded the officials with tracts and engaged in a neoclassical poster campaign, pasting propaganda on historic buildings in Edinburgh. After the battle, which Finlay called

*Ian Hamilton Finlay, with David Ballantyne.*
THEIERE (TEAPOT), *1987.*

the Little Sparta War, a medal was struck and a monument erected. The Saint-Just Vigilantes carry out spectacular actions against the modern bureaucratic state in defense of their own revolutionary values, of which the guillotine and its blade are emblems.

Continuing the aphoristic tradition of Lichtenberg and Lec, Finlay has composed a number of brief sayings on the subject of revolution and the guillotine.

> *The blade stained with blood is no more the French Revolution than the altar*
> *stained with blood is Greece and Rome.*

> *The life of Saint-Just was a duet between a blade and a flute.*

> *The death of the King drew a congregation, that of Robespierre a crowd.*

> *1794*
> *The steeples fell silent.*
> *The guillotine tolled.*

*Rue de la Roquette, 1990. Photo by Stéphane De Barros.*

## AFTERWORD:
## LAST WORDS, FINAL GESTURES

RATHER THAN PROVIDE a eulogy for the countless thousands killed by the guillotine, I prefer to let the victims speak for themselves. Many of those about to be guillotined made memorable and eloquent statements before going to their death. Especially during the Revolution, when standing high on the scaffold before huge crowds, political victims of the Terror managed to use the final occasion to defend their cause and attack their enemies. In the nineteenth century the most heinous criminals often showed the greatest bravado, and an initially hostile crowd would applaud an effective exit line. Here are some notable gestures and last words made facing the guillotine.

Marie-Antoinette went to the guillotine bravely, without a word, her lips moving in silent prayer.

Charlotte Corday, led to the scaffold in a red dress usually reserved for parricides, threw herself on the plank and asked, "Is this what I have to do?"

When during the *toilette du condamné* the scissors that the executioner Sanson were using got caught in his hair, the Girondist Jean François Ducos winced in pain. "Look here," he said, turning to Sanson, "I hope the edge of the guillotine is sharper than your scissors."

Pierre Vergniaud, chief spokesman for the Girondists, was given the honor of leading all the condemned members of his faction to the tumbrils. Pointing to the corpse of Charles Valazé, who had committed suicide but was to be guillotined just the same, the leader said, "He preceded us in death, he must show us the way."

The Comte de Sillery, who was lame, had trouble climbing the steps of the scaffold. When Sanson told him to hurry, he replied: "Can't you wait a minute? After all, it is I who am going to die. You have plenty of time."

Vigié sang the "Marseillaise" at the top of his lungs as he ascended the steps, and he kept singing the stirring words as the blood-soaked knife fell and cut them short.

Philippe Egalité, the duke of Orleans who had voted in favor of the death of his cousin Louis XVI, went to the scaffold clad in a blue dress coat, a white piqué vest, and leather culottes, his boots polished to a high gloss. To the assistant who wanted to take his boots off he nonchalantly suggested, "They'll be much easier to remove afterward."

When the king's sister, Madame Elisabeth, was being thrust on the plank, the fichu covering her breast was torn off. "For pity's sake," she cried to Sanson, "cover my breast!"

The Duc de Châtelet attempted suicide by cutting his veins with a piece of broken glass and had to be carried to the tumbril. When Sanson offered to dress his wounds to stop the bleeding, Châtelet responded, "Don't bother, I will be losing the rest of it just now." Carried to the scaffold, he dragged himself to his feet and cried out, "Vive le Roi!"

General Baron de Biron regarded his trial and condemnation as an enormous joke and was greatly amused from start to finish. Just before being taken to the tumbril, he treated himself to a huge dish of oysters. "Ah!" he exclaimed as Sanson made his appearance, "You really must allow me to finish this last dozen of oysters!"

"At your command," Sanson answered.

"No, *morbleu*," the general replied. "It's just the other way about. I am at yours."

As it was the last day of the year, he remarked, "I will soon arrive in the next world—just in time to wish all my friends there a Happy New Year!"

Malesherbes was winding his watch when Sanson asked him to sit down for the *toilette du condamné*. "One moment, my friend!" he said, and he finished winding his watch and put it back in his pocket. After his hair had been cut, he put his wig back on because he disliked the cold air on his head.

Jean-Sylvain Bailly, the first president of the Constituent Assembly, the first mayor of Paris, and a distinguished astronomer, was traveling to the scaffold in a tumbril when it was suggested that he put his coat on to avoid the cold November rain. "What's the matter?" he asked. "Are you afraid I might catch cold?"

Catching sight of the statue of liberty opposite the  scaffold, Madame Roland exclaimed, "Oh, Liberty, what crimes are committed in thy name!"

Madame Du Barry, screaming and begging for mercy, turned to Sanson and implored, "No, no, it can't be. You're not going to let me die."

The day after Du Barry's death Jean-Baptiste Noel was executed. "I hope you have cleaned the knife well after the Du Barry woman yesterday," he told Sanson. "It would be disgraceful for the blood of a good republican to be fouled by the blood of a prostitute!"

The journalist Jean-Louis Carra remarked to his executioner, "It annoys me to die. I should have liked to see what follows."

When Giuseppe Fieschi,  who had attempted to assassinate Louis-Philippe, was told by the executioner to put his coat on to keep from shivering in the cold, he replied, "I shall be a lot colder when they bury me."

Executed in 1808 for luring men to her hotel room and murdering them with a hammer as revenge for being deserted by her lover, Manette, who wore men's clothing as a disguise, asked her executioner, "Don't you think it a pity to cut off a head as beautiful as mine?"

On the scaffold, Danton commanded the executioner, "Show my head to the people. It's worth looking at!"

# BIBLIOGRAPHY

I N THE INTEREST OF compactness and serviceability, most of the readily accessible novels, plays, and poetry discussed in the text are not included in the bibliography.

## THE GUILLOTINE, CAPITAL PUNISHMENT, EXECUTIONS, AND THE EXECUTIONER

Arasse, Daniel. *La Guillotine et l'imaginaire de la terreur*. Paris: Flammarion, 1987.
———. *The Guillotine and the Terror*. Translated by Chris Miller. London: Lane, 1989.
Badinter, Robert. *L'Exécution*. Paris: Bernard Grasset, 1973.
Bessette, Jean-Michel. *Il Etait une fois . . . la guillotine*. Paris: Editions Alternatives, 1982.
Boatto, Alberto. "On the Guillotine as Bachelor Machine." Translated by Maurizio Viano. *Differentia: Review of Italian Thought* 3–4 (Spring–Autumn 1989): 337–54.
Bryan, Geoffrey. *Off with His Head*. London: Hutchinson, 1934.
Cabanès, Docteur. *Cabinet secret de l'histoire*. Paris: Albin Michel, 1920.
Caillois, Roger. "The Sociology of the Executioner." In *The College of Sociology (1937–39)*, edited by Denis Hollier. Translated by Betsy Wing. Minneapolis: University of Minnesota Press, 1988.
Callandraud, Gilbert J. *De l'exécution capitale à travers les civilizations et les âges*. Paris: J. C. Lattès, 1979.
Camus, Albert. "Reflections on the Guillotine" In *Resistance, Rebellion and Death*, translated and with an introduction by Justin O'Brien. New York: Alfred A. Knopf, 1961.
Chereau, Achille. *Guillotin et la guillotine*. Paris: Bureaux d l'Union Médicale, 1870.
Cortequisse, Bruno. *La Sainte guillotine*. Paris: France-Empire, 1988.
Courtois, Martine. "Le Bourreau familier." In *Les Mots de la mort*. Paris: Belin, 1991.
Degaudenzi, Jean-Louis. "Adieu! La Veuve." *Penthouse* (French edition) 54 (July 1989): 63–67.
Delarue, Jean. *Le Métier de bourreau*. Paris: Fayard, 1979.

Devoyod, R. P. *Les Déliquants*. Reims, France: Matot-Braine, 1955.

Domeniconi, Antonio. "L'uso della ghigliotina a Cesena nella seconda metà dell quattrocento," *Studi Romagnoli* 9–10 (1958–59).

Elliot, John. *The Way of the Tumbrils*. New York: Reynal and Company, 1958.

Evans, E. P. *The Criminal Prosecution and Capital Punishment of Animals*. 1906. Reprint. London and Boston: Faber and Faber, 1988.

Favre, Robert. *La Mort dans la littérature et la pensée française au siècle des lumières*. Lyon, France: Presses Universitaires de Lyon, 1978.

Fleischmann, Hector. *La Guillotine en 1793*. Paris: Librairie des Publications Modernes,1908.

Froidcourt, Georges de. *La Guillotine Liégoise*. Liége, Belgium: G. Throne, 1934.

*La Ghiglottina del Terrore*. Exhibition catalog. Documentazioni di Valérie Rousseau-Lagarde, testo di Daniel Arasse. Florence: Instituto Francese, 1986.

Goulet, Jacques. *Robespierre, La Peine de mort et la terreur*. Pantin, France: Le Castor Astral, 1983.

Grenier, Roger. *Les Monstres*. Paris: Gallimard, 1951.

Imbert, Jean. *La Peine de mort*. Paris: Armand-Colin, 1967.

Ker, Jean. *Le Carnet noir du bourreau. Mémoires d'Andre Obrecht, l'homme qui executa 322 condamnes*. Paris: Editions Gerard de Villiers, 1989.

Kreshaw, Alistair. *A History of the Guillotine*. London: Calder, 1958.

Laurence, John. *A History of Capital Punishment*. New York: Citadel Press, 1960.

Lecherbonnier, Bernard. *Bourreaux de père en fils. Les Sanson. 1688–1847*. Paris: Albin Michel, 1989.

Lee, Simon. "Artists and the Guillotine." *Apollo* 130, no. 329 (July 1989): 14–18.

Levy, Barbara. *Legacy of Death*. Englewood Cliffs, N.J.: Prentice-Hall, 1973.

Longoni, J. C. *Four Patients of Dr. Deibler*. London: Lawrence and Wishart, 1970.

Loye, Paul. *La Mort par le décapitation*. Paris: Lecrosnier et Babé, 1888.

McManners, John. *Death and the Enlightenment: Changing Attitudes to Death among Christians and Unbelievers in Eighteenth-Century France*. Oxford, England: Clarendon Press, 1981.

Montarron, Marcel. *Le Veuve ou l'histoire des châtiments*. Paris: Plon, 1973.

Naud, Albert. *Tu ne tueras pas*. Paris: Table Ronde, 1963.

———. *Les Défendre tous*. Paris: Robert Laffont, 1973.

Przybos, Julia. "Le Tribun, ou le comedién de l'échafaud." *Esprit Createur* 29, no. 2 (Summer 1989): 16–25.

Rossa, Kurt. *La Peine de mort*. Translated by Roger Chateauneu. Paris: Plon, 1986.

Sanchez, Guillermo C. "Fatal Edge: Dr. Guillotin and His Non-Invention." *Harvard Medical Alumni Bulletin* 64, no. 1 (Summer 1990): 48–53.

Sanson, Charles-Henri. *La Revolution française vue par son bourreau. Journal de Charles-Henri Sanson*. Edited and with a preface by Monique Lebailly. Paris: l'Instant, 1988.

Savey-Casard, P. *La Peine de mort*. Paris: Droz, 1968.

Soubiran, André. *Ce bon docteur Guillotin*. Paris: Perrin, 1962.

Thibault, Laurence. *La Peine de mort en France et à l'étranger*. Paris: Gallimard, 1977.

Wald Lasowski, Patrick. *Les Echafauds du romanesque*. Lille, France: Presses Universitaires de Lille, 1991.

# THE FRENCH REVOLUTION

Bindman, David. *The Shadow of the Guillotine: Britain and the French Revolution*. London: British Museum Publications, 1989.

Blanc, Olivier. *Last Letters: Prisons and Prisoners of the French Revolution, 1793–1794*. Translated by Alan Sheridan. New York: Farrar, Straus and Giroux, 1987.

Croker, John Wilson. *Essays on the Early Period of the French Revolution*. 1857. Reprint. New York: AMS Press, 1970.

*Chronicle of the French Revolution*. Adapted and translated by Louis Nevin et al. London: Chronicle, 1989.

*French Caricature and the French Revolution, 1789–1799*. Exhibition catalog. Los Angeles: University of California, 1988.

Godineau, Dominique. *Citoyennes tricoteuses*. Aix-en-Provence, France: Alinéa, 1988.

Gooch, G. P. *Germany and the French Revolution*. New York: Russell and Russell, 1966.

Goncourt, Edmond, and Jules Goncourt. *Histoire de la société française pendant la révolution*. Paris: Fasquelle, 1918.

Huet, Marie-Hélène. *Rehearsing the Revolution: The Staging of Marat's Death, 1793–1797*. Translated by Robert Hurley. Berkeley: University of California Press, 1982.

Karmel, Alex. *Guillotine in the Wings*. New York: McGraw-Hill, 1972.

———. *My Revolution: Promenades in Paris 1789–1794, Being the Diary of Restif de la Bretonne*. New York: McGraw-Hill, 1970.

Lagueunière, Pierre. "La Révolution française: théâtrilité de ses héros et martyrs." *In La Légende de la révolution*. Actes du Colloque International de Clermont-Ferrand, June 1986, 271–79. Clermont-Ferrand, France: A.D.O.S.A., 1988.

Michelet, Jules. *Histoire de la révolution française*. Vols. 1 and 2. Edited by Gerard Walter. Paris: Bibliothèque de la Pleiade, 1952.

Nodier, Charles. "Euloge Schneider, ou la terreur en Alsace." In *Oeuvres completes*. Vol. 8, *Souvenirs and Portraits*. Geneva: Slatkine Reprints, 1968.

Outram, Dorinda. *The Body and the French Revolution*. New Haven: Yale University Press, 1989.

Ozouf, Mona. *Festivals and the French Revolution*. Translated by Alan Sheridan. Cambridge: Harvard University Press, 1988.

Paulson, Ronald. *Representations of Revolution (1789–1820)*. New Haven: Yale University Press, 1983.

Pernoud, Georges, and Sabine Flaissier. *The French Revolution*. Translated by Richard Graves. New York: G. P. Putnam's Sons, 1961.

Salmonowicz, Stanislaw. *Sylwetki spod Gilotyny*. Warsaw: PWN, 1989.

Schama, Simon. *Citizens: A Chronicle of the French Revolution*. New York: Alfred A. Knopf, 1989.

Starobinski, Jean. *1789: The Emblems of Reason*. Translated by Barbara Bray. Charlottesville: University Press of Virginia, 1982.

Thompson, J. M., ed. *English Witnesses of the French Revolution*. Oxford, England: Basil Blackwell, 1938.

## FRENCH SOCIETY AND CULTURE IN THE NINETEENTH AND TWENTIETH CENTURIES

Appelbaum, Stanley. *French Satirical Drawings from "L'Assiette au Beurre."* New York: Dover, 1978.

Clunn, Harold P. *The Face of Paris*. London: Spring Books, n.d.

Flanner, Janet. *Paris Was Yesterday: 1925–1939*. New York: Penguin Books, 1981.

Rearick, Charles. *Pleasures of the Belle Epoque: Entertainment and Festivity in Turn-of-the-Century France*. New Haven: Yale University Press, 1985.

Royer, Jean-Michel, ed. *Le Livre d'or de "L'Assiette au Beurre."* Vols. 1 and 2. Paris: Jean-Claude Simoën, 1977–78.

Seigel, Jerrold. *Bohemian Paris 1830–1930*. New York: Penguin Books, 1987.

Weber, Eugen. *France Fin de Siècle*. Cambridge: Harvard University Press, 1986.

## THE MACABRE, FANTASTIC, AND GROTESQUE

Breton, André. *Anthologie de l'humour noir*. Paris: Jean-Jacques Pauvert (Livre de Poche), 1966.

Chapman, Pauline. *Madame Tussaud's Chamber of Horrors: Two Hundred Years of Crime*. London: Constable, 1984.

———. *The French Revolution as Seen by Madame Tussaud, Witness Extraordinary*. London: Quiller, 1989.

Dijkstra, Bram. *Idols of Perversity: Fantasies of Feminine Evil in Fin-de-Siècle Culture*. New York: Oxford University Press, 1986.

Leslie, Anita, and Pauline Chapman. *Madame Tussaud: Waxworker Extraordinary*. London: Hutchinson, 1978.

Murdoch, Tessa. "Madame Tussaud and the French Revolution," *Apollo* 130, no. 329 (July 1989): 9–13.

Praz, Mario. *The Romantic Agony*. Translated by Angus Davidson. London: Oxford University Press, 1970.

Roberts-Jones, Philippe. *Beyond Time and Place*. Oxford, England: Oxford University Press, 1978.

Schneider, Marcel. *La littérature fantastique en France*. Paris: Fayard, 1964.

Sullivan, Jack, ed. *The Penguin Encyclopedia of Horror and the Supernatural*. With an introduction by Jacques Barzun. New York: Viking, 1986.

## WORKS ABOUT AUTHORS AND ARTISTS

Abrioux, Yves. *Ian Hamilton Finlay: A Visual Primer*. With an introduction and notes by Stephen Bann. Edinburgh: Reaktion Books, 1985.

Alfu. *L'encyclopédie de Fantômas*. Paris: Alfu, 1981.

Barzun, Jacques. *Berlioz and the Romantic Century*. Vols. 1 and 2. New York: Columbia University Press, 1969.

Bellour, Raymond. *Mademoiselle Guillotine*. Paris: La Différence, 1989.

Brombert, Victor. *Victor Hugo and the Visionary Novel*. Cambridge: Harvard University Press, 1984.

Brooks, Peter. "The Novel and the Guillotine, or Fathers and Sons in *Le Rouge et le noir*." In *Reading for the Plot: Design and Intention in Narrative*. New York: Alfred A. Knopf, 1984.

Brown, Nathalie Babel. *Hugo and Dostoevsky*. Introduction by Robert Belknap. Ann Arbor, Mich.: Ardis, 1978.

Carlson, Prudence. "The Garden on the Hill: Ian Hamilton Finlay at Little Sparta." *Arts Magazine*, February 1990, 38–53.

Decottignies, Jean. *Villiers le taciturne*. Lille, France: Presses Universitaires de Lille, 1983.

Echevarría, Roberto González. *Alejo Carpentier: The Pilgrim at Home*. Ithaca, N.Y.: Cornell University Press, 1977.

"Fantômas." *Europe* [special issue] 590–591 (June–July 1978).

Gaudon, Jean. *Ce que disent les tables parlantes. Victor Hugo à Jersey*. Paris: Jean-Jacques Pauvert, 1963.

Hugo, Victor. *Les Fantômes de Jersey*. Edited by Francis Lacassin. Monaco: Editions du Rocher, 1991.

Janion, Maria and Remigiusz Forycki. "L'Apocalypse laique," *Lettre internationale* 21 (Summer 1989): 29–32.

Kott, Jan. "La guillotine, héros tragique," *Lettre internationale* 21 (Summer 1989): 21–24.

Lebois, André. *Les Tendences du symbolisme à travers l'oeuvre d'Elémir Bourges*. Paris: Le Cercle du livre, 1952.

Lombroso, Cesare: "Genio e pazzia nell'opera di Wiertz." *Emporium* 5, no. 25 (January 1897): 3–8.

Miannay, Régis. *Maurice Rollinat. Poète et musicien du fantastique*. Châteauroux, France: Martin Clavier, 1982.

Moerman, André A. "Wiertz ou les egarements d'un talent." In *Antoine Wiertz 1806–1865*. Paris and Brussels: Jacques Damase, 1974.

Simon, Gustave. *Les Tables tournantes de Jersey*. Paris: Conard, 1923.

## WORKS BY AUTHORS AND ARTISTS

Allain, Marcel and Pierre Souvestre. *Fantômas*. Introduction by John Ashberry. New York: Ballantine Books, 1986.

Belbenoit, Rene. *Dry Guillotine*. New York: Dutton, 1938.

Buravsky, Alexander. "The Second Year of Liberty." Translated by Michael Heim. Unpublished translation.

Busson Paul. *The Man Who Was Born Again*. In *The Golem and The Man Who Was Born Again: Two German Supernatural Novels*. Translated by Thomas Moult. New York: Dover, 1976.

Carpentier, Alejo. *Explosion in a Cathedral*. Translated by John Sturrock. New York: Noonday, 1989.

de Charmoy, Cozette. *The Colossal Lie/Le Colossal Mesonge*. Editions OU, 1974.

———. *Exposition rétrospective 1961–1985*. Martigny, Switzerland: Le Manoir de la Ville de Martigny, 1985.

Chavette, Eugène. *Les Petites Comédies du vice*. Paris: Marpon and Flammarion, 1882.

Clarke, Jeff. "Sweet Liberty." Unpublished.

Dickens, Charles. "A Public Execution." In *Dickens in Europe*. Essays selected and introduced by Rosalind Vallance. London: Folio Society, 1975.

Dumas, Alexander fils. "Une Exécution capitale." In *Thérèse*. Paris: Michel Lévy frères, 1875.

Dupoyet, Pierrette. *Madame Guillotin*. Paris: Actes Sud-Papier, 1989.

Elder, Lonne. *Charades on East Fourth Street*. In *Black Drama Anthology*, edited by Woodie King and Ron Milner. New York: Meridian, 1986

Finlay, Ian Hamilton. *Poursuites Revolutionaires/Revolutionary Pursuits*. Paris: Foundation Cartier pour l'Art Contemporaine, 1987.

————. *1789–1794*. Hamburg, Germany: Hamburger Kunsthalle, 1989.

————. *Bicentenary Texts*. Little Sparta, Scotland: Wild Hawthorn Press, 1989.

Hino, Hideshi. *Panorama of Hell*. Translated by Screaming Mad George, Charles Schneider, and Yoko Umezawa. New York: Blast Books, 1989.

Hochwälder, Fritz. *The Public Prosecutor*. Translated by Kitty Black. In *Plays of the Year: 1956–57*. Vol. 16. London, 1958.

Jarry, Alfred. *Selected Works*. Edited by Roger Shattuck and Simon Watson Taylor. New York: Grove Press, 1965.

Kesselman, Wendy. *Olympe and the Executioner*. In *Theatre and Politics: An International Anthology*, edited by Erika Munk. New York: Ubu Repertory, 1991.

Maistre, Joseph. *Works*. Selected, translated, and introduced by Jack Lively. New York: Macmillan, 1965.

Páskándi, Géza. "The Hiding Place." Translated by Eugene Brogyani. Unpublished translation.

Pazniewski, Wlodzimierz. "Sonety Demagoga." Odra 1 (1989).

Reck-Malleczewen, Friedrich P. *Diary of a Man in Despair*. Translated by Paul Rubens. New York: Collier Books, 1970.

Stendhal. "The Cenci." In *The Abbess of Castro and Other Tales*. Translated by C. K. Scott Moncrieff. New York: Boni and Liveright, 1926.

Tisserant, Jean-Hippolyte. "Le Dernier jour d'un condamne." In *Le Théâtre érotique du XIXe siècle*. Poitiers, France: Editions Jean-Claude Lattes, 1979.

Tolstoy, Lev. *Tolstoy's Letters, Volume 1: 1828–1879*. Edited by F. F. Christian. London: Athalone Press, 1978.

Turgenev, Ivan. "The Execution of Troppmann." In *Turgenev's Literary Reminiscences*, translated and with an introduction by David Magarshack. New York: Minerva Press, 1968.

Wiertz, Antoine J. *Oeuvres Littéraires*. Brussels: Parent et Fils, 1869.

Wikoff, Henry. *Reminiscences of an Idler*. New York: Fords, Howard, Hulbert and Co., 1857.

Witmer, Theodore B. *On and Off Soundings, Being Leaves from a Private Journal*. Philadelphia: T. B. Peterson and Brothers, 1872.

## CABARET AND GRAND GUIGNOL

Gordon, Mel. *The Grand Guignol: Theatre of Fear and Terror*. New York: Amok Press, 1988.

*Le Théâtre* 2 [Grand Guignol issue]. Paris: Christian Bourgois, 1969.

Segel, Harold B. *Turn-of-the-Century Cabaret*. New York: Columbia University Press, 1987.

Senelick, Laurence. *Cabaret Performance, Volume 1: Europe 1890–1925*. New York: Performing Arts Journal, 1989.

Till, Wolfgang, ed. *Karl Valentin: Volk-Sänger? DADAist?* Munich, Germany: Knaur, 1982.

## FILM

Bonnet, Jean-Claude, and Philippe Roger, eds. *La Légende de la révolution au XXe siècle. De Gance à Renoir de Romain Rolland à Claude Simon*. Paris: Flammarion, 1988.

Brasch, Thomas. *Engel aus Eisen*. Frankfurt: Suhrkamp Verlag, 1981.

Braucourt, Guy. *André Cayatte*. Paris: Seghers, 1969.

"Fantômas." *L'Avant-scène Cinéma* [special Feuillade issue] 271–272 (July 1–15, 1981).

Frazer, John. *Artificially Arranged Scenes: The Films of Georges Méliès*. Boston: G. K. Hall and Co., 1979.

Guidez, Guylaine. *Claude Lelouch*. Paris: Seghers, 1972.

Hammond, Paul. *Marvellous Méliès*. New York: St. Martin's Press, 1975.

Jeanne, René. *Cinéma 1900*. Paris: Flammarion, 1965.

Icart, Roger. *La Révolution française à l'écran*. Toulouse, France: Editions Milan, 1988.

Lacassin, Francis. *Louis Feuillade*. Paris: Editions Seghers, 1964.

———. *Pour une contre histoire du cinéma*. Paris: Union Générale d'Editions, 1972.

Lefevre, Raymond. *Cinéma et révolution*. Paris: Edilig, 1988.

Mitry, Jean. "Ferdinand Zecca et l'école Pathé (1900–1908)" in *Les Premiers ans du cinéma français*. Paris: Collection des Cahiers de la Cinémathèque, 1985.

Quéval, Jean. *Jacques Becker*. Paris: Seghers, 1962.

Viry-Babel, Roger. *La Victoire en filmant, ou la révolution à l'écran*. Nancy, France: Presses Universitaire de Nancy, 1989.

## CRIME AND *FAIT DIVERS*

Chevalier, Louis. *Laboring Classes and Dangerous Classes in Paris During the First Half of the Nineteenth Century*. Translated by Frank Jellinek. New York: Howard Fertig, 1973.

Delarue, Jacques, and Robert Giraud. *Les Tatouages du "milieu."* Paris: La Roulette, 1950.

Drachline, Pierre, and Claude Petit-Castelli. *Casque d'Or et les apaches*. Paris: Renaudot, 1990.

———. *Le Crime de Pantin: l'affaire Troppmann*. Paris: Denoël, 1985.

———. *Le Fait Divers au XIXme siècle*. Paris: Hermé, 1991.

Irving, Henry B. *Studies of French Criminals of the Nineteenth Century*. London: William Heinemann, 1901.

Lacenaire, Pierre-François. *Mémoires*. Edited by Monique Lebailly. Paris: L'Instant, 1988.

———. *Mémoires et autres écrits*. Edited by Jacques Simonelli. Paris: J. Corti, 1991.

———. *The Memoirs of Lacenaire*. Edited and translated by Philip John Stead. New York: Roy Publishers, n.d.

Locard, Edmond. *Le Fiancé de la guillotine*. Paris: Editions de la Flamme d'Or, 1954.

Monestier, Alain, ed. *Le Fait Divers*. Paris: Editions de la Réunion des Musées Nationaux, 1982.

Romi. *Histoire de faits divers*. Milan, Italy: Pont-Royal (Del Duca-Laffont), 1962.

# INDEX

# ILLUSTRATIONS

p. 68:   Louis Deibler, chief executioner from 1879 to 1898, with his wife. Photo by Jacques Delarue.

p. 70:   Exiting la Roquette, *Le Petit Journal*, 1891.

p. 72:   Louis Lefèvre, arrested May 20, 1915, guillotined April 10, 1916, in Tours, France.

p. 76:   The execution of Eugène Weidmann, June 16, 1939, Versailles.

p. 80:   Wax models of the guillotined heads of Marie-Antoinette and Louis XVI. Madame Tussaud's, London.

p. 84:   Louis Boulanger. Lithograph depicting a scene from *The Last Day of a Condemned Man* by Victor Hugo (1829).

p. 87:   Anonymous. Satirical etching depicting Robespierre guillotining the executioner, late eighteenth century.

p. 88:   J. J. Grandville. Illustration pour Jérome Paturot.

p. 94:   Drawing of Pierre-François Lacenaire, c. 1835.

p. 99:   Henri Monnier. *The Execution*. Drawing, 1829.

p. 103:  Erotikon Puppet Theatre, 1862.

pp. 104, 110: Antoine Wiertz. Panels one (p. 104), two, and three (p. 110), *Thoughts and Visions of a Severed Head*. Oil on canvas, 1853. Photo © A.C.L. Brussels.

p. 113:  Julien Deladoès. *L'exécution capitale*. Drawing, india ink and watercolor. Photo by Roland Beyen.

pp. 114, 122: Tony Johannot. Illustrations for *The Dead Donkey, or The Guillotined Woman* by Jules Janin (1842).

p. 118:  Artist unknown. Illustrations for "The Adventures of a German Student" by Washington Irving (1824).

p. 125:  Honoré de Balzac.

p. 127:  Eugène Sue.

p. 129:  Lord Byron.

p. 131:  Charles Dickens.

p. 133:  Leo Tolstoy.

p. 136:  Jean-Baptiste Troppmann.

p. 141:  Alexandre Dumas *fils*.

p. 147:  Fyodor Dostoevsky.

p. 148:  Drawing of execution scene.

p. 154:  Dirk Bogarde in *A Tale of Two Cities* directed by Ralph Thomas, 1958.

p. 160:  Jacket illustration for *The Man Who Was Born Again* by Paul Busson (1921).

p. 162:  Artist unknown. Political cartoon, late nineteenth century.

p. 164:  Artist unknown. Political cartoon, late nineteenth century.

p. 170:  Pierre Lagueunière. *Le prie-dieu-guillotine*, 1987.

p. 172:  Scene of priest with prisoner approaching guillotine.

p. 176:  Aristide Bruant. "A la Roquette," illustrated by Théophile Steinlen.

p. 179:  Drawing of Yvette Guilbert.

p. 180 top: Photograph of Maurice Rollinat; bottom: Alfred le Petit. *Maurice Rollinat*. In *Le Charivari*, January 6, 1883.

p. 184:  Adolphe Willette. Satirical drawing, 1887.

p. 187:  Scene from *A L'Ombre de la Guillotine* by Jean Bastia, 1930.

p. 190:  Scene from *Let 'Em Eat Cake* by George S. Kaufman and Morris Ryskind, 1933. Performing Arts Research Center, New York Public Library.

p. 192:  *Fait divers* depiction of the capture of Ravachol, c. 1892.

p. 195:  French lithograph depicting Ravachol in triumph over the guillotine, late nineteenth century.

p. 198:  *Fait divers* illustration of the arrest of Emile Henry in the Café Terminus, c. 1894.

p. 204:  Alfred Jarry. Drawing for the cover of "The Song of the Disembraining," from *Ubu Roi*, 1898.

p. 206:  Dimitrios Galanis. *"We Must Go On Guillotining Because . . . "* In *L'Assiette au Beurre* no. 310, March 9, 1907.

p. 210:  Gino Starace. Cover illustration for *Fantômas in Custody* by Pierrre Souvestre and Marcel Allain.

p. 214:  Photograph of Henri-Désiré Landru (l), and of Charles Chaplin (r) in *Monsieur Verdoux*, 1947.

p. 219:  Harry Kellar poster, 1897.

pp. 220–22: Seven wax-figure tableaux from the Musée Grévin, Paris, c. 1889.

p. 222, bottom: Scene from *A Desparate Crime* directed by Georges Méliès, 1906.

p. 224: Lillian Gish in *Orphans of the Storm* directed by D. W. Griffith, 1921.

p. 227: Poster for *Napoleon* directed by Abel Gance, 1927.

p. 228: Abel Faivre. Satirical drawing in *Le Rire*, 1898.

p. 235: Scene from *The Marat/Sade* directed by Peter Brook.

p. 236: George Lichtenberg. Drawing, 1793.

p. 238: Artist unknown. Illustration of Karl Valentin's Panoptikon, c. 1934.

p. 244: Antonio Recalcati. Detail, *31 Janvier 1801*. Oil on canvas, 1975.

p. 252: Scene from the filming of *Life, Love, Death* directed by Claude Lelouch, 1968.

p. 256: Photograph of Casque d'Or, c. 1900.

p. 260: Albert Naud in *Life, Love, Death* directed by Claude Lelouch, 1968.

p. 269: La Guillotine Belgian beer. Photo by Scott Lindgren, 1991.

p. 270: Illustrations from Louis Tannen, Inc.'s magicians' supply catalog.

p. 272: Aurora Plastic Co.'s toy guillotine model and assembly instructions. Courtesy of Joe Coleman, photo by Scott Lindgren.

p. 274: Alice Cooper in "Billion-Dollar Babies," 1973. Photo © Mark Weiss.

p. 279: George Tsypin's set design in Robert Fall's production of *The Misanthrope* by Moliere, 1989.

p. 281: Gustav Völpel in mask, c. 1948.

p. 282 : Scenes from *Steel Angel*, directed by Thomas Brasch, 1981.

p. 284: Hideshi Hino. From *Panorama of Hell*, 1982.

p. 286: Pierrette Dupoyet in *Madame Guillotin*, 1988. Photo © Pierre CAO.

p. 290: Scene from *The Second Year of Liberty* by Alexander Buravsky, 1988.

p. 294: Drawing for *Sweet Liberty* by Jeff Clark, 1989.

p. 296: Gerard Depardieu in *Danton* directed by Andrzej Wajda, 1983.

p. 298: Set for *La Guillotine* by Théâtre de l'Unité, 1989. Photo: E. Berthelot.

p. 300: Small-animal decapitator, *Harvard Apparatus Bioscience Catalog*, c. 1989.

p. 302: Wicar. *François Topino-Lebrun*. Drawing, c. 1791.

p. 304: Cozette De Charmoy. *The Colossal Lie—swift machine with silver plangent blade*. Drawing, 1973.

p. 306: Ian Hamilton Finlay, with Gary Hincks, Keith Brookwell, Nicholas Sloane, Sue Finlay, Andreas Gram, Markus Gnüchtel. *A View to the Temple*. Installation for the 1987 Documenta, Kassel, Germany.

p. 309: Ian Hamilton Finlay, with David Ballantyne. *Théière (Teapot)*. Ceramic, 1987.

p. 310: Rue de la Roquette, 1990. Photo by Stéphane De Barros.

# RECENTLY PUBLISHED BY BLAST BOOKS

## THE DRUG USER: DOCUMENTS 1840–1960
*Edited by John Strausbaugh and Donald Blaise*

". . . A quietly defiant comeback to the 'just say no' rhetoric of the moment."
—VILLAGE VOICE LITERARY SUPPLEMENT

5 ¹/₄ x 8 ¹/₄", 256 pages • $10.95 pb • ISBN 0-922233-05-5

## MORAVAGINE
*Blaise Cendrars*
*Translated from the French by Alan Brown*

"Rip-roaring fiction and imaginative adventuring on all planes of experience."
—TIMES LITERARY SUPPLEMENT

5 ¹/₄ x 8 ¹/₄", 250 pages • $9.95 pb • ISBN: 0-922233-04-7

## PANORAMA OF HELL
*Hideshi Hino*
*Translated from the Japanese by*
*Screaming Mad George, Charles Schneider, and Yoko Umezawa*

"A brain-scraping, gut-breaking revelation from postnuclear Japan." —METRO

6 x 9", 200 pages • $9.95 pb • ISBN: 0-922233-00-4

## VENUS IN FURS AND SELECTED LETTERS
*Leopold von Sacher-Masoch*

"*Venus in Furs* is the quintessential Sacher-Masoch novel . . . a deviant classic."
—NEW YORK PRESS

5 ¹/₄ x 8 ¹/₄", 224 pages • $9.95 pb • ISBN: 0-922233-01-2

ORDERING INFORMATION— *Blast Books* is distributed to the bookstores, wholesalers, and libraries exclusively by Publishers Group West, 4065 Hollis Street, Emeryville, CA 94608. Call (800) 788-3123, or in California call collect (510) 658-3453.

INDIVIDUALS—Send your order to Blast Books, P.O. Box 51, Cooper Station, New York, NY 10276. Add $2.00 postage and handling for the first book and 50¢ for each book thereafter.